REGRETS, NONE

REGRETS, NONE

DOLLY THAKORE

with Arghya Lahiri

HarperCollins *Publishers* India

First published in India by
HarperCollins *Publishers* 2021
A-75, Sector 57, Noida, Uttar Pradesh 201301, India
www.harpercollins.co.in

2 4 6 8 10 9 7 5 3 1

P-ISBN: 978-93-9032-770-6
E-ISBN: 978-93-9032-771-3

Typeset in 11.5/14.3 Adobe Garamond at
Manipal Technologies Limited, Manipal

Printed and bound at
Thomson Press (India) Ltd

MIX
Paper
FSC FSC® C010615

This book is produced from independently certified FSC® paper to ensure responsible forest management.

Contents

This is the book I never read
These are the words I never said
This is the path I'll never tread
These are the dreams I'll dream instead
This is the joy that's seldom spread
These are the tears
The tears we shed
This is the fear
This is the dread
These are the contents of my head
And these are the years that we have spent
And this is what they represent
And this is how I feel
Do you know how I feel?

– Annie Lennox, *Why?*

Okay.

I admit to resentments. But I have no regrets. None.

I wrote this memoir for my son, Quasar, so that he may understand.

I don't know who you are, ma soeur, ma semblable, but I hope you will understand too.

I was not the first woman to 'steal' another woman's husband.

I was not the first woman to bear a child out of wedlock.

I was not the first woman to bring up a boy alone.

I was not the first woman to be abandoned.

And I will not be the last.

Quasar, this is for you, first and always.

But it is also for my maternal grandmother, Rahael Solomon, and my aunt, Rani Solomon,

two fantastic women whose struggles taught me acceptance and survival.

I owe them everything I am today.

And to my parents, Dora and David Rawson,

who provided for me, were patient with me and accepted me.

Two people I hurt very much by not being their ideal, dutiful daughter.

Sorry, mum; sorry, dad.

I

So Many Homes

1

MY NAME IS Dolly Thakore. I am seventy-eight years old. I live and work in Mumbai, India – a place that used to be called Bombay. When I first came here, I was Dolly Rawson. 'Dolly from Delhi', like I said to Simi Garewal, a very long time ago.

This book was written the way some people quit smoking: it took over thirty years. Friends helped, and they didn't. I relapsed now and again. Brief periods on the wagon – a chapter or two at a time. A process begun in a headlong rush, finished in wry contemplation. Anger burnt out. Resentments tended to with care. The slightly astonished realization that there aren't any regrets after all.

In 1982, my son's father – Alyque Padamsee – left me. Our separation caused a minor storm. We already possessed a degree of notoriety: I'd 'stolen' Alyque away from his first wife. In the process, I'd broken up Bombay Theatre's First Couple. There were children involved. The whole thing was a mess.

Ingrid Albuquerque, the first editor of *Savvy*, conducted a series of interviews with me in the aftermath of Alyque's departure. She then spent some four weeks transcribing those tapes, more than a hundred pages' worth – my tears, my heartbreak, my insecurities, memories I had forgotten, memories I had repressed, experiences that I had excised.

Ingrid was the first – and not the last – to say: 'I could write a book about you.'

Instead, I was on the cover of the second-ever issue of *Savvy*. 'The Power, Passion and Pain of Dolly Thakore', July 1984. Maneka Gandhi had been the first.

Even two years after the break-up, I was half-crazed with grief and would remain so for a long time. Therefore, when *Savvy* put up three massive hoardings to publicise the issue, it became some strange kind of validation. I remember one at Haji Ali, another at Chowpatty, and one in Colaba. There may have been five.

Three days later, the hoardings came down. Why? I don't know.

I have my theories, of course. I had spoken about what *I'd felt*, and what *I'd thought*. There were enough people who had reason to want to avoid publicity of that kind. Brand associations cut both ways.

All I know is that the hoardings came down. Given that they'd just gone up, and given that I was on the cover, *Savvy* must have had their reasons. But the hoardings came down.

I'd have to find validation somewhere else. I'd have to heal for real.

After the end of the relationship, it took me ten years to speak to Alyque again. I don't think I ever forgave him, not really. But we found a way to coexist. I saw him often, up until his death in November 2018. We spoke on the phone. A lot of the celebrations in our lives – birthdays, the kids' birthdays – were shared. And some of my resentment lingered. It still does. We had a long association. The relationship didn't invalidate the resentment.

In those last few months of 2018, I saw him quite regularly – one of a handful of people who did.

Time comes a circle, and yet we're never the same.

He could irritate the hell out of me. And I never idolized him the way I once did. But we had a place in each other's lives. With some form of equanimity.

~

My 'story' remained confined to those transcripts for the duration of the 1980s. Ever so gradually, it began to take on the shape of a larger project: a book that would tell the story of my life. I began writing in earnest on the 27th of April 1998. I had told myself I would. I had promised friends like Dinesh Thakur that I would. In the weeks after Alyque left, Protima Bedi dragged me to a series of astrologers, palmists, shadow readers, tarot-card diviners and clairvoyants. Each of them suggested I make a record of my feelings, that I distil those experiences.

So, I began. But excuses came easy. I set down an account of my early years and paused. That pause became a halt, then a stop and then years passed. I needed a computer, I told myself, so I wouldn't have to retype, cancel, correct, get my hands dirty with carbon. I worried about wasting paper, you see. The computer duly arrived, and I learnt to surf the internet and to send emails.

Dust gathered over the 'book'.

I didn't know if I dared. I didn't know if I could say the things I wanted to say.

I also paused because the 'early years' were fine. There were details in the later years – about myself, about people I love, about people I cared for at one point – that I shied away from. I didn't know how much I wanted to reveal.

So the past remained in the corner. Like a body with a sheet thrown over it.

I came back to the project in 2011. I knew now why I had stopped. Maybe I was still looking for approval back then. Maybe I didn't want to be judged. But now, this book has a simple sense of purpose: time is running out. I feel that keenly. The endgame has begun. There will be no stalling now – there is no opportunity.

So, to those who spurred me to finish, you have my gratitude.

Thank you, Jerry. Thank you, Satya. Thank you, Shanta.

~

I've lived in the same apartment for fifty-one years. I moved in on the 1st of January 1970. Alyque and I shared it for twelve of the thirteen years we were together. When he moved out, he left behind a shell that became a silo, a way-station en route to somewhere else, with only my son and I left to mark the passage of … love, a monument, an accident, something.

We populated it, Quasar and I. The walls – bare when Alyque left, taking his paintings with him – belong to us now. They are a record of our lives: stills from rehearsals and performances, paintings – gifts from visionary friends and artists, and photographs of family. The curtains in the living room used to be banners painted for the shows my son directed in college, repurposed, living history.

This is home. We made it so.

Here is a list of jobs I've held, to make it so: I started my career as a sub-editor with the British Information Service (BIS). Then a sub-editor for the BBC. A radio host along the way, first in England and then in India. A copywriter, a model coordinator, an account executive. A newsreader on television. A columnist. A casting director. A media consultant. An actor for over sixty years.

Also: daughter, sibling, friend, wife, mistress, aunt, mother.

My family and friends will disagree with some of what is recounted here. Maybe even a lot of it. But that's okay. This is *my* life, warts and all (a phrase I first heard from the late Richard Attenborough).

2

THIS IS WHAT I remember:

My name is Dolly Rawson. I am four years old. The year is 1947. I live with my maternal grandparents and my Rani Aunty and Samoo Mamu, my mother's only brother.

'Home' is a two-storey municipal dispensary. The building is yellow. I remember this very distinctly. We live in Deputy Ganj, near Sadar Bazaar and Qutub Road in Old Delhi, pronounced 'Dipti', like tea on trains. Sadar Bazaar is a Muslim area and Dipti Ganj is a Marwari area. I don't need to be told this. It is something that I have just absorbed.

We live in one of the three flats above the dispensary. The doctor, the compounder and the nurse – all Christian women – live in these flats, with their families. My grandmother – Rahael Solomon – is the combination nurse and midwife. We are, therefore, somehow lesser to the families of the doctor and the compounder. This is also something I just pick up.

Many rich Hindus live in Dipti Ganj. Marwari men in crisp, immaculate dhotis and women in starched, billowing organza or cotton sarees, always laden with gold jewellery. I watch them through the scratches in the windows that have been painted dark green. Every single window has been painted dark green. I peep through the same scratches when I see bodies lying on the street during the Partition riots. I scramble from scratch to scratch as a mob chases a victim.

Freedom is not without its costs. No one has to tell me this either.

~

I was born in Kohat, Peshawar on the 10th of March 1943. A Piscean, born into a Protestant family, in what is now Pakistan. Whole thing upside down: wrong sign, wrong religion, wrong country. As a child, I would have happily changed any of those three facts.

My mother, Dora, was my grandmother's second child. My grandmother had four children. Lovey, the eldest, was a private nurse. Over the years, Lovey Aunty worked with a number of VIPs in Delhi, including the then prime minister, Jawaharlal Nehru. She earned a great deal of money and goodwill – by far the strongest currency in Delhi. Lovey Aunty *felt* rich. She was a 'sethani', arrogant, with a sharp tongue. She worked very hard but most of what she made, she spent paying off the debts her two sons racked up across the city.

Lovey Aunty had five children in all: three sons and two daughters. She was married to Eric Jackson. He was a clerk in the Education Department, an intelligent, well-read man trapped in a dull job. To us, he was 'Moon' Uncle – the life and soul of every family gathering. One Palm Sunday, he refused to hail a taxi for Church. He insisted on riding a donkey because 'that's the way Jesus did it ...' He was the first truly irreverent man I ever met. Moon Uncle made me laugh, even when he was being vindictive or vulgar, and he was both, a lot.

He had a nickname for everyone. I was 'Badi Dolly' and Cynthia – his daughter, born three months after me – was 'Chhoti Dolly'. There was a routine, an entire sequence of abhinaya that accompanied either name, every single time he addressed one of us. The man should have been in the theatre.

He died in 1972. I still miss him.

Of my Nani's children, only Rani Aunty went to university. She graduated with a bachelor's degree in Hindi from Indraprastha College, Delhi and then went to the Lahore Christian College for her teacher's training. She returned to do her prabhakar (basically, a postgraduate degree) in Hindi. Of course, we had a rather dim view of her expert knowledge of Hindi in those early post-Independence years because it was, you know, *Hindi*. What can I say? I never claimed we weren't idiots.

My mother was also a trained nurse, but she never practised. My father, David, married her in 1939 and marched her off to the distant wilds of Air Force camps. For the majority of the Second World War, they were classified as 'non-family' and posted to remote locations because they didn't have any kids yet.

~

My mother had four children in five years. I was the eldest, born in 1943, and my sister Pam was the youngest, born in 1948. In the time-honoured Indian tradition, I was farmed out to my maternal grandparents. My parents had to send me away because there were, eventually, too many kids to look after.

I'd love to report an idyllic childhood, but the truth is I was a rotten kid. I threw tantrums constantly. I was 'ziddi' in the worst way. I terrorized my grandparents and my aunt. I wouldn't go to bed unless my aunt rocked me to sleep, even when I was five or six years old. She painstakingly put my hair in curling pins every night, so I could go to school with my best Shirley Temple hairdo. I kicked plates of food I didn't like. My grandfather worked as a tailor. He was prosperous, and he brought home baskets of apples or grapes because I demanded them. I didn't know, or care, that these were items of great luxury – food for the rich or the well-connected. In India, in those days, the two were interchangeable.

I adored my grandmother. Every day, she made me little utensils from the mud left over from layering her oven. I sat beside her as she stitched – and sometimes made rag dolls for me – or as she cooked, squatting on the kitchen floor.

I can't remember her *not* working. She was always busy. Nani didn't waste her time. Ever. Every moment was accounted for. Maybe that's what freedom meant to her: time. Time that was *hers*.

She ran a tight ship. The house in Dipti Ganj was spotless. Shoes were discouraged indoors. There was a huge mattress on the floor in the living room, covered always with a pristine white sheet. There was also a single table and two chairs for those 'special' (or 'spoilt') visitors who couldn't – or wouldn't – sit on the floor. My father was one of these exceptions.

In addition to the living – or 'outside' – room and the kitchen, there was the 'inside' room. Two beds, trunks (with bedding folded and draped atop them) and a large, incongruous mirror in an ornate frame on a wooden stand. Years later, I would see something similar in a production of Jean Genet's *Maids*. The kitchen opened out onto a veranda with jharokhas and a tiled courtyard. When the sun came through the jaalee, the floor would become a glittering latticework of shadows. Every evening, we stole my grandmother's flat 'washing' stick and played cricket on the terrace. It drove her mad. Nani did all the chores herself. We had no domestic help. We ate with our hands – we had no cutlery.

When my grandfather returned from work in the evening, his hookah would be waiting for him. If I close my eyes, I can still see Nani in her white cotton saree, bent over her ornate 'paan daan', with its compartments for paan leaves and betel nuts, cracking and splitting supari with her sarauta. Her gleaming brass 'peek daan' (spittoon) was the one thing my grandmother would have killed for, apart from shoes in the kitchen of course. Chewing supari and spitting that thin, dark red stream into the 'peek daan' was her only real indulgence, the only luxury she allowed herself. It was eventually oral cancer that claimed her life at the age of eighty.

But those are the sounds I remember: the burble of the hookah and the crunch-clack of the sarauta. My grandmother spitting into the 'peek daan' occasionally. My Nana reading Hindi, haltingly. It was the only language he could read, in contrast to my Nani and her children, all of whom read and wrote Urdu fluently.

~

Rani Aunty never married. There were always tragic stories of a doomed romance – some handsome young man who married another – but details were scarce. So I don't know how much of it was true.

She was the good daughter, the gold standard. She looked after her parents. She looked after my ne'er-do-good Samoo Mamu, who abandoned his life with a pretty nurse-wife, Pauline, and settled down instead with Suzie, the (admittedly) livelier, attractive daughter of a cook, and sired three sons in rapid order. Samoo Mamu's (new) family was brought into the fold and gladly accepted, but it was Rani Aunty who supported them financially. What happened to Pauline, I never did find out.

Rani Aunty taught Hindi at the Convent of Jesus and Mary School for over thirty-five years. She was a revered teacher, everyone's favourite. After she retired, she tutored Priyanka and Rahul Gandhi at 1, Race Course Road, during their father's tenure as the prime minister. She continued to live in Delhi, but her family was slowly bleeding her dry monetarily. Finally, when she turned eighty in 2004, I convinced her to move to Mumbai. It wasn't possible for me to set her up in any of our homes, but we got her a lovely room at the YWCA in Andheri. She lives there, teaching students and helping strangers, loved by all and visited by her 'real' family as often as is possible. She remains that unique, unaffected woman, and my earliest, longest-serving inspiration.

~

Every once in a while, we were herded into a tonga, which took us to the Baptist Mission Church in Chandni Chowk, near the Red Fort. Apart from this visit to the church, we were almost a Hindu household. We never cooked beef or pork at home. Our lifestyle was simple, the tonga ride was a luxury.

Nani was born Muslim. Her father converted the family to Christianity. My grandfather, on the other hand, was born Kishen Singhand, near Ajmer in Rajasthan. He was separated from his family during a famine when he was about twelve. Christian missionaries were the only people who offered him shelter. They first named him Suleiman and then anglicized it to Patrick Solomon.

Who I was – a Christian – and where I came from – a lack of privilege – were both sources of great embarrassment to me when I was young. Being 'Christian' meant we were either cooks or bearers, or anti-nationalists who had sold out to the British for a tin of milk or rice. In North India, they bestowed us with the derogatory terms 'Native Christians' or 'Rice Christians'.

Within the Christian community, it was another story. Dr Mrs Sinclaire, who lived in the same building as we did, and her husband, a professor at St. Stephen's College, and – by extension – her two daughters were superior to us because of their professions. Next to them lived the compounder, Mrs Dennis, and her family (two daughters and a son, and a husband with a perpetual, benign smile). They muttered 'Praise the Lord' constantly and hosted religious gatherings in their flat. And we'd see and hear people raising their arms and performing a 'bottom's up' routine by touching their heads to the ground, chanting (yup) 'Praise the Lord'. They were Presbyterians, and their *faith* was better than ours. Another story, same ending.

I've always had a profound sense of *un*-belonging. I was on the wrong side of the class divide. I was insecure, I was embarrassed about who I was, and I was embarrassed about being embarrassed about my family. I had a need for constant affirmation. For approval. For acceptance. I reinvented myself constantly. I found things that made me the centre of attention.

I was always going to be susceptible to a certain kind of relationship, to a certain kind of man. I've chased love. I've chased love, had it taken from me again and again, hunted it down to the place where the rainbow ends.

And then I think of my father.

~

Daddy *was* David Copperfield. Dickens, not the magician.

His parents were hounded out of Peshawar, because a Pathan had married a Christian girl. So my grandfather, Dr Roshan Khan, took up an assignment on a tea plantation in Burma and attempted to restart his medical practice.

My grandparents were happy, maybe, for just a brief while. They were expecting their first child when Roshan died, much too young, the victim of a snakebite.

His pregnant widow, Ummed, travelled some eight hundred miles to India, in a caravan from Burma. She collapsed somewhere near the arid plains of Palwal – about thirty miles out of present-day Delhi – and was taken to the nearby Christian Mission Hospital run by Miss Evelyn Rawson.

Daud Roshan Khan was born a few months later, on the 1st of December 1912. Mother and newborn son lived in an area that was mostly jungle. Hearsay has it that Ummed was bitten by a jackal and succumbed to the wound when my father was just a few months old. She had crossed into India a refugee and, with her death, we lost all links with my father's antecedents in Peshawar. All my father inherited was the tin trunk his mother had brought with her. A handful of belongings and a fistful of stories that may or may not have been true.

Miss Rawson took over Daud Roshan Khan's upbringing with the limited resources at her disposal. She never adopted him. He went to the Gange High School in Delhi, where he remained until the age of five, then to the United Christian School (also in Delhi) and then finally to the Baptist Mission High School in Agra for his matriculation in 1931.

Daddy told us stories of his youth when we were a little older. The orphaned kids were admitted to the Gange High School, and made to work in the hostel to earn their subsidy. Part of their duties included serving in the dining room. He and some of the other orphans would wait for the rich girls to throw away half-eaten mangoes or pieces of melon, and then descend on these to savour what little could still be squeezed out.

Once, because of some petty misdemeanour at school, he was locked up in the kitchen pantry. During his brief incarceration, he ate mountains of jaggery and ghee because they were things he'd only heard about but never tasted. He was six years old.

His punishment escalated as a result. The matron tied him to the veranda railing as one would a dog. He found some shards of glass from a broken window within the radius of his leash. He whiled away his sentence doodling on sand, creating whorls and patterns and designs. Later that evening, the principal of the school stumbled upon this mandala on his way home and was so impressed he ordered my father's immediate release.

In Agra for his matriculation, at the Baptist Mission High School, young Daud watched aeroplanes take off and land at the Air Force base and dreamt of being a pilot. He answered a recruitment advertisement in the paper and joined the Air Force as a Non-Combatant Apprentice Labourer, on a salary of twelve rupees a month. His first job was stencilling number plates on planes and defence transport.

That was in 1932. He put down Miss Rawson as his guardian on the application form. And to make his name easier to pronounce, he readily agreed to change it to 'David'.

Daud Roshan Khan became David Rawson.

He excelled at field hockey and football, and represented the Services in both. He never spoke of his academic prowess. He drifted by on sport and on his affability. It was that kind of a world back then.

Daddy was always very skilled with his hands. Maybe because it was all he had as an orphan – his hands, the scraps around him and his imagination. So he manufactured these minute, magnificently detailed worlds. Every year in school, I always had the best maps and charts, illustrated and coloured by my father. After he retired, he whittled model aircraft out of cigar boxes to pass the time. Everyone in the family has these intricate, hand-carved Tiger Moths, Spitfires, Harvards and helicopters, with each of our birth dates stencilled in place of registration numbers.

~

In 1933, my father applied for a transfer from the Royal Air Force to the newly established Indian Air Force. The request was granted, but there had been a large number of applications and until the transfers became effective, the British government decreed that all Indian Apprentices in the RAF would have to wear a 'cullah', a mandatory turban. At that time, my father was a Learner in Lahore, the lowest rank in the Air Force. But he refused to comply. Eventually, four men had to hold him down while a British sergeant grappled with him, trying to get the turban onto his head. My father socked the sergeant in the jaw and was promptly rewarded with a seven-day detention in the Punjab Regiment. The guards called him 'O-Quaidi' as they walked him out, barefoot, in December, to work on their vegetable garden.

Daddy had his fans, even in detention. He was a hockey champ for the RAF, he sketched and drew very well, he spoke English and he was the first literate Indian to join the ranks. He was a firm favourite of the officers in his Regiment. The man who'd been forced to discipline him sent him magazines and sweets during that week.

For six days, my father turned to his work in the way only he could. His locker and its meagre contents – his shirts, socks and 'kerchiefs – were always meticulous. And now he'd been handed a larger canvas. The vegetable patch bloomed. Rows of carrots and cauliflowers acquired Teutonic order. The landscaping may as well have been laser-cut. His efforts earned him a day's reprieve from his detention. He had his Saturday night on the town.

Unbeknownst to all and sundry, he returned to the garden late that night to put the finishing touches on his project.

On Sunday morning, a truckload of friends, admirers, supporters and colleagues turned up to escort Daddy back to camp after a detention well-served. They were greeted by a scene of devastation.

My father had either half-eaten, or severed and destroyed, every carrot and cauliflower. And he had replanted turf over the soil he had so carefully weeded and cleared over the past six days. He walked out, detention served and point made.

We may not have inherited his skill with his hands, but we all inherited his cussedness and his determination. The Rawsons are Olympic-level obstinate.

~

Daddy eventually rose to chief equipment officer in Cochin, Delhi, Secunderabad and Kanpur. He retired as wing commander from the Air Force Headquarters in Delhi. He was in charge of tenders. He could have amassed a fortune if he'd wanted. All he would have needed to do was ensure that certain suppliers were awarded certain contracts. In return for a few 'favours'. Those 'favours' might have been a car, radiograms, refrigerators, carpets, holidays to exotic hill stations or just plain cold cash.

As kids, we *yearned* for those things – any or all of them. But Daddy was resolute, much to the chagrin of several commanding officers, many of whom would have welcomed 'cuts' from the huge supply orders he commissioned over the years – be they trucks or tyres, or regulation socks for the Air Force, rations and household items, or spares for aircraft and furniture for the officers. (This is, after all, the country that had a *fodder* scam – tens of millions of rupees spent feeding countless herds of *imaginary* livestock.)

Our home remained spartan. We didn't even have a bank account. Honesty and integrity were drilled into us like we were an unruly vegetable patch.

Daddy had Mum, and that was enough for him. Wilson Samson, the principal of his school, was my mother's cousin. He brought Daddy home to Nani's one Christmas. And there David met Dora and fell in love. Thereafter, my mother made all the major decisions: schools, choice of subjects, pocket money, clothes, hand-me-downs, films to watch, suitable friends, and – incredibly, and crucially – our visits to the theatre. She was also the sociable one. Daddy was a loner. He was a handsome, respected, somewhat feared officer with few friends. He simply came home and handed over his princely pay packet to my mother. That was it. They were devoted to each other. They never argued. There was no dissent.

That was the idea of marriage and togetherness I inherited.

When my sister Esmie was born in 1944, my father received his commission to become an officer of the Royal Indian Air Force. Some might say that it was just (and long overdue) reward for his unflinchingly honest work ethic. But, because we were Indian, the credit was all Esmie's. She was the 'lucky' one.

My parents and I were never close. It was my grandmother and my aunt who became my role models while I was out on loan.

3

MY REGULAR COMPANIONS in Dipti Ganj were my cousins Cyril and Cynthia, who lived a ten-minute tonga ride away in Sadar Bazaar, and Uma and Enid Dennis, the compounder's children. I played 'Doctor-Doctor' with the Dennis kids, usually receiving injections in the buttocks while Uma pressed paisa coins into my belly button by way of diagnosis.

Things were a little less scientific with Cyril, who, at ten, was four years older than me. There was some feverish activity under the blankets, and during tonga rides to the Christmas and Easter melas at Roshanara and Qudsia Gardens. It was basic, healthy curiosity. And it felt good. We tried again when I was twelve. I was living with my parents in Kanpur by now and I was visiting Rani Aunty in Delhi. Cyril would have been sixteen. The charm had worn off. We were more mature. The Church had plonked itself in the middle of our thinking. A healthy interest in the opposite sex had become problematic.

Guilt is a strange thing. As a mother, I understand it's a powerful deterrent, second only to fear. But as a woman, I also know how easy it is to exploit. In India, the words 'what will people think' can be very persuasive.

Guilt can also be a damn good motivator.

At the age of four, I smuggled home a hymn book from Presentation Convent School, hidden down the front of my tunic. I liked the morning assembly and the songs we sang. I don't think I could read. But I wanted to own that book. And lo and behold, God sent one of Samoo Mamu's friends, a police inspector, home that very evening. And lo and behold, I was struck down by high fever and hot flashes until I worked up the courage to confess my crime to my aunt, and the priceless book was produced and duly returned.

~

Holidays meant the reappearance of parents and siblings. My family would inevitably have become strangers in the three months I hadn't seen them. And for the period of the vacation, I would cease to be the centre of attention. If my parents came visiting, my grandparents and aunt encouraged me to buy presents for them. I was always possessive about my things – we didn't have much growing up, and my toys were my bully's spoils in Delhi. One Diwali visit, within hours of her arrival, a three-year-old Esmie – then called Pilloo – gave the tablecloth a cheerful yank and destroyed a bunch of clay toys I loved.

I didn't like her. I didn't like my family. I didn't want to be with them.

At other times, I would visit my parents. In '48, I went to Cochin, where my father was the station commander of 11 MTSU. The compound or the house, I don't remember which, had huge barrel-shaped gates topped with barbed wire. Our idea of fun was to either get a running start and hop onto a gate and 'ride' it, or to find someone who'd give you a push. There was something exhilarating about those few seconds. We clung on and whooped for joy as the heavy metal gate swung closed or open. In a child's imagination, you were practically flying.

When it was Esmie's turn, I pushed too hard. It might have been an accident. I doubt it. She fell and cut her nose. She carries the scar to this day, although it's much less prominent now, a charming little feature that you'd strain to notice. The blood probably alarmed me. But there was also satisfaction. She was the fairer one, the lucky one, the pretty one, the one close to my mother, the good one, the gentle one.

I was the dark one. The other one.

~

It's strange, the things we remember.

A picnic to Alwaye, in a three-tonne truck, with senior officers and their families. At some point during the day, the kids peered through the hatch into the cab of the truck to find the well-built South Indian driver masturbating.

There was a sheen to him. His urgency excited us. We wanted to watch this strange ritual. But we knew, instinctively, that this action, what he touched and how he touched it, was private. We kept it a secret from our parents.

~

It was during the same trip to Cochin that we received news of Mahatma Gandhi's death. I remember rushing out of the house, almost as if we'd heard the air-raid siren. Everyone in the camp streamed towards the only radio on the compound. I remember the hush that descended on the huddle as the news was relayed to us. Grief radiated from the transistor, like a stain, like a stone had been dropped into still water.

~

I began living with my parents again when my father was posted to Palam Air Force Station, Delhi. The year was 1950 and I was seven years old. My Shirley Temple curls were the first thing to go, followed by every other one of the habits that Nani and my aunt had pandered to. I spent most of my time at home being told that I was a spoilt, ungrateful little girl. While that was certainly true, it didn't do very much for my relationship with my mother. I was scared of her. I never came to love her in the way she expected. And never had her love me in the way *I* wanted. I know now I craved her approval. But she preferred my siblings. They were closer to her. And much easier to handle.

Rani Aunty had laid a solid foundation as far as schoolwork went. I never topped class, but I was always in the running for it. My mother boasted about my marks and my rank outside the house. At home, it wasn't ever good enough.

She kept an immaculate house. Our uniforms were always crisp, white and starched. We seemed to glow when we left for school in the morning. We drove to the Convent of Jesus and Mary, near the New Delhi Gol Dak Khana from the Air Force Camp in Palam (near Dhaula Kuan) in a three-tonne truck. We were always the first kids there.

All the students lived in terror of Miss Pauli. She was an Irishwoman – stiff hair dyed jet black, a slight, bent figure who ruled the school with an iron fist. They were strict, those Irishwomen, and Miss Pauli was the strictest of the lot. She was also in charge of the annual PT display. Early one morning, walking down the corridor to class, I heard that voice boom out: 'You! Come here.'

I went.

'What class are you in?'

I probably couldn't get an answer out. Just as well …

'Why are you not in the PT display?'

I was still speechless, but I suddenly wasn't so afraid any more.

'Your uniform is perfect. I want you to come for practice from today.'

I was in the first standard, and I was leading the march-past soon after. Life with my mother wasn't all bad.

~

Our barracks were squat, U-shaped buildings, with four families to a four-room unit. So our living quarters were cramped, but around us was the entire universe of the Air Force base. And being the children of officers, being middle class, we had the run of the place.

I remember playing 'King and Queen' with the other kids at camp. As the eldest, I was always Queen Elizabeth, while Esmie was Princess Margaret, and our brother and the other kids were guards and ladies-in-waiting, members of the court.

The window ledges of our living quarters would then magically become the deck of a ship. Again, as the eldest, I was the captain of a merchant vessel or a brave naval mission, trying to rescue the unfortunate victims of a shipwreck (see: the aforementioned members of court) from the raging seas four feet below me. One such enthusiastic victim, heavy for his age, managed to topple the Captain off her bold perch as she attempted to pull him aboard. I crashed headlong into the gravel and opened up an enviable gash on my forehead. That was the first time I needed stitches (not the last, alas), and the resulting scar has been a lifelong identification mark on admission forms and on my passport.

Palam is also where I discovered the theatre. My first performance, ever, was as Krishna in an Independence Day function at the

Officer's Mess at the age of seven. I was painted the right kind of blue and was wrapped up in the right kind of saree, and my heart was *pounding*.

The curtain opened, slowly. And I took my first-ever step on stage.

The saree promptly unravelled.

The curtain closed so my costume could be tidied up. The start of the performance remained in limbo – the greatest pregnant pause you could imagine. And the audience, realizing that they'd just witnessed a seven-year-old girl suffer a wardrobe malfunction, began to applaud. They did it in solidarity, to show their support.

I didn't hear it that way. I just heard applause. For me. I was hooked.

~

Our parents made it abundantly clear that there was plenty we couldn't say or do. But our parents, in typical Indian fashion, also neglected to tell us there were things that we should never put up with.

Our cook, Devi Ram, often masturbated in our presence. Our bearer, Kishan Singh, often 'played' with our private parts on the pretext of lulling us to sleep when our parents were out.

A Flight Lieutenant lived with his wife and three sons in one arm of 'U' Barrack. His great passion was restoring cars and watches. As kids, we'd crowd around him, fascinated by this big man delicately probing these machines, gently figuring out ways to make them work. You might say he was a fiddler. The big treat, for all of us, was when he'd favour one of the girls with a piggyback ride. He'd swing us onto those broad shoulders and chat with our parents, as easy as you like, while he tinkered with our clits and vaginas.

I was eight years old. So, less favoured than the younger ones.

But, my goodness, we vied to be chosen for that special ride.

He'd often pack a whole lot of us into his antique convertible and then 'test-drive' down deserted camp roads. Esmie once returned from one of those 'adventures' bruised and crying and very shaken. The Flight Lt said she'd fallen out of the car. I suspect he tried to molest her and she'd leapt out of the running car. Scared, he brought her home.

Upstanding pillar of the community, he was. Very well-respected.

We were all under the age of eight. Not one of us felt secure enough to tell our parents.

Guilt. That wonderful thing. Victims become perpetrators, because eight-year-olds shouldn't be vying for a special ride. It must make *them* bad somehow.

Those little girls were asking for it, weren't they?

Weren't they?

~

In August 1952, my father was transferred to Begumpet – the Air Force Base in Secunderabad. We trooped along to St. Anne's English High School for a ritual that would become very familiar: entrance tests. I was in the third standard, as far as I can recollect. As part of the admission process, I was taken to Miss Queenie Gilbert's class and asked to read out a page in English. She waved me quiet after a few sentences and turned to the class.

'That is the way to read English,' she said. The students applauded dutifully. I was admitted to the school and we swapped Miss Pauli for Miss Gilbert.

The tradition of march-pasts continued at St. Anne's. On the 24th of October 1952, the school celebrated United Nations Day. (This was before the UN had become the sad little side-show it is now, sort of like a drunken uncle who's loud but comfortably tuned out.) I led the school contingent that year, carrying the UN flag and wearing the UNO logo over my uniform.

I have to admit, I liked the attention. But, also, my generation was unabashedly political. By this, I mean we were interested in governance and identity – in the decisions that affected the way we lived and who we were as a young country. We felt like we had a stake in the whole enterprise. 'Politics' wasn't the dirty word it is today.

I remember, vividly, the day in 1954, when Prime Minister Nehru's motorcade drove past the school. And although we were prompted to wave, I don't think we needed much encouragement. Panditji was in an open-top car, and he waved back. Then he tossed his garland towards us. I raised my hand, as if in a dream, and caught it.

I've been to some extraordinary places. Met many remarkable people. Had a rich, varied life. The memory of catching that garland still sends a chill down my spine. It remains one of the most important experiences of my life.

School went well. I secured the fabled 'double-promotion' in my second year at St. Anne's, graduating from standard four to standard six. But that also meant I was an eleven-year-old in a class full of thirteen-year-olds. A lot of them were Anglo-Indians – just a tad more 'liberated' than I was. The hushed conversations in class were generally about three things I knew very little about: dance socials, boys and periods.

I'd started menstruating at nine years and three months. But I was still embarrassed by the fact of my 'chum' and pretended to know nothing of the gloriously inaccurate theories that were brandished about, like the spoils of war. So that meant a few more years of soiled uniforms and bruised groins and thick homemade pads. Expensive, imported Kotex sanitary napkins were available but it was another five years before we could afford them and were sophisticated enough to use them.

~

Secunderabad was a proper, time-honoured introduction to show business. Or whatever they call that kick in the teeth.

Auditioned for the lead in *Snow White and the Seven Dwarfs*? Played a dwarf.

Auditioned for the St. Patrick's Day Fete? Played the hour hand of passing time.

Longed to play Titania in *A Midsummer Night's Dream*? Watched the very European Pauline Speechley play it much worse than I would have, to my mind at least.

I remained on the fringes, but I was well and truly smitten. Debates, plays – I did it all. I'd recite 'O Captain, My Captain' or 'Casablanca' or William Wordsworth's 'The Daffodils' at elocution contests, word perfect, but unsure about what the poems *actually* meant. Inevitably, I came second or third, never first, still looking up, looking in, at people who were just better than I was. I loved it all – the warmth of the applause and the little attention these activities got me.

There was no *plan*, not back then. Just getting *in* was great. It got you recognition. I couldn't depend on sports, I had zero aptitude for it (although I was made Captain of the Gold House at St. Mary's Convent in Kanpur much later, but that had nothing to do with my sporting prowess). I knew by then that I came from a background, a family, that would never put me centre-stage simply because of *who* I was. We were very middle class, and we were just *getting on with it*, with our lives.

We were everything that was right *and* wrong with Nehru's India. Hopeful, upright, educated. Hopelessly naive, unconnected, timid. A minority to boot. Socialist fodder.

We dreamt of the mundane. Because mundane would be a step-up. That was it. That was what our mother expected of us. That was what we expected of ourselves.

Drama and elocution and all, that was all right but it wasn't going to *lead* to anything.

~

The Air Force Base in Secunderabad was miles from anywhere. We lived in a bungalow in Sanat Nagar, and the journey to school and back was a four- or five-step process, a cross between twenty-four hours at Le Mans and a triathlon. Required about the same kind of stamina too.

We had to be presentable in the mornings, so we left with my father in his pale-blue Vauxhall. He drove us to his office in Begumpet, the halfway mark, checkpoint one. A Sergeant then drove us to school in Marredpalli.

The return journey was more complicated.

The car would bring us back to the Begumpet office. And then an unfortunate sepoy would make *two* trips on his bicycle, ferrying two Rawson kids at a time. One of the shortcuts on the return trip was crossing a wide, dry culvert, where we'd dismount and walk. If we'd only had to ski, we could have advertised the trip as an adventure holiday.

So, of course, despite the strenuous physical activity getting to and returning from school, I fractured my foot in innocuous fashion while on the playground *in* school. We were rehearsing for the Republic Day Parade. The PT Teacher, the rather shapely Miss Witherspoon, who was Anglo-Indian but claimed to be white, and whose mother (legend has it, so *of course* it was gospel truth) was a lady-in-waiting for Queen Elizabeth, blew her whistle to start the march-past. I suddenly found that I couldn't lift my left foot.

I was rushed to the infirmary, my father was summoned and I was sent home. And then promptly dispatched to the Air Force MI Room. The hospital was spotless, and it hummed with order and efficiency. I can't remember the exact diagnosis – I had cracked something near my toes? – but I had to wear a cast for three months. We resumed the trek through the culvert on the way home while my foot was encased in plaster of Paris. The bottom of the cast quickly wore away.

~

I can almost reach out and touch that house in Secunderabad, and our time there. For some reason, I have a crystal-clear memory of collecting pods from the row of cotton trees in the backyard during the long summer holidays. We'd separate the seeds from the silk wool and, all year round, we'd sleep in soft pillows, only to repeat the exercise the next summer.

My grandparents, Cyril, Cynthia and Rani Aunty came to visit. We even took a trip to Aurangabad, travelling 'unreserved' in a third-class compartment, pushing and shoving, cramped and dirty, while our co-passengers spat out of the windows. It was all rather horrific. When Daddy was on duty, we shared the status that the Air Force accorded him. Off-duty, we were poor.

It rained all the way to Aurangabad. We arrived damp and sweaty, that unlovely combination, as if we'd emerged from a humid cave. And then had to wade to our accommodation – a dark, dank little 'dak bangla', which did little for our mood – through waist-deep water, luggage balanced on our heads like we were bearers in a jungle.

The trip to Ajanta and Ellora made it worthwhile. The Daulatabad Fort, with Ram's cannon (the Mendha Tope), on which we all posed for photographs. Bibi Ka Maqbara, Aurangzeb's Tomb – they all remain so vivid in my memory. Those trips made history a living thing. In retrospect, I'm glad my parents insisted on those excursions. They showed us the world, as best as they could. And, through their example, they made it okay that we weren't rich. We couldn't do five-star trips, but that wasn't going to stop us from heading out.

~

I remember a cool summer afternoon indoors, sitting on my father's lap. I rubbed my hand against his cheek.

'You bloody bastard,' I said to him. I had no idea what it meant.

He slapped me hard. I peed my knickers. More than anything else, I had caught him by surprise. It was the only time he ever hit me.

~

Secunderabad also witnessed one of the strangest, darkest passages of our childhood. My youngest sibling, Pam – named for Pamela Mountbatten – was born in Cochin in 1948. My parents finally got it right. Pam was calm, bright and sweet, the best of the Rawson siblings.

We lived in a four-bedroom house in Sanat Nagar. About five hundred yards down the road was the Sanat Nagar Club, with its perennially dry swimming pool. Our parents occasionally played an evening game of badminton with some of the Nawabs and their wives. As a matter of course, we'd spend that time running in and out of the pool. The pool was a ship, a cave, a strange land, an enemy hill – anything we needed it to be.

One summer evening, Pam wouldn't come out to play. We thought it was because my mother was a little under the weather. But my parents insisted I take Pam to the club. Halfway there, she stopped. She turned around and ran home, crying and mumbling. It took us a while to understand what she was saying: 'I can hear the dham-dham coming.'

She'd jammed her fingers into her ears. Even my father, who was very strong, couldn't get her to let go.

Pam ran a high fever – a hundred and four degrees – for a day or so. She began to slur. She'd stare at the person talking to her like she didn't know them. She insisted that every door, every window, every crevice and keyhole in her room be blocked. Sunlight, on no account, could be allowed to enter.

And Pam saw snakes. Snakes and rats, everywhere. Red snakes and green rats. Red snakes and green rats that slithered up cupboards, under beds, into clothes on pegs.

We emptied the room of all furniture. We stuffed paper and cloth into every gap we could see. Still, Pam was fearful. She wanted every single member of the family by her side, holding her tight.

The fever broke, but Pam wouldn't step out of her room, not even to go to the hospital. So, the doctors came to her.

To this day, I'm not sure what happened. Whatever it was that waited in the darkness, it terrified her. Pam didn't blink for over a year. She slept with her eyes wide open. All her tops and tunics had to be re-stitched, with slits up the back so she could slip her arms through the sleeves instead of pulling on the garment over her head. She couldn't risk that one moment of not knowing what was in front of her. She couldn't stand water, even to drink. A bath, or even a sponge bath, became a major hurdle. Inevitably, she became severely constipated.

By now, my parents were frantic. They tried every suggestion anyone had. The staff decided that Pam had been possessed by a spirit from the swimming pool. A few of them passed a chicken around her thrice, trying to cast the 'nazar' into the animal. The chicken died. Someone else tied a live frog to Pam's hand. The frog died. A few others passed a coconut around her, only to discover that the water in the coconut had dried up.

Friends brought charms and talismans. One of Daddy's colleagues, a fellow officer named Lancy Joseph, returned from Paris with bottled water from the shrine of Our Lady of Lourdes. A drop was duly added to the little water Pam drank or bathed in.

Very gradually, Pam made some progress. Twelve months passed before she could be persuaded to step out of her bedroom and into the adjoining room. Then the drawing room, and then the veranda. In the meantime, my father had applied for another bungalow in a different locality, on medical grounds. By the time the allotment came through, Pam had made a complete recovery and we moved to Begumpet.

~

The new house was called 'Astridoon', built by an Englishman for his daughter, Astrid, and it was the best house we ever lived in. Twenty-eight rooms on the ground floor, and twenty-three on the first floor, including servants' quarters; a practically infinite number of bathrooms, go-downs, pantries and dressing rooms. We even had a billiard room! I remember parquet flooring and a painting of Atlanta's Race on one of the walls.

We had the ground floor to ourselves. Outside, there were three fountains in the garden. Lotuses bobbed in the water like exquisite embroidery. And trees … trees all around, massive, comforting, heavily scented – pomegranate, mango, custard apple, guava and tamarind. On a hot, still, summer afternoon, lying in the garden, surrounded by the trees and the prize-winning roses, the cocktail of scent was enough to make you feel drunk.

Astridoon was a Gothic fever dream, as imagined by children. Much later, I would learn the term 'magic realism', slightly bemused that the two might be separate.

On Monday evenings, we'd gather round the radio to hear Hamid Sayani, who was the only Indian with an English show on Radio Ceylon, the *Ovaltine Amateur Hour*. On Friday nights, it was Preminda Premchand's 'A Date with You'.

~

Sweetie and Bobby Johnson were regular visitors at Astridoon. The Johnsons were old family friends of Rani Aunty. Their sister Dolly (also called Honey) was my aunt's best friend from college, and I'm told that I was named after her. Sweetie was an engineer with Deccan Airways, and Bobby was a cadet in the Air Force, a trainee pilot.

Although I called Sweetie 'Uncle', he replaced my cousin Cyril as the object of my affection. I must hasten to add this was all in my head. Sweetie always held my hand tight and showered me with gentle kisses on my forehead, and we took walks together, arm-in-arm, but he was very respectful, and it was all (heartbreakingly) *not* amorous in the least. I was eleven and totally smitten.

That was until Sweetie brought Marie home one evening. She was his landlady's daughter, and a few years my senior.

Sweetie's visits became infrequent, although we'd occasionally come home to find him and Marie cuddling somewhere on our extensive lawns. Bobby and the third brother, Robbie, (lovely as they were, I don't think anyone was putting *too* much thought into their names) continued to visit us. They were both twelve or thirteen years older than me, and my memory of that time is tinged with a desperate, aching sweetness. They were the world we wished to inherit – these strong, handsome, upstanding men – and yet, we were just a tad too young. Our infatuations were guileless and naive, deeply romantic and frustrating in just the right way.

Eventually, their term came to an end, and Bobby came to spend his last night with us.

In summers, we slept out in the garden, mosquito nets ranged over the beds, under the stars. Mummy, Daddy and Pam, two beds under one net; Esmie, Ritchie and I under the second; and Bobby, as the honoured guest, had a bed and mosquito net to himself. Our beds were a foot apart. He and I stuck our heads out from under the nets, held hands and whispered to each other all night, under that diamond-encrusted sky. God knows what we talked about. We were young.

He was gone the next morning. But I have never forgotten that night.

Pam returned to school. Life returned to normal. In the months leading up to August 1955, I was aware of a great deal of speculation about Daddy's next posting.

When his term in Palam ended, in 1952, I remember there were murmurs of London, Bombay or Secunderabad.

We got Secunderabad.

And towards the end of his term in Secunderabad, London and Bombay were mentioned again, along with Kanpur. By now I was old enough to understand what 'lobbying' meant. And old enough to understand that Daddy wouldn't lobby, that he *couldn't* lobby, for a post – he lacked that set of skills.

In August 1955, we moved to Kanpur.

4

ONCE AGAIN: A new city, mid-year. And again: the admission dance. As a stop-gap, we were all admitted to the Methodist High School, my first 'co-ed', in September 1955. I was twelve years old. Two months in, I received my first love letter. Terence Mendes, the hero of the class, slipped the note into my hand as I waited to board the Air Force Coach that would carry me back eleven miles to the Air Force Camp in Chakeri.

I read the letter on the way home. Terence was in love with me and wanted me to become his steady girlfriend. Holding that letter, I realized, was like holding a ticking bomb. First adrenaline, and then shock. Only bad girls received letters of this sort. By the time I got home, the hot flush had become a fever. I didn't tell my parents, but I never returned to Methodist High School. I was ill, and then we were into the Christmas holidays and I never saw Terence again. It was, perhaps, an early lesson in romance.

In January 1956, Esmie and I were admitted to St. Mary's Convent High School.

Almost immediately, I made friends with Purveen (Pisoo) Khory. I was in seventh standard, and Purveen and Esmie were both a year junior. The next year, I had another double promotion and Purveen's sister, Denaz, and I became classmates.

This set of friendships has lasted over sixty years, right to this day.

We had much in common: the mythical 'matches' that mean so much to kids. Both families had three sisters and a brother, in the same pecking order. And because Parsis followed two calendars, the usual one and the Zoroastrian one, my mother and Jeroo Aunty shared a birthday, Esmie and Purveen shared a birthday, and even our dogs shared a birthday with their brother Rustom.

Twelve years later, on the 16th of May 1969, when Denaz came to Bombay to attend my wedding, she pulled me aside.

'D'you know what day it is?' she asked. 'It's Cyrus's and my wedding anniversary.'

It was things like that.

We lived out of each other's homes. Their friends became our friends. We picked up that well-meaning sense of superiority that Parsis can possess, that hint of Gosh-Goodness-but-we're-just-telling-the-truth prejudice. But we also dropped some of our inhibitions. I'd never seen my mother in her bra, never less than fully dressed. I'd never seen my sister take a shower. It strikes me that we were embarrassed about our bodies and the fact that those bodies had needs and functions. We would never admit in public that we needed to use the toilet. Meanwhile, bathroom doors were never bolted at the Khorys. And Denaz, Purveen, Esmie and I all bathed together.

Pam and Ritchie were very much part of life at home. But we'd reached that juncture when our horizons had begun to expand rapidly. And the younger Rawsons were just 'kids'. Consequently, I was living two lives – one in the house and a different one outside.

Our summer distractions were Zarine and Froggy (Farrukh) Dhondy. Their parents were in Kanpur on an Army posting, and they'd come visit every summer from Wadia College in Pune. Every year, they hit the city like a last-ditch cavalry charge, the good guys showing up when it was almost too late.

They were the smart Poona Pack. They knew the good songs, the new ones. They introduced us to the culture of 'mixed' parties. They taught us to Jive, Cha Cha, Charleston, Rock 'n' Roll, and the euphoria of 'rockin' around the clock'. Zarine, in her starched buckram petticoats and hair pulled back into a ponytail, was the toast of the city. Froggy, in contrast, was knock-kneed, with extra-thick spectacles perched on his nose, but he machine-gun-quoted

Keats and Shakespeare. He was the first person who got me to look at the world differently – to see that there was more to it than the living-by-rote we were engaged in.

Those friendships, too, endure to this day.

Somewhere on the distant horizon, a new world glittered. I remember I became very self-conscious about my mother's English. Every time she said 'that was she said' at the end of a sentence, I died a little. And I hated myself for feeling that way. I knew *precisely* the sacrifices she made in order for us to have the best possible life. She balanced the budget, and her generosity, friendliness and charm allowed us to keep an open house for all our friends.

~

The Air Force Camp in Kanpur was called Chakeri. It had been culled from an area occupied by some twenty-two villages. None of the villagers were displaced, but the camp permanently altered the area. All of our domestic help came from the villages.

On summer afternoons, at the age of twelve or thirteen, I'd sneak out of the house while my parents took their afternoon siesta. I'd walk down to the village nearest the house and spend two or three hours playing teacher to the village kids. They lacked reading and writing. Also, I could boss people around. That seemed like a fair deal.

The villages were the archetype of rural India: ranged around a central pond, shaded by large neem and mango trees. Cool, airy huts with floors of packed earth; every other hut had layers of cow dung on the ground as well as the walls. Those homes always smelt familiar and genuine somehow – warm and slightly earthy. This was a time before the proliferation of plastic. Brass vessels gleamed everywhere. No sign of poverty, malnutrition or dirt. Bright, hard-working people. It was so simple, it was beautiful. And, in my memory, always, it is almost dusk, and the pond a pool of silken gold as I turned back one last time to wave to the kids before heading home.

Rani Aunty came to visit every summer. Much as we loved her – and she came with a suitcase loaded with beautiful gifts, without fail – her popularity always took a hit the morning after her arrival. We'd have to pull out our books and sit at lessons with her (on vacation, mind you!), apart from the two mornings a week when Esmie and I 'cycle-rickshawed' to school for piano lessons.

Afternoons, we devoured *Woman & Home* and *Woman's Own*, culled from the Officer's Mess. We were ardent fans of the serial 'Stairway to the Stars' and missing an issue, even a single issue, was cause for great despair. So much so, we regularly forgot we were supposed to mind the evening meal. We'd usually surface from that breathless dream to the smell of burning meat. And then get yelled at.

Early evenings during the vacations were spent watering the plants and the lawn. My mother was very proud of her garden. Inevitably, the chore ended in a water fight. We'd get properly drenched, knowing that we'd have to change into our evening wear. In summer, the beds would be laid out in the garden after we were done. The rest of the evening we recited poems and psalms and elocution passages such as 'the Lord is my Shepherd' and the Beatitudes.

Meals were a time for family. We ate together, around the dining table. Breakfast was easily the best time of the day. My mother read to us from the morning paper before we left for school, so that we'd be up-to-date on current affairs. We even had a forty-minute period set aside for current affairs every Saturday morning at school. Kids were encouraged to bring in a news item from the week's events and discuss it in class.

At lunch, especially during our holidays, we listened as my mother listed every last one of our considerable faults and flaws, and complained about tasks or chores we hadn't performed, or had performed badly. If Daddy was in, and my mother had his attention, these lists were works of art – cleverly constructed, wonderfully paced, devastatingly effective. There's a reason none of us trusted her very much.

Dinner was never exciting. We made do with meat curry and vegetables. Ironically, most of my friends would have killed for Ma's meat curry every night. They loved my mother's cooking. Denaz was a huge fan.

What *we* wanted, though, was to settle down to a feast from an Enid Blyton story. We wanted sausages. And bacon. And ham. And cutlets. And cheese and baked beans and chocolates. We grew up with two eggs between four at breakfast and two bananas between four after lunch.

One afternoon, Ritchie (then ten years old) grabbed one of the bananas on offer and clambered up to the corrugated tin roof of the NI barrack and gobbled the whole thing. I raised all hell. The ruckus woke Daddy from his afternoon nap. Daddy threatened to cane Ritchie. That shut us up. Daddy seldom lost his temper, but when he did, we were all afraid of him. Ritchie climbed down, shamefaced.

We never went hungry. We were safe, looked after and cared for. But we yearned for the little joys of wealth. We curated envy. We tended to it with great care and watched it blossom.

When friends came over, we swapped out frayed and faded sheets and bed covers for the ones in better condition. When Parvez Karangia, an eligible bachelor who visited us often, dropped in suddenly one summer evening, my cousin Cyril tried to embarrass us. We were laying out the beds in the garden, and Cyril dragged out the torn mattress on purpose. Parvez didn't even notice, but I could have died of shame.

We were quick to take offence, because we believed ourselves lacking, minus some intangible quality that made special people special.

~

Esmie fell ill. She had kidney trouble and missed a lot of the school term. Rani Aunty prevailed upon my mother to let Esmie study from home, rather than waste the year. My parents would save a year's school fees to boot. And so Esmie was packed off to live with Rani Aunty in Delhi.

This was a terrible decision. By this time, my aunt was living with her no-good brother, his wife and their three children, and her father, in a single eight-by-ten room. That was it – that one room. That was where they lived, cooked, bathed, studied, fought, wept. They had a veranda and access to a courtyard, but no proper bathroom – just a raised platform enclosed by a tin door, with a hole for 'deposits' into an open drain. The drain ran down the narrow lane, collecting other 'deposits' along the way.

Esmie went from the comfort of the Air Force Camp to the squalor of Delhi. She survived it, but she carried that bleakness inside her for a long time.

My mother, though, just wouldn't learn. For all her sacrifices, she was blind to the importance of higher education. To her, making money meant independence. And independence meant success. One had to get through school to be able to make money. That was it. That was the ultimate goal. University education was a pipe dream, an unimaginable luxury.

Unless you ranked in the top five in school, like I did. I was lucky because I formed my study habits under Rani Aunty, while my grandmother was in charge of my well-being. And I was damn obstinate. Esmie, and later Ritchie, never had a chance.

Ritchie was marched off to Rani Aunty's Gulag because he just wouldn't concentrate on his studies. My mother thought it best that he get through his matriculation as quickly as possible. As a consequence, Ritchie never had an extra-curricular life – the place where so many of us found our true calling. I also believe that being around a variety of teachers would have helped him. He passed his matric privately and returned to Kanpur for his intermediate. He failed, and my mother – in her haste to turn us all into breadwinners – didn't allow him to repeat the year.

Between the two sisters, Ritchie's mother and his aunt, they drove him away from education like they were on a mission. They terrorized him until all he had left was dread.

Ritchie first took up a job as a junior salesman. He then bounced from job to job, and ultimately took off on a Merchant Navy ship as a deck passenger (which meant he didn't have a cabin and was at the mercy of the elements). He left Bombay in 1969. He eventually settled in Los Angeles and continued to shuffle through professions. After many semesters in various courses in school in the US, he finally discovered he had a learning disability.

~

What of the other one, then? The dark one?

I grew up. Suddenly, it was the summer of 1957. A letter arrived from Bobby Johnson. He'd earned his 'wings' and would be passing through Kanpur en route to Calcutta. Rani Aunty agreed to take Esmie and me to the station to meet him and wave him through on his journey, as if he were a war hero. I wore my smartly tailored green Peter Pan Collar dress. Nothing else accentuated my 26-inch bust line and my 18-inch waist quite as well.

On a crackling hot summer day, we rickshawed to the station, twelve miles from the camp, through dust (endemic to Kanpur) that hovered like a cataract. I still remember the date. It was the 2nd of July. We waited on the platform. It was one of those afternoons that mark adolescence, a waking dream, burning with secret fever – waiting for someone we hadn't seen in years, aglow in the knowledge that I'd had a childhood crush on him. Of course, that made it easy to forget I was thirteen years and three months old.

The train pulled in. Bobby took one look at us and decided that he would break his journey for the night and continue the next day. And so we made the twelve-mile trip back to Chakeri, Bobby and I in one rickshaw, Esmie and Rani Aunty in the other. We held hands and sat glued to each other. Nothing unusual in that – the seats were thirty inches wide!

When the rickshaw pulled up at the house, squeals of surprise and delight rang out. Bobby was grabbed, pulled, hugged, pushed, pinched and passed from family member to family member like he was a special present. His unexpected arrival had upset the sleeping arrangements, though. The Officer's Quarters in Chakeri were essentially a line of eight rooms, all leading to a common veranda. A wall divided the eight rooms into two residences of four rooms each: two bedrooms, a dining room and a living room. One of the bedrooms was for our parents and one for the four of us. Each bedroom had an attached bathroom and a dressing room, which allowed for a degree of privacy. We had *two* extra guests that night – Rani Aunty and Bobby. But since Bobby was the chief guest that evening, he got the bed in the centre of the room, the one that Esmie and I normally shared.

By and by, the others fell asleep. Bobby inched towards my side of the bed. We held hands, and they must have been slick with sweat. We didn't care. Our fingers intertwined and we conversed all night in fervent whispers. God knows what we talked about. It must have felt incredible – adult and epic, and deeply personal. I doubt I heard much of it. My heart beat loudly, with his hand in mine, skin on skin, and blood coursed through my ears like never before.

At some point, he leant over and we kissed. My first kiss. Proper. Romantic. Intended. Not play.

I loved him then. Immediately, and forever. He had my heart.

Dawn crept up on us. In that light, everything was different. I wasn't a little girl any more.

Time changes when you're in love. Each moment stretches out like an eternity. But when you add up those moments, they're gone in the blink of an eye. Years pass, and yet everything retains that fantastic clarity, every minute, every smell and every colour, like today is the day after.

Dawn became mid-morning, and then it was time for Bobby to leave. As luck would have it, I went to bathe when Bobby walked into the dressing room to pack for his departure. We snatched a few more kisses and tight hugs – precious and life-changing. I was thirteen and he was twenty-six. It was a brand-new day, and it was also the end of the world. I still remember Bobby on the 10th of November every year – his birthday.

~

Every letter we wrote was first composed in 'rough', corrected by my mother and then copied onto ruled paper. Pretty soon, the contents of the draft I showed my mother began to differ from the actual letters I sent Bobby. There was, however, one insurmountable problem. The letters I got in return were read by all. Declarations of love were unlikely to be well-received around the dining table. What to do?

In a moment of inspiration, I sent Bobby my school's address. I urged him to write openly about his feelings. A few weeks later, I was summoned to the Principal's office. I wasn't allowed to receive any mail on the school premises, began Mother Rosalind. My heart sank, and I stammered my apologies. My life flashed before my eyes. But when Mother Rosalind handed me the letter, it was unopened. I barely heard her warning that it could never happen again.

I hid the letter inside the brown paper cover of Sir Walter Scott's *Quentin Durward* – my Senior Cambridge literature text. By now, I had a little more privacy at home. A six-by-eight veranda had been boarded up and served as my study-cum-bedroom. And it was here that I read and re-read Bobby's letter while the world slept. I relished every word. I read 'If I wait for you as I wish to, my life will be ruined' over and over again, enthralled and grief-struck. We had – like idiots – talked about getting married in 1965, after I'd completed my MA. That was eight years into the future. But this … this was doomed love, and that made it the best kind of love. I daydreamed about Bobby, night after night, undisturbed, with the dedication of a monk. That my love was also secret made it even more romantic.

That's all it should have been. Some star-gazing. A delightful story to tell people over a drink, twenty years down the line. But for one thing: a few months later, Bobby was transferred to Kanpur. He lived five hundred yards down the road.

We saw him almost every day. He passed our house on his way to work and would invariably pay us a visit on his way back home. I dare say we were a more welcome sight than the Officer's Mess. There was always my mother's meat curry. He became a member of the family.

It was the perfect con. Bobby wasn't an outsider, or a stranger. Everyone at home knew him, trusted him, loved him. And he was much older than me, which made even the prospect of a burgeoning romance seem absurd. My parents were usually a formidable unit. Bobby sat squarely in their blind spot. We became invisible.

Bobby would accompany us to the movies. I'd be 'allowed' to sit next to him, and he'd fondle my breasts while I covered my chest with my handkerchief. We stole kisses as we passed each other on the way to the bathroom, we brushed past each other in the house, just a little too close, we hugged a little too tight and too long.

Occasionally, we managed to get away. Bobby would pick me up on his motorbike, and we'd thunder down the narrow lanes to a secluded spot under a large neem tree. There was always a moment, after I hopped off the bike and Bobby swung the kickstand into place and turned off the ignition, just a moment when the two of us looked into each other's eyes in the sudden silence, aware that we were alone, even if it was for a handful of seconds. Just a boy and a girl, under a neem tree, somewhere far away.

Bobby would sweep me into his arms and kiss me.

We could have been the paperback cover of *Forever Amber* or *Wuthering Heights*.

It couldn't last. We'd get caught. Or life would intervene. Something. And we must have sensed it. Because every encounter began to feel desperate, like it might be the last.

One evening, my parents had walked across to the neighbours for dinner, and I had permission to go to the local Majum Cinema with Bobby to watch an English film. We timed it so that we left before the end. Not that I could have told you what the first part of the film had been. We sat at the edge of the veranda, hidden from view by my father's Landmaster. We had a window of a few minutes before my parents returned.

That was the only evening of heavy petting I had with Bobby. We kissed for hours, it seemed. I began to feel some hardness. I couldn't understand the wetness in my panties, but I loved every minute of it. I was only fourteen.

I loved him. God, I loved him.

I don't think I've loved anyone quite the way I loved him.

~

Once a month, we gave in to my mother's demand that we visit the Shaws. They were a Christian family who lived nearby. One of their daughters, Rani, adored my mother. She was about six years older than me. She'd failed her matriculation exam three or four times. She had a long, prominent chin, and she always hid it under a handkerchief. She loved dogs, I remember. Their house always smelt of dog. Her sister, Maya, was less friendly. Also less attractive, even with a normal-sized chin. She always seemed to be at war with her acne.

I didn't like them much. I felt superior – I was better-looking and always ranked in the top five in class.

One Sunday evening, as we trooped into the car to go visit the Shaws, Bobby arrived on his motorbike, impossibly dashing and – secretly – all mine. My cousins were visiting from Delhi, and my mother insisted that Bobby come with us. Bobby was duly introduced to the Shaws, and Rani – bless her and her long chin – took him to see her dogs. On the way home, Cyril made fun of both the sisters. We joined in. It seemed like a good opportunity to remind Bobby that we (I) were much better, really.

Too late. Too little.

The frequency of Bobby's visits dwindled, then became erratic and then stopped altogether. Meanwhile, the whispers all around were driving me crazy. Bobby and Rani Shaw were 'going together', and they seemed serious. He didn't say anything to me – no clarification, not so much as a by-your-leave. We had been a secret, and we died a secret. He was confident, perhaps, that a fourteen-year-old girl would never admit to the things we'd done. Or the things she thought they shared.

That was my Senior Cambridge year. I was distracted and distraught. I functioned in a state of near-hysteria for months, tightly suppressed, like a scream behind a closed door. I cried every night.

Bobby Johnson married Rani Shaw that November.

Dolly Rawson, the brilliant Dolly Rawson, managed a Second Division in her Senior Cambridge exam.

No one died. The world kept turning.

Look, I was thirteen when we met again. And he was twenty-six. It was never going to happen, not in the way I saw in my dreams. If he'd never come back to Kanpur, Bobby would have remained a sweet, adolescent crush.

But I wonder what went through his head. Being with someone much younger can be attractive to a certain kind of man. I've been in relationships with a significant age difference – enough for there to be an element of worship, of moulding an ingénue to your liking, that collision between Daddy and Lover – to realize that it's a real thing: sexy and satisfying. Whatever works for people, as long as it doesn't damage either party.

Too little, too late.

Perhaps what affected me so deeply was this: Bobby Johnson dismissed a set of my choices and decisions because *he felt like it*. And he didn't bother with an explanation.

~

I nursed that heartbreak through the rest of my teens. There were other boys. I fancied some of them, and some of them fancied me. Arvind Rikhe was one I liked. He was the son of an Air Force officer who rode in the coach with us every morning. He paid no attention to my feeble attempts at conversation and/or flirtation. So I paid no attention to Vijay Raina, another Air Force kid, who fancied me. He came home one afternoon to tell me of his feelings. Poor boy was so nervous that he walked straight into what he thought was an open door and shattered the pane of glass.

Instead, in the aftermath of L'affair Johnson-Shaw, I acted in plays like *Pied Piper of Hamelin Town* and Gilbert and Sullivan's *The Mikado*, and in the monthly class revues, where we dramatized our textbooks. I remember playing Betsey Trotwood in *The Pickwick Papers*. I also captained Gold House on Sports Day, and winning anything there was always sweet. It 'outfaced' my mother, who always called me 'ghodi' – horse – because I wasn't demure, because I was the boisterous one. Life was what it had always been. We were a little older, a little wiser. Just enough to hurt.

The only other real highlight was my parents' membership of the Cawnpore Club. Yup. Cawnpore. Like the British spelt it. The year we joined, I was cast as the lead in the club's Independence Day musical, written and directed by the impossibly elegant 'Toshy Aunty' – Santosh Mahendrajit Singh.

5

MOST OF THE girls who'd passed their Senior Cambridge went to Loreto Convent College, Lucknow, for their Intermediate. So, off I traipsed. Although I didn't know it then, it marked the start of my life as a nomad, all the way until the ripples came to rest in Bombay, some twelve years into the future.

Denaz and I shared a cubicle the first year, but we soon made friends outside of the Kanpur lot. By the second year, I was asked to share a room with Usha Soota. She was a year senior to me – bright, clever, and quite the star on campus. She was the secretary of the Dramatics and Debating Society. I'd already begun to participate in debates and inter-college elocution competitions, and we became friends.

At a debate held in honour of a visiting Mother Provincial, the topic was the time-honoured 'The Rebellion of 1857: Mutiny or a War of Independence?' I had my prepared script of arguments. I learnt it by heart and thought I delivered it beautifully: heartfelt, poignant, with just the right amount of patriotic fervour. That bubble of positivity lasted until the end of the debate. I had, as the Mother Provincial pointed out, been very vocal about the 'cows of fat and pigs'.

Usha had had a string of boyfriends, and one handsome university Romeo had just broken her heart around the time we became roommates. As a consequence, we exchanged confidences about love and life late into the night. Of course, 'late' is a relative term because lights went out at 9 p.m.

Shireen Bobb from Dehradun was the curviest girl on the block. Bra size 36" while the rest of us despaired between 28" and 30". Unsurprisingly, she had a stock of pretty explicit anecdotes and Shireen had elevated the telling of these stories to performance art. By turns, we 'skipped' the after-dinner study period between 8 and 9 p.m. and snuck out onto the deserted terrace to receive instruction from Shireen. This was, um, education of a different sort – necessary and infinitely more interesting.

One time, it was my turn to partake of Shireen's lascivious selection of stories and the two of us hid in a classroom, waiting for an opportunity to get onto the terrace. Another Senior Cambridge student stumbled into the classroom, looking for a textbook or something. Shireen and I crouched in the dark. Our escape attempt had hit a roadblock. Shireen's 'sex education' classes had been imperilled.

Shireen had as much discretion in that dark classroom as she did with her boyfriend. The situation – this poor girl, blithely unaware of our presence, stumbling around for the light switch – proved too much of a temptation.

In the dark, Shireen snorted like a pig. Sharp and loud. The other girl took off like a rocket, screaming, running straight down the darkened corridors to Mother Superior's quarters, while I followed in hot pursuit, trying to explain that the whole thing had been a joke, a misunderstanding … just one of those things.

By then: general mayhem. People spilled into the corridors. One screaming girl plus two running girls equals a delightful break from the boredom of study hour.

In due course, I was paraded before Fanny Mike. Sorry. Mother Francis Michael.

'You will be penalized!' she said.

I trembled. I had no idea what the word meant.

Ultimately, I was 'gated' for a week. This meant that I couldn't accompany the rest of the girls on the excursions to Hazrat Ganj on Tuesdays and Thursdays. This was a (mild) disaster because we went to the Ganj to surreptitiously stare at the university heroes out of the corners of our eyes. They either strutted down the Ganj in gangs or hung around (and in some cases, owned) the shops there. Our ambitions were modest in those days.

Of course, we were on no account to *talk* to them. Or go to a restaurant. Or the cinema. We were allotted the hours between 4 and 6 p.m., like we were prisoners in the yard. In fact, about the wickedest thing a girl could admit to was her fondness for 'Ganjing'.

We were allowed two films a month, nun-approved. And, inevitably, the choice of those films revealed the baffling logic of some Christian thinking.

A large group of hostel girls, across the first and second years, were dying to watch *Gigi*, starring Louis Jourdan and Leslie Caron. We couldn't get a block-booking for ninety girls, so the second-year lot were dispatched to the 3 p.m. matinee on a Saturday. The first-years would then go and watch the film on Sunday morning. The seventeen-year-olds returned, shaking their heads. *Gigi* was unsuitable for the tender sixteen-year-olds. Why? Because when Jourdan asked Caron to marry him, she asked: 'Does that mean that I have to sleep in the same bed as you?'

The horror.

Of course, the bastard seventeen-year-olds had already seen it.

Instead, we were packed off to watch Yash Chopra's *Dhool Ka Phool.* In which, Mala Sinha:

a. has consensual sex with the hero.
b. runs through the rain in a salwar kameez that clings seductively to her (enviable) hips and her (enviable) breasts.
c. gives birth to an illegitimate child, who she then *abandons* in the forest.

Now. Nothing wrong with any of the above, narratively speaking. But *this* over the suggestion of sharing a man's bed? On moral grounds? Just because it was a 'Hindi' film?

Oh, Fanny Mike.

Fanny Mike was also the Preserver – if not the Originator – of a curious little custom. Many of the girls at Loreto came from the landed gentry, the Zamindars and Rajwadas of Uttar Pradesh. Tekraj, the granddaughter of the legendary cricket commentator Vizzy of Vizianagram, was in my year. When their parents came to visit, they were ushered into a lounge and plied with tea and scones, served on silver platters. When our parents, the parents of rather more ordinary stock, came to visit – having driven down from Kanpur, through the dust, under the scorching sun – they stood around in the corridors until we were summoned from our rooms. No tea, no scones, not even a glass of water.

We were being told about a New India. We were living somewhere else.

~

What else in Lucknow, that place at that time in my life?

I got my first haircut by torchlight. Stylist: Usha Singh. Heartily approved of by my friends: Roshnak Khan from Morar, Gwalior; the very sexy Anjali Patnaik, also an Air Force kid; the simple, sweet, tall and awkward (at that age, those two always go together) Nandini Narain, daughter of the chief secretary of UP; and the gorgeous Vinita Behl, who wore the most daring tiger-print one-shoulder or off-shoulder kurtis, breaking every rule at the Convent.

These girls were my friends. They were also everything that I aspired to.

The annual play that year was *Charlie's Aunt*, the legendary three-act farce. I played timid Ela Delahey, one of the supporting characters. She too found love at the end of the play. I remember the show because, at fifteen, I had already started to measure time in productions – a uniquely theatrical affliction.

Lucknow was also the first time I encountered the word 'lesbian'. In a girl's hostel, there were always bound to be 'special' relationships, but this new term cast some of those relationships in a different light. A classmate from Kanpur, I'll call her X, always had very close relationships with girls. In the ninth standard, X seemed to be Usha's special friend right up until the very smart and rather brilliant Dipti arrived from Delhi. And suddenly, X was carrying and fetching for Dipti. Stuff like that is radioactive in school – it glows in the dark.

Maybe she was just the kind of girl who needed to look up to another in her closest relationships. It's an impulse I know well.

At Loreto, X shared a room with another girl. And whispers about their 'closeness' wouldn't quit. I was duly interrogated by

Mother Damien. After much prodding, I confessed that I had seen them giving each other head massages.

I'm still deeply ashamed of tattling on X. I don't particularly care whether she was a lesbian or not. And when have *any* rules ever affected what goes on in hostels, from the good to the horrific? But I did contribute to that typically Indian situation: two and two adds up to seventeen.

There was a very attractive professor of psychology who taught at Loreto for a few months. She brought a burst of colour and vitality to the college. I even invited her to Kanpur during a mid-term break. She duly accepted and paid us a visit. One afternoon, after lunch, she caressed my stomach. It wasn't a kind of touch I'd encountered before. It certainly wasn't the touch of a teacher, even though she couldn't have been that much older than me. The touch left me uncomfortable, and I made sure to keep my distance from her. She left college soon after.

I've, perhaps unfortunately, never been attracted to women. Not even as a passing curiosity. Sometimes I wonder why. I've been surrounded by phenomenally sexy, supremely interesting women all my life.

Our biological clocks were ticking. Hormones had arrived and announced themselves. We were on a Church-approved assembly line. One only fell in love once. And one kissed the man one was going to marry. 'Sex' was a dirty word. Desire meant downfall. Above everything else, we needed to worry about what people would say.

As if the barometer determined the weather, and not the other way around.

It took me a long time to throw that yoke off my back.

I was sixteen years old, going on forty-two, and just a little confused by the contradictory signals I was getting from everyone around me.

Adolescents. What a thing.

And religion. What a thing indeed.

After the Intermediate, it was back to Kanpur and higher education proper; the hallowed corridors of Christ Church College.

We were three or four girls to a class of thirty boys. We never mixed; it was off the bus or the rickshaw and straight to either the common room or to class – shoulders tucked in, heads down, eyes to the ground. The walk from the gate to class was pure torture. Boys leered at us from either side, every step of the way. Insidious whispers followed us up the stairs. So did catcalls, bad poetry, pure obscenity. Every single morning.

I'd returned from Lucknow with hard-won fashion cred, and I wasn't about to let that go. I wore figure-hugging kurtas, my bags and my shoes always matched, my hair was styled short and I wore lipstick. I represented college and university in theatre, debates and elocution for a long time. I was outgoing and carried myself well.

Some of the loitering heroes sat for the same set of exams three or four years running. They failed with flair. They'd saunter into the examination hall, pull out textbooks to cheat from and then make a show of putting them away. They'd hand over pristine, blank answer sheets to the invigilators and say, 'Agra University *kaunsi bhaagi ja rahi hai*? (Where's Agra University going to disappear to, then?)'. They knew – at least – that Kanpur colleges were affiliated to Agra University at that time. Then they'd loiter in the corridors the whole year, only for this ritual to repeat itself.

~

Because I had already spent two years away from home, my parents were much more amenable to outstation trips. I represented Agra University at the All India Inter-University Youth Festival, held at the Talkatora Gardens in Delhi. I can't remember what the debate was about.

This is what I *do* remember: all the participants were invited to tea with the prime minister. Pandit Jawaharlal Nehru moved amongst us. He shook hands with some of the participants. He chatted with a few others. He spoke to you like you were an equal. The man was *there*.

Inevitably, tea on the lawns of Teen Murti ended with a photo-op. I crouched near the prime minister's feet for the photo. When it was time to leave, Panditji put his hands on my shoulders as he rose from his chair. It was months before I allowed that choli to be washed.

I went to Dehradun for the All India Declamation Contest at the Indian Military Academy. I held forth on William Wordsworth's 'Our birth is but a sleep and a forgetting …' if memory serves me correctly. True to form, I came third (so close, Dolly, but no prize). Wajahat Habibullah, later the chief information commissioner of India, placed first, while Ambika Soni, later president of the Youth Congress and cabinet minister for Information and Broadcasting, was second. At least I had the consolation of losing to two people who'd influence national policy!

I acted in my first Hindi radio play, *Trikon Ka Chautha Kon*, written by Gyandev Agnihotri, who was then a professor at DAV College, Kanpur. He later moved to Bombay, where all the theatre people go, and wrote screenplays for the Hindi film industry, which a lot of theatre people also do.

I travelled to a number of smaller cities in UP – Moradabad, Nainital. This was when Nainital *was* in UP. I attended a Student's Christian Camp in Sat Tal. We had a fabulous time – we worked in the fields all day while we sang hymns. In the evenings, we acted in little skits around the bonfire. When I look back, even in the midst of what must have been a hundred hurried heartbreaks, connections made and lost, it all feels so *innocent*. Whole and pure and uncomplicated.

I had a sweet little crush on Romen Mukherjee, an MA student from Allahabad. I even took him – and his friend Jaswant Brown – home, thinking that my parents would be thrilled that I was bringing home good Christian boys.

I mooned over Romen for a few days, and then all was forgotten. Bobby still had the shattered pieces of my heart, but I wasn't immune to attention. I even had a small celebrity encounter that left me thrilled.

Cricket stars were ascendant, and the Indian cricket team was in town. The Parsis of Kanpur lionized the Parsis of Indian cricket – Nari Contractor, Polly Umrigar and Farroukh Engineer. But the biggest sports heartthrob in the country, bar none, was M.L. Jaisimha. He was a polite, courteous gentleman, devilishly handsome, and he moved like a tiger on the field.

I hit my emergency Parsi button. And the Khorys responded magnificently. Suddenly, I had tickets to the best seats in Green Park and personal invites to the Indian team's celebrations. We accompanied Jaisimha, Farroukh Engineer and Budhi Kunderan to the only decent restaurant in town – Kwality on the Mall – and feasted on cold coffee and chicken sandwiches. These were the days before cricketers had private taxis to ferry them around on their rest days, and before they got paid outrageous sums of money. So we moved around Kanpur in two-seater cycle rickshaws. And I have a treasured, very vivid memory of riding in a rickshaw with M.L. Jaisimha.

Two decades on, I renewed my contact with the Jaisimhas because my Australian brother-in-law, Hartley Anderson (my sister Pam's husband), is a cricketer from the same era. Jaisimha and his wife, Junie, became friends of mine. We reminisced about my crush on him, all those years ago, with great joy. Jaisimha, sadly, is no longer with us, having passed on in 1999, but I visit Junie every time I'm in Hyderabad.

~

Perhaps the most significant thing to happen in those two years was Shakespeareana's visit to Kanpur. This was the theatre company founded by Geoffrey Kendal. They performed *Arms and the Man* in the Air Force Camp. Naseeruddin Shah writes of watching the

Kendals in his memoir, and of how important that experience was for him as a schoolboy. Over the years, I've run into dozens of people who remember watching the Kendals perform on one of their extensive tours through India. I too was totally smitten.

Shashi Kapoor played Bluntshil to Jennifer Kendal's Raina. For weeks, I fantasized that Jennifer would fall ill at the last minute, when the show couldn't possibly be cancelled, and they'd have to hunt through the camp for someone, anyone, who could fill in at such short notice.

Young Dolly Rawson, someone would say, when the hour was late, and hope almost lost. She acts, she does some stage, some elocution. She may be your last hope ...

Not that it ever happened, thankfully. Jennifer and Shashi became friends in my Bombay life and, up until not too long ago, I'd sit with Shashi every time I went to Prithvi. In later years, he'd be in his wheelchair, under the tree. Sometimes, I'd hold his hand.

Esmie and I were now of an age when we were allowed to accompany our parents to Air Force Balls. It felt like we were living through a modern-day *Pride and Prejudice*. We were a gaggle of girls – maybe four of us around the same age? All we needed was a dark, handsome, brooding (but not *too* brooding) pilot to ask us for a dance and sweep us off our feet. Anjali Patnaik and I were the two great dancers. And although swathes of young pilots inevitably queued up to ask us for the next number, we preferred dancing with each other. We'd perfected our steps while at Loreto, and we were just *better* together. I fancied a couple of the pilots but, on the whole, considered myself far too superior. I was also flattered by the attentions of Anand Mohan, a young MA student who dutifully stood outside the window of whichever classroom I was in and sketched me in whatever I'd worn to college that day. But all of them were still boys, really.

This is what I remember best from that time: worrying about what to wear, on a non-existent budget, for weeks and weeks before a ball. But nothing compared to the morning after, when we crowded around my mother's bed to dissect the previous evening for *hours*. That's what I remember. Being vitally alive, stuffed full of hope, aware and present in every second of our lives. We practically *glowed* from it.

Later, I found they had a name for 'it': youth.

II

Delhi-London Local

6

WITH BOBBY JOHNSON two years in the rear-view mirror, I'd graduated with good marks. I applied to the University of Delhi LLB programme and was admitted. Law seemed like a solid choice until I was ready to marry and settle down. But I'd done well in English literature, scoring 76 per cent. I allowed myself to dream a little. Miranda House was *the* institution for English in Delhi. They attracted the best students. They had the best teachers – Mrs Krishna Esoloff, Kamala Achaya. They took theatre seriously – it wasn't just an extracurricular activity. The Miranda House Play was a major university event, and because the male parts were filled with boys from neighbouring colleges, there was added interest. That play was on *Delhi's* cultural calendar.

So, I applied. Almost on a whim. And was accepted.

Off I went.

~

My roommate at the hostel was the very pretty Jasbir Singh from St. Bede's, Simla. She was a General's daughter, and she wrote letters in French. I was very impressed by this. I'd tried to pick up French at Christ Church but had never managed more than 2 per cent in French theory in the two months I'd attended class. All I wanted to do was to be able to sound sophisticated and a little exotic – 2 per cent Bardot would have been fine, thank you.

Being at Miranda House was a bit like that, like being around a finishing school for future world leader-type people. You think I exaggerate? Here's a list of the people I debated with or elocuted against while representing Miranda House: N.K. Singh, Nigam Prakash, Aftab Seth, Montek Singh Ahluwalia. Senior IAS officers, bureaucrats, members or heads of the Planning Commission of India, ambassadors, the lot.

I was a Rawson. So I gave as good as I got.

~

My most memorable experience at Miranda House was, unsurprisingly, the Annual Play.

We performed Benn Levy's *The Rape of the Belt* that year. Despite being a (comparative) theatre veteran, I was simply too terrified to audition. All of it – Delhi, Miranda House, all these elegant, worldly people – overwhelmed me. I was happy with the debates. Or when I placed second or third in the elocution contests.

Junie Das was the lead, and Jasbir herself had a part that was almost as important.

One afternoon, I had to get a book to Jasbir urgently. I knew she was in rehearsal. With some trepidation, I trudged along to the auditorium. I sidled in and lurked around the entrance for a bit until I noticed Jasbir. I walked closer to the stage, turned to address Authority, somewhere in the darkness, and asked: 'Miss, can I give her this book?'

From the dark, a husky voice bellowed a question in reply. 'Do you act?'

Except it sounded like 'Do-hoo a-youuuu acct-ah?'

All of them spoke like that, those teachers at Miranda House. 'Acct-ah'.

I didn't know to whom the question was addressed, so I timidly said, 'Yes, Miss.'

From the darkness, Authority emerged. Mrs Esoloff peered at me and then tossed me a script.

'Read,' she said.

Just like those little quirks of fate in school – reading a passage out loud, and carrying the flag on sports day.

I read. A single paragraph. Mrs Esoloff turned to Jasbir – beautiful Jasbir, my best friend Jasbir, the General's daughter Jasbir – and said, 'Thank you very much, Jasbir. Dolly will play the part.'

I was elated and horrified. This was like my fantasy about *Arms and the Man* come true. But Jasbir wasn't just my best friend. She was also my roommate. And she could easily choose to believe that I had visited her on purpose, to get noticed.

She never did. We remain friends to this day. But I'm sure there was a slightly strained atmosphere in the hostel room that evening.

Three boys rounded out the cast. Kenneth Maharaj Singh and Anwar Abbas from St. Stephen's – which was boys-only at that time.

And from Kirori Mal College, one Amitabh Bachchan.

Yup. *Him*.

~

He wasn't Amitabh Bachchan back then, of course. He wasn't *Amitabh Bachchan*. He was just another middle-class kid.

Amitabh later wrote an essay for the *Telegraph*, talking about his memories of that time. It was mostly about Junie Das, who died far too young, and her sister Brinda (Karat, née Das, Member of Parliament). He writes of how those three boys in the cast were the envy of their colleges because they'd accessed the Forbidden Kingdom that was Miranda House, where the mysterious opposite sex got up to mysterious things.

I played Antiope, the Queen of the Amazons, and he played Zeus.

I remember him being shy and laconic, a well-mannered, very tall and very thin young man. There's a photo of all of us lined up for our curtain call. Amitabh's head is bowed, looking steadfastly at the floor. He says that it was because he'd fluffed his lines, and his mother had come to watch.

If I may, here's an extract from the book *To Be or Not To Be*, released to commemorate his sixtieth birthday:

> At college I was an unknown entity. I may have been selected for the Miranda House performance of Benn Levy's *The Rape of the Belt* but it was in the insignificant part of Zeus.

Dolly Thakore was the Miranda House girl who dominated the show.

~

We've run into each other since. He's always been unfailingly gracious.

I remember meeting him at Regal Cinema, after *Saat Hindustani* had just released. No one knew him back then, and no one knew of him. Oddly enough, that film was written and directed by K.A. Abbas, the uncle of Anwar Abbas, also from *The Rape of the Belt*.

Once, we were on the same flight from Delhi to Bombay. We ran into each other at check-in and planned to sit together. By then, however, Indian Airlines had given up its token nod to socialism and introduced business class on some of its sectors. Bachchan was flying business, of course, and I wasn't, of course, and we were foiled by the class barrier, as it were. He couldn't schlep his way to Bombay in economy; he'd have been harangued for autographs.

However, he made his way to baggage claim to apologize for not having sat next to me. I thought it was very sweet. The other passengers gawped at him.

Much later, when I was a casting director, I went to see him with a script for *Nine Tiger Man*. He politely declined.

On the 17th of July 1982, Quasar and I were in a terrible car crash – two people died. How we survived, I do not know. A touch of grace – *someone* was certainly looking out for us. I was in a coma for twelve days. The initial recovery took four months. The after-effects lingered for almost ten years.

Ajitabh, Amitabh's brother, came to visit me in hospital during that first week. He carried a handwritten note from Amitabh wishing me a speedy recovery. Amitabh himself was in Bangalore shooting for *Coolie*. Every Indian above the age of forty knows what happened next.

On the 26th of July, a routine stunt on the sets of *Coolie* went horribly wrong. During a fight with Puneet Issar, Amitabh was supposed to land on top of a table. Instead, the corner of the table hit him in the abdomen and caused massive internal injuries. He was airlifted to Breach Candy Hospital. He was in the ICU for months and eventually required something like sixty bottles of blood. The country ground to a halt. His fans alternated between prayer and sending death threats to Puneet Issar. They say Indira Gandhi, the then prime minister of India, detoured on her return from an official trip to be at his bedside.

Weeks later, when I was released from Jaslok Hospital, my first stop was Breach Candy Hospital. Amitabh was still in the ICU, so I wasn't allowed to see him. I was ushered in to see his mother, Teji. She brushed aside my greeting because she was aghast at my appearance. She made me lie down in the room that had been booked for the family and plied me with chocolate cake and coffee.

It was with that in mind that I went to see her when she was very unwell, sometime in the middle of 2007. I was allowed into Prateeksha, but Teji was too ill to receive visitors. So I chatted with Amitabh for a while.

I was genuinely touched by his chivalry at the end of that visit. As I took my leave, he said I was welcome to call my driver and tell him to drive in. I didn't *have* a driver, much less a driver with a mobile phone. So the 'Superstar of the Millennium' gallantly accompanied me to my little Alto, parked on the street outside, and held the door open for me.

Our paths cross occasionally. He was supposed to play Kaderbhai in the film version of my friend Greg David Roberts' book *Shantaram*. That project fell through.

And during the launch of Nandita Puri's *Nine on Nine*, Amitabh and Jaya Bachchan were to read a chapter. At the very last minute, Jaya failed to show up at the Grand Maratha and, much to my delight, I was asked to read alongside Amitabh.

On stage again, after so many years. All that remains is for us to share some screen-time together. It's fool's gold, that wish, but stranger things have happened.

One of the earliest memories of my time at Miranda House was marching down Rajpath on Republic Day 1963, representing Delhi University. The Indo–China War had ended in 1962. And after all the knitting we had done for our soldiers, it was time to show our appreciation. We were full of patriotic fervour and expressed our nationalism by participating in the Republic Day Parade. I marched to India Gate, holding my college flag.

The nationalistic feeling receded somewhat once we resumed classes. Our postgraduation lectures were held at the university campus. Some of us had to leave the guarded precincts of Miranda House and walk five-hundred yards to get to our classrooms. We dreaded that walk the same way we dreaded the walk from the rickshaw to the building in Kanpur, except it was worse in Delhi. Invariably, eve-teasers and 'Romeos' would cycle past and thump us on our chests and yank our chunnis or dupattas, making us cringe every time.

This is how they asserted their bravado.

~

Some of the positives of being at Miranda House?

We were the only residential women's college in the university. And some of us were invited to join the Wednesday Challenge Club – membership restricted to *only* fifty university intellectuals. What an extraordinary citadel of pseuds!

But what better place than university to be a pseud? It was, after all, an intellectual hub, and I felt privileged to be invited.

The Club was housed in a British Quaker House on Ridge Road. And every Wednesday, there would be readings of plays and poetry, and debates and discussions. I made friends with Kabir Bedi and Navin Bratt Chawla. Over the years, Navin had the more chequered career. He became notorious as part of the Sanjay Gandhi Family Planning Project, wrote a book on Mother Teresa, was appointed secretary for Information and Broadcasting in the UPA government, and rose to become the chief election commissioner. More recently, he authored *Every Vote Counts – The Story of India's Elections*, recounting those experiences.

In 2019, almost fifty-seven years after I met him, I was delighted to host a dinner for thirty guests at my home after the launch of his book in Bombay!

~

The Little Theatre Group was the most sought-after theatre company in Delhi at the time. Joy Michael invited me to join her group and cast me as Malini in Rabindranath Tagore's play of the same name. Three times a week, I'd take a bus to Shankar Market after college to attend rehearsals. Miranda House had given me special permission to work with Joy because the hostel gates shut at 7 p.m. And it was performed in the veranda of her home in Sunder Nagar, with the audience sitting on the lawn below.

On another very ordinary day, the college peon shuffled down the corridor calling out my name – usually not a good omen. I nervously hurried across to the office. The person on the other end of the line announced that they were calling from Indira Gandhi's office and I nearly jumped out of my skin. At the time, Mrs Gandhi was the president of the Indian National Congress. She would later become prime minister.

They wanted to know if I was ready to perform a one-act play for an African delegation at the Constitution Club in two days' time?

The caller didn't have to ask twice!

I suggested *Square Pegs in a Round Hole* – something I had performed in Loreto a few months ago with Manju Vyas, now Sampat, who happened to be visiting Delhi at the time … and we still remembered the lines.

We were asked to report to Congressman Sadiq Ali's house in Lutyens' Delhi. They sent the car for us.

We went, like two country bumpkins ushered into a palace.

Sadiq Ali's friend Shanti Bhatnagar played host. She even took permission from Miranda House to let us stay overnight at their place. Time was short, and we'd lose too much of it in transit otherwise.

Those forty-eight hours were one of the most surreal experiences of my life.

I was passionate about politics, and here I had courtside seats.

Sucheta Kripalani – India's first-ever woman chief minister – fussed over our meals. Her husband, Acharya Kripalani, lounged in his easy chair under a sprawling banyan tree and rehearsed my lines with me. He was interrupted occasionally. The UP government was in the midst of a crisis, and he would huddle with C.B. Gupta, then chief minister of UP, as they tried to resolve the issue.

Rumour had it that Pandit Nehru was to attend our performance the next day. He didn't. But Indira Gandhi did … and we performed before an audience of diplomats and politicians.

~

That much distraction was bound to have repercussions.

Kamla Achaya decided my grades weren't good enough. I would have to repeat the first year of my MA.

This was a bitter blow, after so many years of being a conscientious student.

I lived under a dark cloud for a few days. It was my first real academic disappointment, and there was no one to blame but myself. How would I face Rani Aunty and my parents?

But I didn't get much time to wallow in my agony. My friend Nandini Narain from Loreto came to my rescue. She had just received a scholarship to Stanford to study journalism and communications. She'd be giving up her job with the British Information Service.

There was a vacancy … was I interested?

7

I TOOK TO the job like a duck to water. My first task was marking out the BIS release by-lines in press cuttings. Also, hanging out with white people – being on first-name basis with them and being invited to their parties – was still a thrill. The afterglow of the Raj hadn't completely faded.

Delhi had expanded my horizons. Preminda Premchand, the redoubtable voice of 'A Date with You' (on air every Friday night) ran an open house at her Defence Colony residence. Anyone who was a friend of her two sons, Sushil and Suneel, was free to drop in.

I adored Aunty Preminda. She was a single mother, she was a legendary radio host, and she directed plays. She was smart and funny, and threw the best parties. In short: everything I wanted to be. Aunty Preminda had an appetite for life and an understanding that she was a global citizen, much before the term became fashionable.

Every once in a while, she'd pick a random country. Say, Greece. And on Greece's Independence Day or National Day, we'd all get together at Aunty Preminda's. But the décor and the food were all Greek. And we'd listen to Greek poetry and music and wear Grecian clothes.

She entertained ambassadors and diplomats on a regular basis, and made sure we were invited. I'd been forced to overcome my awe of VIPs even before I started work for the BIS. One night, I met Melville D'mello, the Voice of India, and was properly star-struck. Whether it was a state function or a diplomatic meet, for years, his was the voice we'd heard it in. We saw the world through his eyes. He relayed Mahatma Gandhi's funeral to us as we huddled around our radios in Cochin. He'd been the voice of my childhood.

Aunty Preminda gave me my first break in broadcasting. I reviewed books for Voice of America and earned a little extra pocket money. That led to a few announcements for the External Service of All India Radio. This was around 1963. These were my first baby steps in media. At least all that elocution came in handy. Not for the last time, either.

Auditions at All India Radio were rigorous. It felt like we'd mistakenly applied to join the army instead. Kabir Bedi, Shakti Maira (who became an internationally renowned artist) and I celebrated our first successful AIR audition at La Guffa in Connaught Place. We split a cold coffee between the three of us. It was all we could afford!

~

At work, I was now writing captions for photographs. The first one I crafted was for a shot of Pandit Nehru, flanked by Motilal Kothari and Richard Attenborough. It was 1963. Attenborough was keen on making a film on the life of Mahatma Gandhi.

Seventeen years later, Richard Attenborough would walk into my living room in Bombay accompanied by my friend Rani Dube. I was breastfeeding my son, sitting on a mattress. A few days later, he would ring me to ask if I'd be the Indian casting director for *Gandhi*, his long-gestating magnum opus.

Things move in circles, I think. Like the world. Or maybe the world moves in a circle because everything else does. It's just a question of what comes around when.

While at the BIS, I was asked to accompany a guest from the British Council around some of Delhi's tourist sites. At the Qutub Minar, a group of young men offered us a series of unsolicited opinions, the gist of which was: if I was willing to guide a white man around Delhi, I must be a whore.

I wish I could say I just shrugged it off. Instead, the incident hung over me like a cloud. I felt guilty and ashamed, and complicit in some way. I had done nothing and yet had been made to feel like I'd done something wrong. The only thing I *could* do was question myself, my choices, my clothes, my behaviour. That's how shaming works. I felt the same way when I visited five-star hotels alone. The British High Commission, where I worked, was right across the road from the Ashoka hotel. And its coffee shop became the natural, convenient location for meetings.

The Punjabi 'Durbans' and the drivers who hung around the entrance leered at me knowingly. I was a stylish young woman who walked into the hotel unaccompanied and walked out a little while later, unaccompanied again.

I knew what they were thinking. And I had to force myself to ignore it – *what will people think*.

Luckily, I had little opportunity to let that fester.

~

I made friends with the people who lived in the British High Commission Compound in Chanakyapuri. There was Lilius, the fiery Scotswoman. She constantly rang me up to mediate in disputes with her domestic help. If they hadn't used a steel ladle on a non-stick pan, they'd used the wrong shoe polish on the wrong shoe. These things sounded exotic to me – one didn't encounter Teflon much in 1964. Lilius was married to Bill Freeman, the passport officer. And there was Alec Goldsmith, the third political secretary, who was also a good friend.

At a birthday party for my old friend Usha Soota, I met Kris Srinivasan. At that time, he was an under-secretary in the Ministry of External Affairs. He would eventually rise to the position of India's foreign secretary. He asked me out pretty soon after. I imagined myself in love with him, but it was an uneven match. He was far too sophisticated and I was in awe of him.

I could have trademarked the t-shirt: 'Susceptible to Charismatic Older Man'.

Kris had been to Eton, and then Oxford. He was erudite, Western and irreverent. He was an iconoclast by religion. He would've been supremely obnoxious if he hadn't been so funny. In truth, he was a very generous man, but he was deeply insecure because he came from a broken home. He just wouldn't let things – *anything* – slide. He had to upset order. He supplied chaos.

We spent a lot of time with each other, at social engagements and alone. I must have driven him to distraction. I knew nothing about sex. All I knew was that I would – could – only ever sleep with the man I was married to. In retrospect, I wonder if that added to his general abrasiveness. It couldn't have been fun for him. He must have really liked me though, because we continued to spend time together. Or maybe I had become a real challenge.

When Kris's transfer to Beirut came through, a number of his seniors advised me: 'Don't let him go alone. He should get married.'

Before I could reply, Kris would jump in. 'I'm not marrying someone I've never been to bed with.'

I'd just look down, hoping the earth would open up and swallow me.

But time spent with him was exhilarating. I remember one particular gathering. A roomful of foreign services people spent an entire evening arguing about the comparative merits of *Dr No*, the very first Bond film, versus those of Ian Fleming's novel. I couldn't believe that smart people could debate something so prosaic, and yet sound so intelligent doing it. And all about a film I hadn't seen, but was now dying to.

~

Strangely, my grandmother became part of this rotating cast of characters, this immersion in the Delhiness of Delhi – everyone knows someone who knows someone. She was a midwife and moved from job to job. She had a horror of being dependent on anyone. I can't even remember where she lived after her retirement from the dispensary. She looked frail, this little old lady, draped always in a crisp, white cotton sari, a blur in silver and mahogany, but she was made of sterner stuff. Her thaila always had supari, and her sarauta and a box of sweets for whoever she was visiting. And she always had a silver one-rupee coin for each of the grandchildren she might encounter on these visits.

In those days, a rupee went a long way.

Around 1962-63, she took up an assignment as the live-in caretaker for Raka – the six-year-old daughter of Tarakeshwari Sinha. Mrs Sinha was the finance minister in the Nehru government. Because my grandmother finally had a fixed address, and because I was a shameless opportunist, I visited her often. Almost always, I was asked to join Mrs Sinha for lunch or dinner, along with her cabinet colleagues. For a nineteen-year-old curious about politics, this was a bit like winning the lottery. I suddenly found myself on first-name terms with an assortment of ministers, state ministers and politicians. If Mrs Sinha requested, I was always happy to accompany her to social engagements or official functions. And I sat and watched, slack-jawed, as the Kamaraj Plan was hatched around her dining table.

The Kamaraj Plan was a far-sighted political strategy named after K. Kamaraj, freedom fighter and three-time chief minister of the Madras Presidency. During his third term, Kamaraj observed that the Congress Party was an institution on the decline, out of touch with its roots. Despite his stellar track record as chief minister, Kamaraj proposed that senior Congressmen voluntarily resign from their national or state posts and dedicate their energies to rebuilding the Congress party, particularly in the aftermath of the 1962 Indo-China War.

Kamaraj duly resigned. He paved the way for five other senior leaders to resign as well. This was, if it's unclear, at a time when politicians put the party and the country before themselves.

~

Picky – Nandini Narain – returned from Stanford, armed with her degree in journalism, and joined *Hindustan Times*. Immediately, the matchmaking cartel went into overdrive. I don't mean to suggest that we, her friends, looked on, aghast, as the aunties made merry. We were *in* there. The Loreto mob traded in their novels and magazines for the IFS, IAS and IPS red directories. We scoured those indexes for prospective bridegrooms and then descended on Nandini's mother, Chandra Mausi, with our carefully compiled 'research'. And she'd play along, checking off the Mathurs (Kayastha, 'of Mathura', but also some Brahmins and Banias) and their like for Picky and Anjali Patnaik, good Muslim boys for Roshnak Khan and, inevitably, Christians for me.

We laughed a great deal, just sitting around, trying to plot our futures.

In due course, all that conjecture threw out a name: Tibbu Daulat Singh. He was a devastatingly handsome young man, and Nandini fancied him. But he was excited about his first external services posting in Paris and didn't want to be tied down.

So the marriage market machine whirred for a bit and sent out Bachelor #2: Sushil Dubey, another young IFS hotshot. Worryingly, his mother seemed much more interested in marriage than he did. She might have married Nandini herself. Also, Sushil Dubey was already 'escorting' Brinda Jaswant Singh. And there was yet another candidate: Yogesh Chandra (codename: Chirpy), quite the intellectual hero from St. Stephen's College. He was another attractive, brash, ambitious IAS brat.

It was all very exciting. But we had reached an impasse. What to do? How to choose? How to pick one of these eligible young men?

Well? What would Jane Austen do?

~

The Narains threw a tea party on the lawns of their Wellesley Road Home. And the only friend of Picky's who was invited was yours truly. Why? Because, as a Christian, I wasn't a 'threat'. Even Jugnu, Nandini's thirteen-year-old sister, was hidden away at her uncle's place.

Tibbu was patently bored. He had no interest in being there. Sushil, on the other hand, was restless. He had an 8 p.m. date with Brinda. He needed an escape plan because, as per cliché, his mother disliked Brinda. As the evening dragged on, Sushil sidled up to me and tried to convince me to call Brinda for him, to apprise her of the delay. Mrs Dubey, who must've *really* hated Brinda, because she would have married Sushil off to simply anyone who *wasn't* Brinda, drifted past us during these negotiations for the emergency phone call. She beamed at both of us. Then she pinched my cheeks a couple of times and went to speak to Chandra Mausi.

'Your younger daughter is very sweet,' she said.

'Who?'

'Your younger daughter.'

Chandra Mausi must have panicked at this point. This was exactly the kind of thing she'd hoped to avoid.

'My younger daughter isn't here.' I imagine her tone was fervent.

'That girl talking to Sushil,' Mrs Dubey volunteered. It was her turn to be puzzled.

'Oh, *her*.' Chandra Mausi must've sagged with relief. 'That's Dolly Rawson.'

And then, casually, the grenade: 'She's a Christian.'

Mrs Dubey looked like someone had slapped her. She made her excuses, strode down to Sushil and I (still in negotiations over updates for Brinda) and 'rescued' her son.

~

So much for our educated 'elite'. So much for the 'secularism' bandied about on college campuses. I wish I could say that I made my peace with this kind of sneaky discrimination. God knows it happened often enough. But it was dispiriting. Wasn't rich, wasn't connected. Now the fact that I'd been born Christian, one more thing I had no control over.

~

On the 27th of May 1964, Pandit Jawaharlal Nehru died.

Teen Murti was a half-mile from the British High Commission. Brigitte Braithwaite, the political secretary, asked me to accompany her and I did. Within minutes, we were next to Panditji's body. He looked at peace. He was still beautiful.

I knew a lot of the people huddled in the room. They were all acquaintances from Tarakeshwari Sinha's house. Many of them greeted me. We stood, united in grief.

He was a beacon. He was *my* beacon. He gave us an idea – this country – that I still believe in. I remembered those things that afternoon, when time stood still, tears running down my face.

Later that evening, I took my parents to Teen Murti. Security in those days, even at the prime minister's official residence, wasn't what it is today. My parents and I walked towards the gate, uncertain of where to join the endless queue. As we were being directed to the end of the line, out of sight, the staff at Teen Murti recognized me and ushered us in. We walked to where Panditji's body lay in state.

Our childhoods, I thought – India's and mine – were over.

~

On the 16th of April 1965, I accompanied an acquaintance to Good Friday Service at the Redemption Church in Delhi. My friend said she needed to make a stop on the way home, to say hello to a friend of hers. I tagged along. And that's how I met Shatrushalyasinhji of Nawanagar – Sat. He was a light-eyed charmer and an old-world flirt. And an honest-to-goodness prince. Like, really. Capital 'P'. He was royalty – had a princely state and everything.

Sat was one of the nicest people I ever met. He was great company, moved in enthralling circles, and somehow got along with everyone, everywhere. We spent a lot of time at the Delhi Zoo. He was a keen naturalist. His knowledge of gems was immense. It had to be. He had a lot of them! Every time I went to see him, his room would be littered with topaz and emeralds and rubies and pearls. He was interested in politics and could argue for hours. He made it very easy to forget that he was, you know, a *prince*.

His status was a little harder to forget when he showed up in a twenty-foot-long limousine. Or when he sent the car to pick *me* up or drop me off, as he did so often.

Sat had been married, once. But he was divorced, totally gorgeous and did absolutely nothing.

Inside of a few months, Sat had adopted my friends and family. He was perfectly at ease in our rather modest Lajpat Nagar home. Ever the gentleman, he responded with a gallant invitation to dinner at the Ashoka Hotel, where he had a permanent suite.

Five-stars weren't really our ambit at the time. But at least I was used to them, despite the gallery of leers. My family were a little more uncomfortable. Remember, this was at a time when people dressed up – and I mean their *best* clothes – to take a *domestic* flight.

My brother Ritchie and his childhood buddy Victor Dey (whose family were tea planters) were promptly barred from the banquet hall because they didn't have dinner jackets. So Sat ordered room service for them. We returned to the suite after dinner to discover a maritime disaster. They'd gone exploring, the two idiots. And encountered a whole lot of fittings they'd never seen before. Including the bidet.

Cue: flooded floor, wet ceiling, soaked shirts, shit-eating grins.

It was all a bit of a fairy tale, really. Prince Charming and Young Dolly. There was no doubt he was sweet on me. I loved him. Not head over heels, but he was a wonderful man and we spent a lot of time together. I felt completely safe in his company. He was a thorough gentleman. Ironically, I would have welcomed greater physical intimacy. That was a source of both frustration and relief. I learnt a valuable lesson, though. A man and a woman could be close, could be intimate, could spend time alone, and it didn't necessarily mean they were making the beast with two backs.

~

Esmie had passed her matriculation and Intermediate privately. In this day and age, we'd say she got her degrees by correspondence. She worked as a receptionist on a salary of two hundred rupees a month.

In 1963, she applied to join Air India as an air hostess and was accepted. Her life changed completely. Within months, she was flying to strange and exciting countries we'd never dreamed of. Our sense of wonder was soon replaced by an ever-growing list of goodies we absolutely had to have, from wherever in the world she was that week. Esmie, good sport that she was, never failed to oblige.

In the fullness of time, she would meet and marry Dennis Jacobs, who also flew with Air India. They were blessed with the most beautiful baby boy – my nephew, Zhya.

Around the time I met Sat, Esmie suffered a slipped disc trying to help a passenger lift a bag. She lived and worked out of Bombay, because Bombay had the only international airport in the country. And while she was in traction at Bombay Hospital, a doctor tried to molest her. Traumatized and out of commission, Esmie considered a shift to Delhi for her convalescence. Sat, ever the prince, heard of the situation and offered his flat on Little Gibbs Road in Bombay's Malabar Hill. Esmie could move into Skylark with her friend and colleague, Mangala Muthalik. She wouldn't have to travel with her bad back, and she'd have someone to help her out and look after her.

~

At some point between meeting Sat for the first time and Esmie's injury, Sir Paul Gore-Booth, the British high commissioner, threw a party to celebrate the Queen's birthday. All the British Council and BIS employees attended. I found myself in conversation with the handsomest Englishman I ever met. This was David Stride, Head of the BBC's Eastern Service, visiting from England.

He asked, casually, if I'd been to London. I told him it was an unimaginable luxury. I didn't have the money or a place to stay. I didn't even have a passport.

We were just talking.

'Well, Dolly,' said David, 'If you ever do make it to London, I'll have a job waiting for you. That's a promise.'

I thanked him and smiled and nodded. Like I said, we were just talking.

Bill Freeman, husband of Lilius and the passport officer, must have overheard the conversation. Because the next morning, he sent me papers for a passport *and* an entry permit, brought to me by a gentleman whose job it was to take my photograph. It was a little bit like being dropped into a hurricane. One minute, talking to David Stride. Two days later, plonked on a pavement somewhere, clutching a passport and an entry permit. People would have *killed* for an entry permit, but here I was.

Still had no air ticket, no money and no place to stay.

Alec Goldsmith, the third secretary, had a cousin, Sally Wigram, who flew with BOAC as a stewardess. He arranged for me to share a flat with her in King's Court South, Chelsea Manor Gardens, until I'd found my feet in London. Alec's father, a General with the Meerut Regiment during the War, would become the first person to take me to Lord's for a test match. We went by bus, and he carried a packed lunch.

All these people just stepped forward, one by one. For no good reason, except they felt they had to. The kindness of strangers, I think to myself. That line. That's theatre. That's life. *The kindness of strangers.*

I still didn't have a plane ticket! But the prospect of a life in London suddenly looked very real. That energy began to infect everything. Esmie could organize a ticket. Seven hundred rupees, though. That was a lot of money back then. And my mother offered it to me.

Out of nowhere, out of nothing, the pieces of a previously unimagined life were falling into place.

~

My first holiday in Bombay was in 1964, and I lived with Esmie in Bandra. During that trip, I'd met Nusli Wadia and Keki Lawyer. We just kind of hit it off; we were young and shared many interests. Nusli would send his car to pick me up and bring me to the action – usually a party in Cuffe Parade, at Kamla Shivdasani's. And it was at one of these parties that I bumped into Simi Garewal.

I can't begin to tell you how striking she was. She'd grown up in England, so she didn't have a lot of the hang-ups that plagued us.

Our first meeting, we looked each other up and down. Simi pointed that sharp nose straight up into the night. 'I'm Simi from the film industry,' she said.

But I was a Delhi University snob, and I hung out with intellectuals *for fun*.

'And I'm Dolly from Delhi,' I said.

We got along fabulously after that.

~

I was scheduled to fly to London on the 7th of September 1965. I came to Bombay at the beginning of the month to spend some time with Esmie. I was madly in love with Sat, although the most we ever got up to was some furious hand-holding. Yet he kept saying, 'Don't go, don't leave, stay back, stay here.'

My response was always, 'No. I'll never have this opportunity again.' It was heart-breaking and thrilling all at once. God knew, if David Stride had only been making conversation, I might be back in three weeks. The unknown exhilarated me, though. There was adventure out there, waiting to be seized. I had a chance at something I'd never imagined possible, a life in another country. And here was a prince, pleading with me to stay.

On the 6th of September, India crossed the international border on the western front, into Pakistan. What had up until that point been a series of skirmishes and escalations had become the war of 1965.

All international flights were cancelled. Sat rushed back to Jamnagar. His palace was being bombed, and he needed to coordinate relief efforts on the ground. Jamnagar – and indeed many places across the country – urgently needed air-raid shelters. Even in Skylark, where we fretted and fumed and mostly just worried, the windows had been blacked out.

Sat came back from Jamnagar a few days later. We were leaning out of the balcony in Skylark one afternoon, and I happened to glance in the direction of Pavlova, the neighbouring building. I did a quick double-take.

'That's Simi,' I said. And in the same breath, 'Simi!'

She turned sharply, looked at me and then grinned a huge grin. 'Dolly!' she screamed.

She was at Skylark in a matter of seconds.

I'd like to be able to report a tussle, but it wasn't even a contest. Simi trained her guns on Sat and it was like watching a deer in the proverbial headlights. Poor boy never had a chance.

They had one of those mad, rip-roaring romances. Those never last, but by God, they leave some memories. He gave her a Jaguar. He gave her diamonds. In fact, many years later, when Sat commissioned a jewellery exhibition, he got in touch with me. I was a model coordinator with S.H. Benson then and sent Phyllis Mendes, Shobha Rajadhyaksha (later De) and Simi to Jamnagar to model his collection.

India and Pakistan declared a ceasefire on the 23rd of September. On the 24th or 25th – I don't quite recall now – I was on a flight to London. I was nursing yet another broken heart, but it was a softer blow this time. Simi Garewal wasn't Rani Shaw. And the relationship with Sat had never quite become an obviously romantic one.

Besides: London, baby!

8

MY OLD FRIEND Manjeet Dayal picked me up at Heathrow. On the drive to Chelsea Manor Gardens, I was confused.

This? This was it? This was the London we dreamt of? Uniform grey sky? Dark, dreary buildings, one after the other? Where was the colour? Where was the noise? Did life not seethe in every nook, every crease, every cranny, like it did back home?

I never thought I'd be homesick.

Sally Wigram had left instructions with her flatmates, Liz Perry and Jane Rutledge. The two of them welcomed me, and I settled in for my first night in England. Later that evening, I saw my first programme on television. E.M. Forster's *A Passage To India*, on a black-and-white television set, directed by Waris Hussein (cousin of Sehba Hussein, a schoolmate from Lucknow and Kanpur) and, of course, a post-colonial nightmare.

We'd only ever seen the news on television. So, to view my first fiction programme, about India, directed by someone I knew, on the day I'd landed, was a good omen, I decided.

The next day, Liz's live-in boyfriend Neil – dark-haired and good-looking – asked me to join him and his radio jockey friend for a drink at the legendary Chelsea Potter Pub on King's Road. Neil made a small fortune driving tourists around in his private taxi. Also, it was okay to be a taxi driver in London. *What* he did didn't define *who* he was.

I had my first Dubonnet. Damn, if it didn't taste like freedom. And it was Queen Elizabeth's favourite drink too. I've never been much of a drinker. Even now, on a good night, one whisky is my limit. But on that day, I knocked back those Dubonnets and smoked my first Gitanes. I remember waking up six hours later, disoriented and now properly displaced.

I was already countercultural.

~

Sat had arranged for a friend of his to loan me three hundred pounds that would tide me over until I had a job. I promptly bought a lovely pink negligee, a dressing gown and a fur coat from Peter Robinson's in Sloan Square and went off to see Froggy (Farrukh Dhondy), my second weekend in London.

Froggy was reading natural physics at Pembroke. I alighted from the train in my best (silk) saree and heels. I was ready for Cambridge, I thought. I expected to be met by an academic sort in a smart suit. Instead, I loitered on the deserted platform until I discerned faint cries of 'Dolla'. It wasn't just the wind, then. The sounds floated downstream, originating near a figure with an untamed beard and wild, shoulder-length hair, dressed in a green sweater that descended almost to its knees.

My friend, Farrukh Dhondy. Cambridge undergrad, impersonating the Abominable Snowman. That weekend, I was to become familiar with the word 'bourgeois'.

We trooped off to his digs. We never wrote to each other much, Froggy and I. Yet, every time, we picked up where we'd left off. Amidst scones and tea, we kinda/sorta made back the last few years. Somewhere in that ramble, Froggy asked me to get a letter of employment for a Mala Sen from my employers. I didn't pay too much attention to the request.

It was 'dinner' night at Pembroke. There's something about Oxford and Cambridge. History breathes, the museum comes to life around you, and it's delicate and formidable all at once. Distinguished gentlemen in robes will wish you good evening at midnight, and as you slip around the corner, someone will tell you that the odd man in the cloak you just met is one of the world's great Heidegger scholars. It's magical. It was magical, that night.

After dinner, I was smuggled into St. Catherine's through a ground-floor window. I was to spend the night with Dick Stokoe, someone I'd never met, never even heard of. Froggy was nervous his landlady might not appreciate a woman in his room. He'd enlisted his friend, the aforementioned Dick Stokoe, whose 'bedder' – it was hoped – would be more accommodating.

I lay in bed all night. I pretended to sleep. I was wide awake, confident that this white stranger would attack the very next instant. Finally, his 'bedder' came by with a bowl of warm water. Night had become morning and I washed up and left. When I got to know him a little better, Dick confessed he'd studied badly the whole night because he was so nervous about a girl from the land of the Kama Sutra sharing his room.

Three days after my arrival, I'd gone to see David Stride. Not only did he remember who I was, but he was also as good as his word. Within a week, I had joined the BBC as an editorial assistant in the Overseas Information Service. My role was to help edit the Overseas Press Bulletin and London Calling. Meanwhile, the Hindi section of the BBC World Service invited me to report on subjects of special interest to women from India and Pakistan.

Suddenly, I was a broadcaster. I had no idea of what the hell I was supposed to do. I only had a lifetime's experience in debates, and in elocution, and in the theatre. I was very good at preparation. The rest was trial and error. I didn't have much of a choice.

Once I'd gotten my start in broadcasting, work began to flow in. I got a call from BBC's English-By-Radio – a guide for people who were new to the language. I went on to play a nine-year-old Indian girl on some hundred and four episodes.

Within weeks, I had a routine. Most Monday evenings, I would take a train to Birmingham. I'd head to Pepper Mill Studios. There, I'd appear on two BBC TV programmes for Indian and Pakistani immigrants, *Look, Listen and Speak* and *Make Yourself at Home*, presented by Mahendra Kaul and Ashok Rampal. Both series attempted to ease the newly arrived into life in the UK. How to use the gas connection, how the NHS worked, precautions for pregnant women, that sort of thing. Those were my first set of TV appearances. I'd stay the night in Birmingham – where I slept on a four-poster bed for the first time in my life. And then head back to London the next evening.

Eight weeks into life in London, I received a call from the Central Office of Information. Would I come to Lambeth North? Well, was I going to say 'no'? When I got there, they thrust half a dozen eight-minute scripts at me. I glanced at the copies of the *London Newsletter*, saw that they had each been marked 'English-Hindi Translation' and panicked.

The COI had rung the BIS in Delhi, asking for a translator. The BIS, in turn, pointed them in my direction. My protests that my Hindi was actually very poor – that I could under no circumstances *translate*, that the best I could do was tell someone what to cook, when to serve it and that the bed needed to be made – were overruled.

The job had belonged to Dr Gaur. He was the Head of the Urdu and Persian Department at the School of Oriental and African Studies, someone with actual qualifications for the job. He'd suffered a brain haemorrhage and the six scripts were the resultant backlog. And while I was trying to figure out whether or not I could do the job, he passed away. The position was open. If I translated the scripts, I could broadcast them. Did I want it?

The COI paid eight guineas a recording. That worked out to about thirty quid extra a month. So I borrowed a Bhargava's English-to-Hindi dictionary and enlisted Froggy. Farrukh's Hindi was horrible – mangled, Parsi, comic. I had to get special dispensation for him to spend days at the BBC library in Bush House, Aldwych. Together, like a duo of intrepid amateur archaeologists, we took the plunge. The first of the scripts arrived just before Christmas. It took us eighteen hours to translate those eight minutes. The following Monday, I recorded the *London Newsletter*, scheduled to be broadcast to the Seychelles, Mauritius, Fiji, Ceylon (now Sri Lanka) and Madras (now Chennai) at 11.30 a.m.

That first morning, the sound engineer asked me to announce my name.

'Dolly Rawson,' I said.

Pause. The voice from the booth clicked on again.

'Um. D'you think you could be more … um … *Indian*.'

Great. I now had to translate *myself* for the job. Also, coming up with a nom de guerre on the spot is not an easy thing. Not when you're worried about getting the Hindi right on the broadcast.

'Kavita' came to mind. Kavita Rohatgi was a friend of mine from Kanpur, a smart and attractive girl. She later married and became Kavita Nagpal, the *Hindustan Times*' long-serving drama critic. 'Kavita' would do. And for the surname, I decided on something nice and non-committal. 'Mehta'. Kavita Mehta. Sounded Indian enough, I thought. So Kavita Mehta I became.

~

Two years after my return to India, some five years into the future from that first broadcast, I barged into the Station Director's cabin at All India Radio, Bombay. I can't remember what for. He was in the middle of a meeting but the door had been shut, so he'd been talking to someone important.

I launched into my tirade but before I could say more than a few words, the gentleman with his back to me, the Station Director's guest, stirred.

'*Yeh toh Kavita Mehta ki awaaz hai*,' he said. (This is Kavita Mehta's voice.)

I was a little stunned. A thin line separates an anecdote about one's broadcasting career from experiences with stalkers.

I asked the gentleman how he knew who I was.

Turns out he was the Station Director of Radio Mauritius and he'd listened to Kavita Mehta, every week for the three years I'd been in London.

~

One night, I was eating a samosa during the interval of a Hindi film somewhere in Southall when two Indian people came up to me. They'd seen me on the television on Sunday morning, in *Make Yourself at Home*, and they wanted to say hullo. I beamed from ear to ear, crumbs of samosa be damned.

I think that was the first time I was recognized because of my television work.

~

The other girls all went home to spend time with their families during the holiday season. I was in London, December 1965, my first white Christmas, in a gorgeous two-bedroom flat, all by myself. The Air Force instincts kicked in. I invited Froggy and his Cambridge set, Darryl DeMonte, Mary Hoffman, John Snow, Ian Lamb, and *their* friends – Adil Jussawala and Farshid Bharucha – to come and spend Christmas with me in London. I didn't mind cooking for them. At least the house was full of laughter and chatter.

A few days later, Farshid telephoned in the morning. He was an artist-visualizer-type person who lived down the road.

'Tell Froggy that Mala left Bombay yesterday. Mala. Left. Bombay. Yesterday,' he said.

Once again, I failed to spot the import of this cryptic utterance. I woke Froggy and relayed the message. He went back to sleep and I left for work, catching the tube from South Kensington to Queen's House.

Froggy eventually showed up. We were neck-deep in translation, and once he arrived, we stumbled off again. After lunch, he came to my office and asked if he could telephone home. He had a brief conversation. Then he dropped the receiver and charged out of the office, running like mad, without a hint of an explanation. The receiver dangled despondently, the only sign that something very strange had just occurred.

I got home two hours later to find a dazzling young lady draped across the couch. Eight or ten young men waited on her. Mala Sen had arrived on the Air India flight from Bombay. She was seventeen, tall, grey-eyed, and from another planet.

I didn't know what to do. So I introduced myself and got busy cooking. Matar pulao and keema aloo for ten people. Once I was done, I walked about for a bit. The clutter near the door had distracted me all evening, so I laid out the (now) ten pairs of shoes in a neat line. I couldn't think of *anything else* to do at that moment. The surviving members of the Cambridge set still rib me about it. 'There was Dolly. I'll cook. And then, in the middle of a transcontinental elopement featuring *a seventeen-year-old*, I'll tidy up the shoes.'

Farrukh and Mala met as teenagers. She was another Defence kid, and they'd had a charmed adolescent romance. He was an Unsuitable Boy, obviously, and she was much too young, obviously. Still, Froggy had been plotting to bring her over to England ever since he'd got into Cambridge.

I picked up this information in bits and pieces as the house slowly settled back to normal after dinner. Mala still hadn't moved from the couch. I fussed over her. I asked if she was okay, if she wanted to unpack and change. I took her to the bedroom. As we shoved her bags onto the bed, Mala suddenly asked if I knew how she'd managed to get to London. I didn't, and I *had* wondered. Those were the days of entry permits, and migration codes were very strict.

With an imperious shake of her head, she flung her passport at me. I blinked. It was a *British* passport. That was odd. I flipped it open and read that it belonged to 'Mala Snow'. I almost fainted.

Earlier that year, back in Bombay, Froggy had run into a white man on Marine Drive. They'd both been caught in a monsoon downpour, and they were waiting out the worst of it under the same building. The white chap was John Snow. He was a Peace Corps Volunteer in India on his summer break. He and Froggy discovered they were both from Cambridge and that they were both due back in a week. They cemented their friendship by hatching the plot to bring the love of Froggy's life down to England by marrying her to an Englishman.

Many months later, I translated the Arya Samaj Wedding Certificate issued to one Mala Sen and one John Snow. Mala filed for divorce so that she could then marry Froggy. I think they might be credited in the Green Card playbook with the invention of that specific manoeuvre.

The fairy tale didn't last. With a start like that, could it ever? Farrukh and Mala divorced seven years later, but remained close. Together, they were responsible for some key advancements in socialist thinking in England. Mala, in particular, was a pivotal figure in the establishment of 'Brick Lane' as a safeguard for the rights of the Bengali community. She wrote *Bandit Queen*, which became the basis for Shekhar Kapur's film. Phoolan Devi believed the film glorified the rape at the heart of the story. And Mala, who had many reservations about the screenplay that eventually emerged from her book, had no choice but to be silent in the face of protests she likely supported. The Indian Woman became her singular preoccupation. *Death by Fire* was an examination of the ritual of sati through the ages, and its socio-cultural-economic-sexual implications.

She became, over time, a dear friend. There were always long gaps – we didn't see each other often, especially once I moved back to India, and we weren't great at staying in touch – but we remained close. Mala was the first of a remarkable set of women who have been my peers and friends. All of them brave, imperfect, glorious. All of them *doers*.

And always honest. With themselves and with me.

Mala visited Bombay occasionally. She loved her father but was indifferent towards her mother. They were both headstrong women. Mala's mother had married again. Mala would land at the airport, go to her stepfather's place and then, at midnight, my doorbell would ring.

'I can't bear it,' she'd say. And she'd stay at mine.

She went through my life like a comet. I'd always remain her emergency port of call. I was there when she landed in England. She spent the first night of the rest of her life, as the cliché goes, under my roof. She also spent her last night under my roof. She drove from my place on Peddar Road to the Tata Memorial Cancer Hospital. True to fashion, she chose the head-on approach of surgery on her oesophagus over the slow death of chemotherapy.

She passed away on the 21st of May 2011.

~

David Stride called one day, asking me to come by his office. He introduced me to a diffident-looking young chap.

'This is Mark Tully,' said David.

'Hullo,' I said.

'Mark's travelling to India for the first time,' said David. 'He had some questions.'

And Mark Tully, who can teach me a thing or three hundred and seventeen about India, asked if he should carry baby food. He and his wife had just had their first child, and he was nervous about the stories he'd heard.

~

The flat in King's Court South belonged to Liz Perry's parents. Her father was vice president with the World Bank. Because he was posted in the Middle East, Liz had sublet the apartment to the three of us. It was now December of 1965 and her parents were due back. That meant, for the first time, I needed to look for accommodation in London.

From Chelsea, I moved into a huge four-bedroom flat in Seymour Street, behind Marble Arch. It was a good address to be at, centrally located and hip. The flat belonged to the ex-Pakistani high commissioner. In a strange quirk, my six (!) roommates were all from Asia or of Asian origin – Gita Singh, the landlady, from Malaysia; Priyani and Beetie from Ceylon; Shama Thakore from East Africa, Diane Seukeran from Trinidad; Monica Wee from China.

Young Dolly Rawson was the only one from India. The move was effortless. Introductions done, suitcase unpacked and popped atop a cupboard, I was now a Londoner.

The next three years would shape the rest of my life. London was a shock – like being plunged into ice-cold water. But, God, it woke me up. I've never been that vitally alive in my whole life, so home in my own skin.

~

Life is what happens to you, Lennon said, while you're busy making other plans.

This is not to be confused with what Lenin said. Which was, basically, 'Go left.'

So much happened in so little time, it left me breathless. The Hindi Prachar Parishad conducted Hindi classes once a week at the India House canteen in Bush House. They got in touch with me because of my burgeoning reputation as an expert in Hindi. I sighed, ordered my personal copy of Bhargav's English-Hindi dictionary from Delhi, and joined as a tutor.

A sizeable part of my broadcast audience were native Hindi speakers. There was always a need for another forum that helped people with their profound sense of dislocation, that helped their transition to another country and that gave them a flavour of home. The result was *Pravasini*, London's first Hindi weekly, published by the Hindi Prachar Prathistan. I was a regular contributor.

One thing led to the other, as it does. Soon, the Indian High Commission called, asking for help in organizing their Republic Day and Independence Day celebrations. Out of the blue, I got a phone call from Hampton College to come and give them a talk on India. This request would become a regular occurrence during my years in England. I gave a few talks to women's organizations in Cambridge – the association with Froggy was a factor there, no doubt.

The questions were, in general, priceless.

Did people in India speak English?

Did I ride to school on an elephant?

Did I live in a tree?

Was I wearing a diamond in my navel *at that exact moment*?

(This is before body-piercings became a fad.)

Yes, no, no and no. Although, if Sat and I had worked out … well, we'll never know, will we?

I was astonished by the ignorance I encountered. Given that the lives of the people asking these questions had been altered beyond recognition by the institutionalized robbery of said country of elephant-riding schoolchildren, it all seemed a bit much.

Almost inevitably, the theatre, like a bad penny or an irresistible ex-boyfriend, became part of my life in London too. Just a gathering. Just a small reading. Just a one-off performance. Another distraction. Another way to make friends. Another way to fill the evenings. Another way to find a community that would sustain beyond the curtain call.

Mid-1966, I acted in *Shoonya*, written by J.P. Dikshit. It was produced and directed by Vinod Pande, who also played the lead. Vinod fancied himself as a romantic hero, à la Dilip Kumar, all quivering lips and mournful eyes. I played his long-lost sweetheart.

In the play, my car stalled in the middle of a dense forest late one night. Seeking shelter from the pouring rain, drenched to the bone, I stumbled upon a hut. Only to discover my childhood sweetheart, living his life as a hermit, on the rebound.

It was an agreeable bit of nonsense. But Vinod – who is now a filmmaker in Bollywood – underlined his artistic integrity with his insistence that I enter in a wet saree. For verisimilitude, you see.

We performed to an audience at the Indian High Commission, as part of the Independence Day celebrations. There was some polite applause at the end. After we took our bows, Chief Guest Saeed Jaffrey, already an established actor by then, bounced onto the stage for the felicitations, found a spot next to me and whispered: 'The best bit was the clinging saree.'

A triumph, clearly.

~

Saeed was in his post-Madhur Jaffrey phase. He went through life like a tornado. A drunken one, sure, listing to the left, but the man had some life force. He lived in a bed-sit in Knightsbridge. We often went to plays and concerts together. That's how his landlady got to know me. And I got used to her phone calls.

'Your friend Saeed has burnt my carpet.' Little increments marked the passage of time. 'This time it's the mattress.' Saeed's new 'friend' Hilary had just broken his heart, and he was drinking himself blind.

One evening, we set off to attend a Vilayat Khan concert at the Queen Elizabeth Hall. Saeed was well-lubricated before we met. He just about managed to get aboard the bus. He found the nearest seat and slumped there, looking weary but undefeated, which was an ominous sign. During the performance, he staggered to his feet at every opportunity, and slurred '*Wah, wah!*' irrespective of whether or not the performers had played a note. At first, the audience was too stunned to do anything but ignore him. But as soon as it became apparent that this was going to continue through the rest of the evening if given the opportunity, the ushers appeared and, with grave courtesy, lifted him up so his feet were off the ground and deposited him on his arse on the pavement outside the theatre.

Saeed was part of a small group of Indian talent that was trying to break into the British market. Aspiring Indian actors were paupers. The only parts for them were crowd scenes that needed a sprinkling of brown faces. Say, for example, a scene set in a hospital.

They were always bit parts, but the equity rate was good – twenty-eight pounds a shift, with a meal to boot. You could survive on that for weeks. And a lot of them did. Zohra Segal, Madhav Sharma, Jamila Massey, Tariq Yunus and Jerry Ram, who metamorphosed into the screenwriter Dharamveer when he returned to Bombay. We didn't have enough to be competitive about, or jealous about. So the bonds we forged have sustained us over decades. We're all still friends, those of us who remain.

On one occasion, Saeed and I went to the Mermaid Theatre where the gorgeous Leela Lean, wife of David Lean, was hosting a dinner for a large Indian contingent. It got late, as it often did those days, and we missed the last train. We couldn't afford taxis, and so Utpal Dutt, a legend of Bengali theatre and Hindi screen, and Ismail Merchant, producer extraordinaire, walked me home.

Every summer, Esmie would find a way to get me a crate of Alphonso mangoes from Bombay. Vivek and Vijay Srivastava, old friends from Kanpur, would inevitably show up two or three days after the fruit arrived. Like migratory birds, they had an unerring instinct.

This was my mother's legacy. I ran an open house. Friends who were studying at London University would drop in unannounced, at odd hours, always hungry. They often stayed the night, sleeping on the carpet or the couch. I yelled at them about their hygiene, I fed them, and I sent them on their way.

By now, I had three distinct, overlapping sets of friends. The first was the Hindi crowd – everyone involved with the radio shows, the classes and the magazine. Then there was the Cambridge crowd – Froggy and his friends. And I now had the theatre crowd as well.

Roshan Seth lived down the road from me, in South Kensington. I knew him from Delhi. We'd been friends, although Roshan was always reserved and a little serious. But it was good to have someone who understood where you came from. Roshan was at the London Academy of Music and Dramatic Art (LAMDA), and he was clear he wanted to live and work in England.

Roshan roomed at #2, Sydney Place, with Rumi Chopra and Umesh Sahai. That was on my way to the tube station, and I saw them almost daily. Cup of tea, drink, quick sandwich, something. Roshan would invite me to come and watch some of the performances at school. One of these was a staged reading of Tagore's *Footsteps in the Sand*. LAMDA had invited Gerson da Cunha – globetrotter, poet, diplomat, all-round legend – to be part of the play. Gerson was the Creative Director of Lintas Bombay but he was on a posting in London. Some girl back home had broken his heart and he was now living in a flat at Sloane Square. Gerson's life was like that – epic, fragile and poetic, all at once. He felt deeply and lived at full throttle. He remains one of the best, most wonderful human beings I've had the privilege of knowing.

I met him for the first time after that performance of *Footsteps in the Sand*. He threw a small party at his place. There I met the exotic Geeta Patnaik, author of *Karma Cola*, another friend of Gerson's, for the first time. She had brought along her husband, Sonny Mehta, who would later go on to head Knopf Publishing.

Lilius and Bill Freeman, my friends and benefactors from Delhi, were close by as well, on Oakley Street. The first time I visited, I experienced a different kind of culture shock. In Delhi, they'd lived in a three-bedroom air-conditioned apartment in Dorset House, in the British High Commission Compound in Chanakyapuri. Here, they were in a single room bedsit. The bathroom was on the first floor, the toilet on the second and the kitchen on the third. No army of full-time servants either.

A little further down the road, at The Vale, lived Sir Paul and Lady Gore-Booth, recently returned from their posting as high commissioner to India. In Delhi, they'd lived at 2, King George's Avenue. Their daughter Celia did a lot of theatre with us and we'd drop her home after rehearsals. When we parted in Delhi, Celia insisted that we continue the Indian tradition of visiting unannounced.

The first time I dropped in, unannounced and unscheduled as requested, I was startled to find Lady Pat Gore-Booth at her sewing machine. She was delighted to see me and insisted that I stay for dinner. At which point, she put away the sewing, got to her feet and cooked us a quick meal of bangers and mash.

I was impressed. It represented the best of England, I thought. Everyone was equal. That was how it should be. Equal opportunities for a country of equals.

9

ONE OF MY new roommates, Diane, was a law student. Her friends dropped by regularly. Amongst them was Dilip

Thakore, brother of Shama, also a roommate. I knew he was trouble the moment I laid eyes on him.

On Seymour Street, Dilip was king. He was in his final year at Lincoln's Inn. His family owned huge plantations in East Africa. He was one of those irreverent, sardonic provocateurs I find irresistible. His parents' money kept him comfortable but fuelled his existential angst. He was smart and he was sharp. He was on the university debate circuit. He was also more British than the British. He was always in a three-piece suit and wouldn't be caught dead without a cravat, even on weekends. He loved good conversation above anything else, but he went looking for arguments. He was a voracious reader who introduced me to Kingsley Amis and Nietzsche. He had a wide, off-kilter set of interests, and he reshaped my view of the theatre by dragging me along to a bewildering range of performances.

He'd stop before every mirror he passed and regard his reflection.

'You handsome devil, you,' seemed to be the standard verdict.

He coined the phrase 'NATO-Nympho': No Action, Talk Only.

Pretty soon, I was under his spell. I enjoyed his company. I was to be his latest conquest. I rather liked the attention.

It wasn't love at first sight, though. While he was a good-looking man, he didn't have a great voice. And he was prickly. He and the Cambridge set argued all the time. They thought Dilip was bourgeois, and he thought they were a bunch of damnfool hippies. Farrukh and Dilip, in particular, fought about everything under the sun while everyone else in the room sat around feeling awkward and uncomfortable. When provoked, Dilip was a bully.

But London could be lonely, and we began to spend more and more time together.

In February of 1966, Dilip became the first man I had sex with. It wasn't a big deal, which was a bit of a disappointment. It precipitated an odd little knot of guilt. Now that I'd slept with Dilip, I was bound to him for life. At least, that's what my upbringing suggested. I had two problems with this. One, that didn't seem like the best idea in the world. It was all right in England, but I didn't know what the future held for us. And I didn't know how he felt. Was I just another notch on the bedpost?

~

My relationship with Gita, my landlady, was rocky from the start. I wasn't home that much during the week. And most weekends, I was away visiting friends.

This seemed to piss Gita off. She expected her tenants to stay in on weekends and follow a schedule she'd set out for them. 'Today, we clean the bathroom' type thing. I was a conscientious objector on many levels. First, this wasn't boarding school. Second, I kept a very neat house and always cleaned up after myself. And third, I felt a little bit superior to Gita and her gang. I'd been to the right schools and the right colleges, I spoke English better than all of them, I worked for the BBC and – unlike everyone else in that apartment – I was a 'genuine' Indian. No second-generation Jane-come-lately, me. I didn't realize until much later that I'd become a little bit discriminatory myself.

An uneasy truce held until my birthday. I'd been in London almost seven months, and I wanted to throw a party and invite everyone who'd either helped me or hosted me or had just become a mate. The final tally was almost ninety guests. This included the Cambridge and Oxford friends, my colleagues at the BBC and the theatre crowd. We'd formed an informal repertory. We rehearsed some of Lorca's *Yarma* at Seymour Street, with the usual suspects in attendance: Gerson, Zohra Segal, Rani Dube, Kusum Haider, Divya Shah, Saeed and Roshan.

I didn't think to ask Gita for her permission. I paid the same rent as everyone else, and I thought I was entitled to throw a birthday party. But Gita didn't feel the same and, on the day of the party, she announced that everyone had to leave by midnight. If they didn't, she'd inform the police. I thought the curfew was a bit much – people were at our place through to the next morning all the time.

Everyone's friends, not just mine. It was an accepted thing. I didn't think her threat was serious. She was just having one of those days. She wasn't going to *do* anything, really. She *wouldn't.*

Just when the evening roared to life – you know, the one moment where *everyone* is on the dance floor, politics be damned – Gita appeared, looking like the Grim Reaper. She switched on all the lights and stood there, her mouth clamped tight, lips almost invisible. She asked everyone to leave.

There was a moment's silence. Everyone looked around, shuffled their feet, looked at Gita, looked around again, saw that no one else was leaving and went back to having a good time.

When I heard the first of the police sirens, I dismissed them. I was seething, but I didn't want to cause a scene in front of all my friends. Besides, the cops had responded to something down the street, surely. Disturbance of peace kind of thing. It couldn't be *us*.

It could. It was.

A bunch of baton-wielding Bobbies charged into the room. This didn't affect my friends in the least. If anything, the presence of policemen made it a better party. They swung into protest mode without missing a beat. For many, politics was the drug of choice. I have a vivid memory of Dilip being carried down three flights of stairs by two policemen.

'I'm a licensee,' he yelled all the way down to the pavement. 'I can sue you!'

~

I moved out the next day. I didn't think Gita was going to wake up thinking she'd made a mistake. I packed my trunks, dumped them at the Paddington Station 'Left Luggage' counter, checked into the Hillway Hotel in Bayswater and started looking for a new flat. The Hillway charged a guinea a night for bed and breakfast. I made eleven guineas a week. I also had to eat at some point during the day.

It was a question of when I'd run out of money.

My fortunes had also become part of the zeitgeist, I thought. They were swinging wildly. London had looked very different twenty-four hours ago.

For a while, my life revolved around the listings in the papers and sending applications to every agency I could find: Share-a-Flat. Ramblers of London. Accommodation Limited.

Each agency, to their credit, sent back long lists, cross-referenced with every available address and the attendant provisions: no blacks, no browns, whites only.

Every day, I'd make enquiries on the phone. The initial conversations were promising. I'd finish work, gather my things and set off to make house calls. And a variety of ladies would open the door, red hair in curlers, blonde hair in curlers, brown hair in curlers, cigarettes jutting from the corners of their mouths, all aflutter.

'We didn't know you were this colour, luv.' Or, better: 'You didn't sound brown on the phone, luv.'

Should I have taken that as a compliment?

I thought back to Lady Pat Gore-Booth at her sewing machine. And about equal opportunity.

~

Dilip and I were fighting. He felt that I should have stood my ground. That I should have sued Gita. It didn't help to be reminded of that while I trudged from house to house, hauling my overnight bag.

The previous year, I'd joined the protests against Enoch Powell, a man who spewed a sentiment many shared but were too afraid to voice. Farrukh had turned me into a Marxist. I took part in the October demonstration against the American intervention in Vietnam ('We shall fight/We shall win/Ho Ho Ho Chi Minh'). During that protest, Brinda Das (Junie's sister) and I marched arm in arm.

My current predicament, much as it pained me to admit, was more personal than Vietnam.

I went to see a beautiful property in Grosvenor Square, off Hyde Park. It had a full-on Christine Keeler/Mandy Rice-Davis vibe.

I walked in through a set of huge doors – more like a triumphal arch. The brass doorknobs were the approximate size of footballs. I waited at the foot of a magnificently carpeted staircase that looked like it went straight up to heaven. An accented voice drifted down from the third floor.

'Come.'

The bedroom had an ornate double bed with an exquisite velvet bedspread. I couldn't believe my eyes. It looked like a film set, I thought, although I didn't really know what a film set looked like.

The spectral voice belonged to the Polish housekeeper. She took care of the property and lived around the back. The rent was five pounds a week; Elizabeth – who I'd be rooming with – had gone to the doctor; and was there anything else?

I was about to ask if I could move in right away when the doorbell rang. A florid gentleman – and only Englishmen can really achieve that degree of florid: floppy hair, just a bit out of breath, the red cheeks of habitual drinkers – walked in. He was in a black pin-stripe suit, with a top hat, a tail-coat and he carried a sheathed brolly. He looked like a villain from a Tintin comic. Or a High Priest of Satan.

I was introduced to him as a potential tenant.

'It's the 26th of March today,' he said. 'Shall I send you twenty-six red roses tomorrow? Twenty-six red roses for the beautiful young lady on the 27th …'

You might as well have cued the violins from *Psycho*.

The man insisted on small talk. He wanted to get to know me. I began to make my excuses. I had to be somewhere, my friend was dying, I'd just remembered that I needed to be at the airport, I'd left the gas on, there was a taxi downstairs … something. I was too nervous to turn around – I was sure the man would murder me sharpish while his Polish accomplice stood by, stoic and deranged – so I shuffled backwards until I felt the doorknob press into the small of my back, turned, let myself out and fled.

I didn't stop when I got to the pavement. I ran into the Wimpy's at Hyde Park. I needed to be surrounded by people. I waited until I had calmed down a little.

Then I called Dilip from a public phone booth and howled. Dilip relented and promised to come house-hunting with me the next day.

We rang a Marion Powers – that was a ground-floor flat, overlooking a garden square, Belgravia. 'Come over right away,' she said. Dilip waited outside as she ushered me in. The flat was filthy, although the lady was on crutches, which may have been why. She sized me up and then plunged into a monologue about how wonderful it would be to have me cooking all these wonderful curries for her and how the two of us would put the place right, make it beautiful, until it was wonderful. I started to get a little uncomfortable. I asked if Dilip could come in. Her enthusiasm waned. She seemed keen on it being 'just us girls'. It was time to go.

During that time, I dropped in on the Gore-Booths on many of the evenings back and forth from potential homes. I needed to vent. Bad luck was one thing. But being turned down because of the colour of my skin was beginning to wear me down. Sir Paul listened with great patience. And during one of my visits, he wrote me a letter on his personal stationery, apologizing to me on behalf of his countrymen. I was touched. He was parliamentary secretary at the time, and he didn't need to go out of his way to make me feel better.

By now, I'd given up on West End. I extended my search to the outskirts of London. Suzie in Chalk Farm asked me to come by after work. When I got there for my appointment at half six, it was dark. A row of semi-detached red brick houses ran down the street, anonymous in the gloom. I rang the appointed doorbell at the appointed time. A tall, very attractive black girl opened the door. Suzie was out, and I'd have to wait. So saying, she slammed the door shut.

On cue, it began to drizzle.

There wasn't even a bus stop where I could shelter from the rain. The street was quiet, abandoned, like a ghost town. Feeling like I'd stepped into an episode of *The Twilight Zone*, I huddled in a telephone booth like I was a sentry on guard duty, on the border of a strange, strange land.

No one went in or out of Suzie's house for well over half an hour. There were barely any people on the street. But all of them glanced a second time at the woman in the saree inside the telephone booth. I was afraid people would think I was living there, so I picked up a stray *Evening Standard* and pretended to leaf through it and dial a series of numbers that I 'found' in the classifieds.

I noticed a listing for High Street Kensington. I dialled WES 4783, and a Cindy Brinston answered the phone. Yes, she'd placed the ad, and yes, the place was still available although girls were still coming around to see it. I was welcome to throw my hat into the ring.

High Street Ken was on my beat. And it was close to the Hillway. What the hell, I thought. I have nothing to lose. So at 9.30 that night, I went.

The place was a charming basement flat, and very well-located. I'd arrived just after Rosemary, another prospective tenant. She perched on the couch with great élan. She was red-haired, she had freckles, and she was asking about parking. I looked at her and then looked at Cindy. White and white. I didn't know what I could do to change that. I went through the motions because I was there. Cindy replied to the questions and finished with the usual 'I'll let you know'. At least she didn't end with 'well, you're *brown*, luv.'

The Hillway wasn't the cheeriest place in the world at the best of times, but it felt like a prison that night. This was the season of grey London and it had infected me, I thought.

The next day, I finished work and sat at my desk and looked at Cindy's number for a while. I was nervous, though I had no reason to be; I was despondent, and I thought myself a damn fool and a poor girl in some distress. It was best to just rip the bandage off, so I called.

'Come over right away,' she said. It took me a while to process what she was saying.

'Now?'

'Now.'

'To move in? As a licensee?'

She just laughed.

Within an hour, I was in a cab, trunks strapped in, en route from Paddington to 26 A, Argyll Road, just off High Street Kensington, between C&A's and Safeway, and home for the next three years.

~

Cindy and I got along right off the bat. Our schedules were also an ideal match.

She and her boyfriend, Martin Langdon, would come home after work. Lincoln's Inn was just behind Queen's House, where I worked, so Dilip would meet me at the end of the day and we'd come home together. We'd dump our bags, I'd change into trousers because I never wore anything but sarees to work, and we'd go across to our local. A drink for Dilip, maybe half a pint for me, then we'd walk home for dinner.

Cindy had two typically chintz sofas. After dinner, she and Martin took one of the sofas, and Dilip and I took the other. We'd watch TV for a while. *Frost*. *24 Hours*. Never *Peyton Place*. Then the two of them would go off to Martin's place, and Dilip would take the last tube home at 10 … 10.30.

On Fridays, Martin would spend Sabbath with his parents and Cindy would come home. And that became a tradition for the two of us – Friday was girls' night.

Cindy and Martin also chased the sun, like white people do. In England, as I discovered, the sun is a rare and precious element. The two of them would hop into Martin's Jaguar and disappear every weekend, after tracking the weather forecast like treasure hunters. They'd return on Sunday evening, showing off their tans if they'd been successful. Martin's Jaguar annoyed Dilip no end, and Martin knew it. They'd argue about everything. But Dilip cautioned them every weekend, without fail – if they got too brown, Cindy and Martin would find themselves evicted.

So I had the place to myself, more or less, Monday through to Thursday. *And* on most weekends. No wonder I loved that house.

Cindy and I got very close over the years. She married Martin and we stayed in touch when I returned to India. They came to visit me in Bombay in 1987. I met them every time I travelled to London. They are now grandparents. Their son – Gavin – stayed with me when he travelled to India in the early '90s.

~

Around about this time, I became close with Rani Dube. Rani had migrated to England with her husband, Hari, and her two small children. She worked as the first female producer on BBC's Hindi Service. She'd been on the radio since the age of five. She was a very attractive woman, and she had a wonderful ability to get things done. People listened to her.

When she complained about casting on BBC television – where actors in blackface were still high watermarks of diversity – it opened the door to a more inclusive policy. One of those who gained from it was Rani herself. She eventually became a television and film producer and a documentary filmmaker. She also had a vast knowledge of Hindu mythology and Hindi literature.

She often came over from Walsall to spend the night. She told the best stories and was a remarkable flirt. Every man she met was in love with her, of course. Lead actors on British television would visit while she was in make-up and ask, 'You're gilding the lily, are you?'

Hari killed himself in 1966. He was an anaesthetist and he injected himself with an overdose.

I can't claim to have known either Rani or Hari very well when the tragedy occurred. She was a close acquaintance who eventually became a close friend. I didn't know the state of her marriage, didn't know if every man *was* in love with her and whether that took a toll on them. I didn't know if a man like Hari understood a woman like Rani – she was forward-thinking, evolved, independent and successful.

Or maybe depression is just depression, and people sometimes just can't find a way back from the brink.

Four of us rushed to Birmingham to be with Rani and the kids: Shivendra Sinha, the man who directed *Phir Bhi*; Kunwar Sinha, who went on to become a producer of English News on Doordarshan Bombay; Dr Amar Varma, a friend of the family; and I.

If anything, Rani and I got to know each other in Birmingham. We talked for three days and we laughed a lot in those three days. I babysat her four-year-old daughter Nira, while everyone else attended the funeral. Rani returned in the most Rani-like fashion possible.

'You just missed Richard Attenborough,' she said. 'He just dropped me off. In his green Rolls Royce.' He'd also sent her a mink coat, she said, which she promptly returned to his wife. I hung on to every word.

The weekend ended badly. Neither Shivendra, nor Kunwar nor I could offer Rani and her kids a place to stay for the next few weeks. Dr Amar Varma could. He was well established and affluent; he had a large house with more than enough room. Except Dr Amar Varma couldn't. He couldn't take Rani home because his wife wouldn't be comfortable looking at a widow every morning.

You could take the idiots out of India …

Rani eventually moved to Richmond Green, in London proper. She married again, soon after. Her husband's name was Paul Davis, and he too was a doctor. I hosted Rani's wedding reception, for some thirty Indian actor friends, at my Argyll Road flat.

10

DILIP BELIEVED IN holidaying abroad. Our first summer together, he went hop-picking in Weil der Stadt, Germany. This was student tradition – cheap labour in exchange for the thrill of manufacturing beer. I decided to spend the weekend with him. Two days wouldn't justify the cost, so I made it a longer trip, starting in Berlin and making my way to Dilip.

I booked myself on a ferry from Dover to Ostend, travelling 'on deck'. Cabins were much too expensive. Dilip had written to say I should eat before the voyage began because prices shot up once the boat left shore. I set off from work, toting my red Samsonite, in a saree and heels.

As instructed, I made a beeline for the coffee shop on-board and wolfed down a hamburger. In a rush to get a good seat on deck, I shoved my chair back and some part of my saree – the hem or the fall, I can't recall – caught on one of the legs and ripped. I asked the steward where I could find a needle and thread and affect some running repairs. He directed me downstairs to the cabins, where an attendant might be able to help.

By the time I'd managed to lug the Samsonite below deck, the boat had set sail. An attendant asked for my ticket. I explained that I didn't have one for a bunk, but before I could get any further, he asked me to sit down on a heap of luggage. I sat.

Moments later, he reappeared and asked me to follow him. Again, I couldn't get through my explanation. The attendant led me to a cabin, told me to take the upper berth and disappeared again.

My cabin-mate was a Dutch au pair – Rosalind. She pulled out a needle and thread, and we fixed the saree in no time. I waited for the attendant to come back, and maybe ask for some extra money because I didn't have a ticket, but he never did. So I changed out of the saree and spent a very comfortable night in a warm bed.

We arrived in Ostend early the next morning. Rosalind had appointed herself my philosopher and guide. She marched ahead of me, carrying my suitcase onto the Rotterdam Express to Berlin. The train went via Osnabruck, which was home for Rosalind.

We took our seats, the train pulled out of the station, we chatted for a bit. An hour into the journey, Rosalind sat up.

'*This* compartment only goes up to Osnabruck. The compartment for Berlin is at the end of the train,' she said. And then she was off again, red Samsonite and Dolly in tow. She put me in the correct compartment, plonked me between two Americans in thick, black-spectacles and Bermuda-shorts, and made sure I was okay.

Even today, I'm not so sure if she was an au pair. She had to have been a secret agent.

We bade our goodbyes. Mine was fervent. What the hell was I going to do now, after my guardian angel had set the trip in motion? Rosalind made her way back to her compartment.

There was a lady in her thirties sitting next to the window.

'My name is Rosemary Panknin,' she said. She was freckled and mousy-haired and timid-looking. She was also scheduled to disembark in Osnabruck. She spent the rest of her journey trying to talk to me. I didn't want much to do with her. She projected none of Rosalind's serene confidence. And I was nervous. I had never been to Berlin before. I didn't know anyone. I was on my own. Most of all, I didn't speak the local language, something that had held me in such good stead in London.

As she gathered her things to disembark at Osnabruck at 11.30 in the morning, Rosemary turned to me. 'I come from Berlin, but I'm meeting my parents in Osnabruck and spending the weekend with them. I return to Berlin on Monday, but I have a sister called Anna in Berlin. I will tell her to help you.'

It sounded like lip-service, something you tell tourists you'll never see again. I thought I'd be better off if I attached myself to the two Americans. They'd studiously ignored me thus far, but they were headed to the youth hostel and I could use the company, even if it meant just tagging along.

We reached Berlin at about 8.30 in the evening. No Rosalind this time, and the Americans weren't interested in being gallant. I must have cut a sorry figure, or a comic one, tottering along on my heels, in my saree, dragging my big red suitcase, trying to keep up with two hulking Yanks in shorts.

I resigned myself to losing track of my silent companions, and having to step onto a Berlin street all on my own when a very attractive blonde in a smartly tailored blue dress glided up to me, like an Aryan Mary Poppins.

'You must be Dolly,' she said. 'My sister Rosemary rang. I am to take you home. Our parents heard that an Indian girl was coming and are driving back immediately.'

And just like that, Berlin was magic.

~

Anna took me to Lichterfelde, on Finckenstein Alle. The Panknins lived in a very modest house, but it was comfortable and safe. Within thirty minutes, a car pulled into the driveway. Mutti and Fatti and Rosemary had abandoned their Osnabruck weekend and come home to look after the Indian girl.

For a brief moment, I had a vivid recollection of growing up with my parents. We had our problems, sure, but they approached life like the Panknins – their door was always open and there was always an extra place at the table.

The whole family fussed over me. We ate in the kitchen and we talked. They were full of questions. Where was I from? What did I do? What was I doing in London? What was I doing in Germany?

For once in my life I could reply that I was here to see my boyfriend. It felt very grown up.

As we tidied the kitchen after supper, the family asked if there was anything I needed.

And being a true Indian, I replied: 'I'd like to have a bath.'

'Sure,' they said. 'Why don't you unpack?'

I thought they'd have to get the hot water going or something like that. So I went, unpacked my suitcase and re-entered the kitchen.

The dining table and the chairs had been cleared away. What I had assumed was a kitchen cabinet, or the place where the Panknins stored their crockery and cutlery, stood open. The bathtub it contained was now in place of the table. Plastic pipes ran from the tub to the taps in the sink. The family beamed at me and indicated that I should go ahead.

I was stunned and a little embarrassed. Even in the West, one man's standard amenity was another man's unimaginable luxury. Everywhere, the shadow of the war. Austerity had become part of people's lives.

I also began to understand the European practice of a good wash.

I didn't have the heart to ask for a bath again that week. So, every morning, I 'bathed' perched on the toilet seat. I pirated hot water from the sink in a glass I'd smuggle into the loo.

I was overwhelmed by their warmth and affection. They introduced me to everyone as their Indian daughter. Rosemary worked in a jewellery shop, and Anna was an editor at a large publishing house. The Panknins were lifelong Berliners and talking to them was better than any history book.

They accompanied me to the museum near the Berlin Wall. They walked through the exhibition, crying silently. They took me to Check Point Charlie, the border crossing into East Berlin. On the drive there, they issued instructions non-stop: don't talk to too many people, don't get too familiar, don't stay in one place too long, keep your head down.

East Berlin was a symphony in grey, bleak and dismal, hurried and bloodless. It felt like someone had, slowly, carefully, very deliberately, leached the colour out of the world.

When I crossed back into West Berlin that evening, the Panknins greeted me like a long-lost relative who had finally managed to defect from behind the Iron Curtain.

The next day they drove me to Kurfürstendamm, which was Berlin's Champs-Élysées, a historic boulevard and the luxury shopping district. We saw the Kaiser Wilhelm Memorial Church, which Berliners call 'The Hollow Tooth', because the spire was badly damaged during the Second World War, but was left to stand as a monument when the church was rebuilt. We also went to the Schiller Theatre, home of the Prussian State Theatre. And we went to a large Saturday dance hall, where they showed me off to all their friends. It's not as if they were babysitters for just that week: by the time we exchanged goodbyes, I had a formidable list of contacts in Munich, Heidelberg and Stuttgart. The Panknins had worked the phones, and I had a guard of honour all the way through to Dilip.

In Munich, I found another Rosalind. She had been commandeered by Frank, an editor friend of Anna's who had, in turn, commandeered Rosalind as part of Dolly's Guard. Much like Dick Stokoe on my first night in Cambridge, Frank got nervous about an Indian girl staying with him. I just hope I lived up to the myth: the Indian women in the heads of these white boys seemed fascinating. But Frank enlisted Rosalind, his secretary. Which is a hell of an entry on the job list.

'Send the two letters and, oh yes, there's an Indian girl arriving on the train from Berlin. She's now your problem.'

Munich Rosalind was understandably nervous and she brought along her friend for support. So here were these two young ladies, both wielding German-English dictionaries. It was all a bit *Monty Python*.

After much pointing and gibbering and nudging and nodding, the girls managed to say: 'Schwabing'. Schwabing was Munich's district of fun. Sort of like Soho, lots of bars, but with more red and a harder edge.

'Yes!' I said. And nodded with enthusiasm. 'Ja,' I said, in case they'd missed my meaning.

Off we went. I gawked at everything around me like a yokel, trying to take in the authentic Munich I'd only ever heard about. We'd barely taken our seats when someone put a hand on my chair and knelt by my side.

'Dolly?'

And there was Veena Luthra, an old friend from Miranda House, studying at the Goethe Institute. I never did ascertain exactly what she was doing at a Schwabing place, but I was thrilled to see someone I knew well in the unlikeliest of locations. We screamed at each other in delight, in stereo, and went straight back to getting along like a house on fire.

For the next three days, I went to Rosalind's to sleep. She was very sweet, but my presence seemed to wreck her nerves. The rest of the time, Veena had the Institute Director's chauffeur-driven car at her disposal and the two of us went everywhere together. Including the beer festival at the Augusteiner Keller Garten, where fantastic blondes carried ten one-litre mugs of beer to a table at one go.

The sights and the sounds, the cities themselves, flew by faster as I got closer to Dilip. In Heidelberg, I was met at the station by the very gentle Monica, another one of the girls enlisted by the Panknins, who showed me around the historic fort and the Brandenburg Gate.

I arrived in Stuttgart, and my vacation paused to draw a breath. I was with Dilip. Everything else receded to the background. The hop-picking camp seemed in no hurry. Dilip and I would picnic in the Black Forest all day. We even made love under a poplar tree. It was exhilarating – in my other life, this was something beyond my deepest, wildest fantasy – even though it was pretty uncomfortable. The movies prepare you for long gazes and quivering lips. What they don't prepare you for is bramble and twigs, poking into your back, leaving you scratched and itchy.

Dilip and I always chuckle over that memory.

~

Our next holiday together was Costa Brava in Spain, in May 1967, on a package tour that cost a grand total of sixteen pounds sterling, each, plus fares. We flew on a Dakota that looked ancient enough to have been refused a part in the Second World War. It taxied for so long at Mansted Airfield that a bunch of our Northern co-passengers set up a chorus: 'Put in a bob (hey!)/ It's running out of gas (hey!)'

Compared to Germany, this holiday was ultra-luxurious. We lived in a clean, modern hotel by the sea. The attendants went a little batty when they saw Dilip. 'El Cordobé!' they kept screaming. We weren't sure if this was a good thing. Further inquiries revealed that 'El Cordobé' was the most popular matador in Spain, rather than a comment on Dilip's corduroy habits. Dilip, of course, was well-chuffed. He always fancied himself the best-looking man in any room, and here was international recognition.

We bought a guitar. We sat around on the beach, in the shadow of an abandoned boat, and sang 'King of the Road', which was about 70 per cent of Dilip's repertoire at any gathering.

After two days of eating Spanish omelettes for breakfast, lunch and dinner, we ventured into town. The place was quaint, like a giant collage of picture postcards, cobbled streets, warm and intimate. Van Gogh on a good day. We walked from cafés to restaurants to corner shops, peering at the menus pasted on the storefront windows. We stopped at a place we thought we could afford, although we couldn't make head or tail of the menu. We'd forgotten our Spanish-English dictionaries at the hotel, of course. So we had to go with the waitress's recommendation – although she could have been speaking Cyrillic.

The 'Calibra' arrived in due course. Two, white, four-inch pieces of *something*, liberally dosed with coriander. Or maybe it was parsley? It could have been white dhokla left out in the sun. We picked up our knives and forks and spent the next few minutes stabbing at the meal in vain. Each piece had the consistency of a rubber doormat. We clinked and clanked and swore under our breaths. Then we decided to stop being sophisticated and went at lunch with our bare hands – the way God intended it.

And chewed. And chewed. Then chewed some more. It felt like we were trying to force down recalcitrant chewing gum, with a distinct lack of character or flavour, spiced with coriander. We rushed back to the hotel room, now bona fide international travellers, and located 'Calibra' in our dictionaries.

We'd just eaten a tentacle of a large octopus. Which, I later discovered, isn't really the best kind of octopus.

Back to the Spanish omelettes we went.

Over the weekend, we went to Barcelona by bus. We didn't speak the language, didn't know the city, but who cared? Through a combination of sign language and three-and-a-half mangled Spanish words, we asked a co-passenger, a little gnome of a man, for some directions. He was a masseur for a football team – at least I think that's what he meant. He might just as well have been in pepperoni manufacture. He asked us to follow him to the International Industries Fair, where they served good Indian tea. We'd conveyed that much, at least.

I was delighted when we got to the tea-board stall. There's something about the faint whiff of home. In a strange country, faces that only seemed familiar made you feel less alone.

We gleefully ordered two cups of Darjeeling. Proper bloody tea. Unlike the watery hot milk we drank in England. The girl who served us did a bit of a double-take and leant forward.

'Dolly Rawson?'

Juhi Tandon, alumnus, the Miranda House Mafia.

Before I could ask any questions of her, Juhi told us to go visit the India Pavilion and then come back. We dutifully went across to the main Pavilion. We peered around and tried to guess why Juhi had sent us here. That's when I felt a hand on my shoulder. I turned around to find Pondy Verma standing there with a huge smile on his face.

Pondy was with the Indian Foreign Service, and his current posting was Madrid. I'd met him in Delhi, but I really got to know him through Kris Srinivasan.

Many of my friends in England found it strange that I could go to these far-flung places and always, somehow, bump into someone I knew from my old life in Delhi. But this was also a time when knowing anyone with marginal influence could make a difference to your life. The old-boy network ran on connections made in school and university. As a consequence, only a select group of well-travelled Indians had the opportunities to work abroad. Girls like Juhi were from the right families. We were still groggy from our colonial hangover. Hostess duties always came to the same group of people. They spoke the right kind of English and had the right bearing.

Plus, I was just plain lucky. Always. Someone watched over me, alright.

In Spain, Dilip and I managed to attend a real bullfight. Matador El Cordobé fought, and won. But we were in the cheapest seats, right up in the nosebleeds, and no matador doffed his hat to me!

~

Between holidays in Germany and Spain, Dilip and I continued to meet every day. We fought more and more. We'd transitioned from mutual attraction to a relationship proper, and we weren't a good match. We came from different worlds. I never really cared for his friends. He thought my Cambridge set was dirty and bohemian. He wanted to return to India after his finals. 'I don't want to remain a second-class citizen here,' he kept saying.

That was fine. Except he wanted to go to India and be a first-class citizen. He believed he could rent a nice room, with electricity, running water and everything, for a hundred rupees a month and live a comfortable life on a minimal allowance. He'd only known India as a student – flying from Kenya to Bishop Cotton Boys' in Bangalore and then flying straight to Europe or Africa at the end of the school term. I tried to tell him that he wanted to go to India to be a white man because, otherwise, he didn't know what he was talking about. He knew it all, though. He'd seen it all.

Dilip always fancied himself a bit of a lion on the prowl, a rotating cast of slow-moving gazelle in his sights. He was popular, and he had a series of special girlfriends. I had first-hand experience of how he could dial up the charm. He'd met a Swedish girl called Merta on an earlier strawberry-picking camp and, when I asked, went blue in the face trying to deny he continued to stay in touch with her.

Then he asked me to help tidy his room. And, of course, a bundle of letters and photographs from Merta fell to the floor, into a convenient patch of sunlight. I felt betrayed. I accused Dilip of two-timing me. I cried. He looked guilty, stared at his feet and mumbled a lot.

Writing this now, I wonder if he'd meant for me to find that bundle? Is that why he'd enlisted my help? That he hoped it would save him from sitting me down and saying, 'Look, it's just not working anymore.'

Like a typical university romance, which is what this really was, we'd begun in a blaze and were limping towards the finish.

~

Kris and I had continued to write each other. Always a trickle, never a flood, the letters back and forth remained a constant. Kris was now Charge d'Affaires in Beirut. He wrote to tell me that he was expected in London on the 27th of September 1967. He was going to visit his estranged father in Sussex, over the weekend of the 29th. The letter ended with a request: when Kris met his father and his new family, it would mean a lot to him if I were there. Would I consider it?

I would. I felt very protective towards Kris. And Dilip had finished his exams and had been called to the Bar from Lincoln's Inn. We'd said our goodbyes. There was some sadness, but neither of us would commit to a future. This was it.

Dilip left for Nairobi on Tuesday, 26th of September 1967.

~

Kris and I were to meet for coffee near my office on King's Way on the 28th. We had to sort out our train tickets – when and where. But we also needed to get to know each other again. I hadn't seen him in over three years.

Late that night, there was a knock on the door. I sat up in bed, alarmed. It could be a stranger. It could be Saeed. There was another knock. I put on my gown, crept down the hall and peered out at the stoop.

Dilip stood there, like a castaway. All flights to Kenya had been suspended. President Jomo Kenyatta had made an entry permit mandatory for all Indians returning to Kenya. Dilip was, for the moment, without a country. He had no one else to turn to. His suitcases surrounded him, like a small fort.

That was as low as I ever saw Dilip. He was stateless, and powerless to do anything about it. He seemed calm, but I thought he was panicked. There was no quick fix for a situation like this. And because he was, technically, an alien, his status in England could change overnight. He'd gone from being a first-class citizen of Kenya to a refugee in a matter of hours.

There was no question of Dilip going anywhere else at that time of night. He'd live with me. And it would have been callous of me to abandon him for the weekend. I had to change my plans immediately.

Kris left for Sussex, alone and angry.

~

It took Dilip two months to get his papers in order. He departed for Nairobi, but things were different between us now – better, but more complicated.

My correspondence with Kris restarted. He invited me to come visit him in Beirut in April of '68.

In March, on my birthday, a telegram arrived.

'From Dilip. Nothing has changed. Stop. I love you still. Stop. Come to India. Stop. Let's marry. Stop.'

I sat with that telegram in my hand for a long time. I was smiling, though my heart beat faster and my cheeks were flushed. But, as much as that telegram meant to me, I knew real life was messy and not the fairy tale I'd been fed as a young woman.

I wasn't just going to fly into Dilip's arms. And I wasn't going to miss the chance to see Kris, and to visit Beirut.

~

Of course, I landed in Beirut just as tensions in the Middle East, in the aftermath of the Six-Day War, began to rise again. Within hours, Air India had closed down its offices and their Commercial Director Bobby Kooka had flown in for talks.

Kris was on call right through the week. His driver, a handsome young man, was the one deputed to show me around – Beit-e-dine, Al Hamra and Tyre. Kris would return home late, always preoccupied. Even though we shared the same bed, he'd curl up in a corner and go to sleep. He'd twitch and toss and turn all night. I never got the chance to find out whether or not we could have been intimate. We didn't even hold hands.

It was a strange week, a fever dream. An eerie echo from my time in Bombay just before I left for London.

Love, travel, war.

Kris managed to obtain leave that weekend. We planned to drive to Damascus and live with Prem Shankar Jha, an old friend from Delhi. We left nice and early and were at the Syrian border by noon. Only to find that I wouldn't be allowed into Syria without special permission because my passport read 'journalist'. So we made the six-hour trip back and Kris got on the phone, calling various friends and sections and ministries.

We tried again the next day. This time, we drifted across the border like we were-on a magic carpet. We decided to drive straight to the Indian Ambassador's residence to thank him. We rang the bell, introduced ourselves and were asked to wait.

A few minutes later, a voice called out: 'There can only be one Dolly Rawson.'

It was Tony Kidwai, the Ambassador's daughter, also of the Miranda House Mafia. I leapt up, and we hugged.

Air India had resumed services to Beirut while I was still there, and Esmie flew in with a letter from Dilip, now in Bombay. He still loved me and went on to say a series of flattering things. The world seemed a little less bleak. I didn't mind Kris being preoccupied. I was too. Once again, it seemed, fate had intervened.

~

Back in London, I began to make plans for my return to India, and my wedding, and setting up a life with Dilip. I had a list of things I wanted to take back, things that weren't available in India – cutlery, crockery, non-stick pans and a washing machine.

I'm not saying it was rational. But it *was* fun. I was playing 'House'.

I looked for work that would bring in a little extra money. I enrolled with an employment agency, and they shipped me off to a variety of odd jobs. I typed up the credit payment lists of the ultra-rich shoppers at Harrods'. It sounds much more glamorous than it was. I sat in a dingy back room, decidedly un-Harrods like, typed like a maniac and hated every minute of it. After a week of that, it was time to move on.

The very next day, I was sent to the offices of the 'Dictionary of International Biography', Victoria Street, St. James' Park. For five pounds a week extra, I quit the BBC and was made editorial assistant. It was a respectable establishment in a quaint building, and a well-worked, well-oiled scam run by the handsome and distinguished Ernest Kay.

We picked American firms from the telephone directory. We called them and explained, at some length, how privileged they were to have been nominated for *inclusion* in the Dictionary of

International Biography. And then, once we had their attention, we made our pitch.

For two hundred dollars, they could have their name included in the Dictionary of International Biography, and they'd receive a bound copy. For four hundred dollars, they could have their name inscribed in gold on a leather-bound edition. And for an *additional* eight hundred dollars, they could attend a weekend conference in New York in April 1968, along with everyone else listed in the Dictionary.

What an august gathering that would have been. And it would have been my first visit to New York.

We did well. The dollars rolled in. But the event was cancelled because Martin Luther King Jr was assassinated two weeks before the event was scheduled to take place.

This was our generation's Nigerian General scam. You know the one: 'You too can partake of the general's secret stash of two hundred million. Just give me your details.' Over the years, I've received many requests to pay up for an award or a certificate. The last one was an American committee who had nominated me for 'International Woman of the Year'. One hundred and ninety-eight dollars for a certificate I could frame and hang on my wall.

I declined. You can't scam a scammer.

~

By August of 1968, Dilip's enthusiasm had waned. The stream of letters dried up. He'd made a great impression on a bunch of young students at the St. Xavier's Social League Camp in Dahanu, and his life in Bombay was looking up. His life-jacket from a few months ago had become a ball and chain.

I needed answers, though. I'd reapplied for the position of story editor with BBC2. This was an assignment I coveted. But my seniors were also aware of my potential return to Bombay. The application remained in limbo. I'd given notice to my landlady. And I had written to my parents: I was considering a marriage proposal from Dilip, and I might return home after almost four years.

My mother had met Dilip on her Christmas visit in ’66 and she hadn’t been impressed. He was caustic and abrupt. He wouldn’t court her opinion; there was no wining and dining, no driving her around. And she was aghast I was dating a postman. I tried to explain to her that students on their winter break almost always worked blue-collar jobs. Dilip’s happened to be with the postal service. In reality, he was a lawyer in training. But, no. Dolly was dating the postman. The daakiya.

By the time I made the trip to Delhi via Bombay, my correspondence with Dilip was at a bare minimum and my parents were worried. But I’d made a promise, London was on hold, and I didn’t have the heart to cancel my trip.

So I got on the damned plane.

III
Bombay Girl

11

I LANDED IN Bombay on the 28th of November 1968. Dilip knew I was on that flight, and he knew that I was expected in Bombay, but there was no sign of him at the airport. I made my way to Ashley House, Colaba, where my friend Denaz (née Khory, now Tata) lived. I was aware Dilip was close by, maybe five hundred yards away, on Wodehouse Road. But two could play that game, so I didn't go looking for him either.

I spent three days in Bombay, and then left for Delhi on the 1st of December.

Except, as I alighted the bus at the airport, who should I run into? The young and dashing Dilip Thakore. He knew my schedule alright. Before I could say a word, he said: 'Miss the flight.'

Damnfool that I was, I might have done it too. But it was Daddy's birthday, so I told Dilip I couldn't. Dilip promised he'd be on the next flight to Delhi. He must have forgotten that promise as soon as he made it because all I got was a series of confusing letters.

In the first letter, Dilip poured his heart out to me. He loved me. He loved me more than I could ever imagine. The next afternoon, I got another letter. This time, he stressed that all he wanted was the best for me. And he did not think that he was the best for me. And out of deference for his feelings for my well-being, etc. The third letter showed up the day after. On that day, he was of the opinion that he *was* the best for me, after all.

On and on it went, for three weeks. We didn't have a phone at home in those days. I had a bunch of hurried (and polite) phone conversations at the neighbours'. And this steady stream of letters. By the end of those three weeks, I was more bemused than alarmed. I just couldn't get a handle on what Dilip was trying to say because what he said changed every day.

As if I needed more fuel to this merry blaze, Kris Srinivasan arrived in Delhi. He was en route to his new posting in Libya.

We did the rounds at parties with old Delhi friends. It was warm, familiar, comfortable. Kris was attentive and affectionate, and that made it worse. I didn't know what I wanted. I knew Kris and I liked him, and I liked our time together. But something was missing. Dilip had a hold on me. I don't know why. Maybe because the relationship never quite ended. Like a bad habit.

I decided I had to see him. I needed to know if I was going back to London and my job with the BBC, or whether I was going to start a life in India with Dilip.

~

I packed all my things and got on a flight to Bombay. Yet again, Dilip failed to pick me up, so I took the airport bus to the Air India office in Kala Ghoda. And then a taxi to 5, Sobani Road, where Dilip shared a charming flat with Rumi Mistry and Shankar Menon.

Dilip answered the door. It was clearly one of those days where he thought he *wasn't* the best for me. I wasn't expecting an apology; I knew Dilip too well. But I thought he might be glad to see me.

'Hello, old fruit,' he said.

I promptly burst into tears. Dilip retreated to the corner of the room and watched me the way one watches a small, unpredictable firework. I tried to explain myself. I had a return ticket, I had a job waiting for me, and I had a life that I loved. If he didn't want me, I would fly out the next day.

Maybe Dilip saw a little of himself in me – a refugee looking for port. In the end, he did the best he could.

'I say, old fruit. Tomorrow is New Year's Eve. And there's a dance at the Catholic Gymkhana. So why don't you go after that?'

Damnfool that I was, I stayed. What else could I have done? Landed in London on the 31st of December? I think about that moment occasionally, though. And, some of the time, I wish I'd got on that plane and landed in the freezing cold. That would have jolted me back to my senses.

Because if I stayed, we'd move in together. And if we moved in together, we'd get married.

~

We both had issues we should have dealt with. Instead, we just clutched at the other person and swept the mess under the carpet, hoping it would go away.

I was twenty-six and unmarried, and a motley collection of aunties and gossip had a permanent residency in my head. I wanted to get married so that I could shut them up. Meanwhile, Dilip was twenty-six, attractive, England-educated and foreign-born. He'd gone and fallen in love with some Parsi girl at St. Xavier's. They'd met at the camp in Dahanu. She loved him, and he loved her.

Then I arrived, and he just couldn't make up his mind. He felt indebted to his 'old fruit', I think. He resented getting married at twenty-six. His father had married at thirty-seven, to someone twenty-two years his junior. Dilip's mother had him when she was barely seventeen, and they were close. She never failed to rib him about marrying so young. And marrying someone who was nine months older than him.

Hindsight, they say, is always perfect. We were terminally unsuited for each other. We were just too scared to see it.

We should have listened to his mother. Mummy was against our union from the start. I wasn't Hindu, wasn't Brahma-Kshatriya, didn't come from money, wasn't fair, wasn't pretty, wasn't thin enough.

She was an attractive Gujarati lady, very elegant. She split her time between Jhinja (in present-day Uganda) and Nakuru (now in Kenya), on the Thakore's five-thousand-acre estate in East Africa. They had timber and coffee plantations. She had a staff the size of an army, drove a Mercedes, kept an excellent table, had really exquisite taste and was invited to royal banquets when the Windsors came visiting. She had a pair of white gloves for those occasions. She spoke the Gujarati-accented English that's so particular to East Africa.

We were always civil with each other – Mummy, Pappa and I. Never fought, and stayed cordial for years and years. I continued to visit them even after Dilip and I got divorced.

~

I moved in with Dilip. Within days, I began to feel a little insecure. I was just ... *there*. I felt like an outsider, an interloper, the rock that had chained itself to Dilip. Our hero was a struggling junior at the Bombay Bar, devilling with Mukund Modi. Law was a gentleman's profession. One sat in the High Court Library all day, reading briefs and case law. Dilip made sixty rupees that first year. The second year was a comparative windfall: one hundred and twenty-five rupees. So, Dilip had to make do on a monthly allowance of twenty-two hundred rupees from his father. It allowed him to live comfortably and nurse his bitterness. His rent at the Sobani Road flat was seven hundred rupees a month – so much for my Marxist boyfriend. He hated the sense of obligation. He hated his lack of self-worth. But he had to live a certain way, up to a certain standard. And when I moved in, he had a target for all that frustration.

He made me sign an Open Marriage Contract, although we weren't married yet. The contract entitled either of us to independent friends, independent holidays and shared expenses – down to the last paisa. We couldn't read each other's mail. It entitled us, in effect, to totally separate lives.

And that was fine. Kind of evolved, actually. But why were we getting married if our lives were to be this exclusive?

~

On my third day in Bombay, already a little overwhelmed by the complexities of Dilip's existential angst, I rang Kabir Bedi. He was the film chief at S.H. Benson's. I wanted to let him know I was in town and looking for a job.

'Come and see me, Doll,' he said. So I did. It was a relief to see a familiar face. We chatted for a bit and he asked: 'Do you want to act in a play?'

'Sure,' I said. A lot of my theatrical work has begun in exactly this fashion.

Off I went, to St. Xavier's college. The show was *The Persecution and Assassination of Jean-Paul Marat as Performed by the Inmates of the Asylum of Charenton Under the Direction of the Marquis de Sade*. Or: *Marat/Sade*. Directed by Alyque Padamsee.

Kabir introduced me to Pearl. I thought she was terrific. Alyque looked right through me – he was yelling at someone. The production was populated mostly by people from the advertising community in Bombay. It was a fairly typical rehearsal.

I knew who Alyque was, of course. Pearl and he were Bombay Theatre's 'First Couple'. I'd watched them in *The Crucible*, at the AIFACS in Delhi. And everyone talked about them in slightly awed tones. They had passed through London while I was there, but I never got to meet them.

I had a bit part – one of the inmates at the asylum. I attended rehearsals for about two weeks. I didn't really get to know anyone. Every night, after we were done, I'd have to take a taxi (which I couldn't afford) or a bus (which could be unpredictable) back to Wodehouse Road, where we lived. I dropped out because the taxi rides became too expensive for me. I didn't even have a job. If I *had* known people a little better, I would have learnt that Alyque and Pearl lived at Bella Terrace, next door to Dilip and myself.

Also playing one of the inmates was Leela Rao, a very fair girl, half-south Indian, half-English. Alyque decided that anyone with the name Dolly Rawson *had* to be very fair, while the dark little thing that Kabir had brought along was Leela Rao. It made no difference that I'd dropped out. Alyque had no idea who I was, and my name stayed in the cast and credits.

It was a brief little passage, of no real consequence.

~

During those two weeks of rehearsal, I wandered onto the first quadrangle of St. Xavier's one evening. Leaning against one of the pillars was an apparition. I blinked and looked again. She could have been an angel but she was too damn sexy. White saree, flowers in her hair, a Jesuit's worst nightmare.

This was Protima, then Gupta. She had come to meet Kabir and whisk him away to wherever beautiful people disappeared to.

We had them over for dinner soon after. Protima and Kabir, and my friend Rani Dube who was down from England. My old friend Randhir Behl from Delhi also came. Randhir was head of film, TV and radio at Hindustan Thompson Associates for the longest time. I had also invited Rasna, who choreographed fashion shows. Randhir and she met for the first time that night and would go on to get married. Which became a theme of sorts that night. Kabir chatted with Rani for most of the evening, while Protima was off being sick in the loo. 'It's my stomach,' she kept saying. Then she'd disappear again. Meanwhile, everyone in the living room talked about the possibility of a film on the life of Mahatma Gandhi. Attenborough, it seemed, was a little closer to making his dream a reality.

Protima was pregnant, of course. She and Kabir married nine days after that dinner. I wasn't invited, but I was happy for them. Kabir and I had known each other a long time. My sister Pam attended the wedding because she and Gulli, Kabir's sister, were good friends from Miranda House. Protima and I would have to wait a few more years before we became close.

~

I was walking down Colaba Causeway early in 1969. A man passed me, and I felt him shove his finger up my arse.

There's always a moment of disorientation: Is this happening? To me? Right now?

There's also a flinch – part-physical, part-emotional. Because, if you're an Indian woman, *you're always expecting it.*

Then anger.

I turned and I screamed. I screamed out and I screamed at him.

Not one person turned to look in our direction. Heads down, people went on with their business.

Welcome home, I thought.

~

In 2014, I did a three-hour archival recording for All India Radio. Jerry Pinto interviewed me. That it was an AIR interview was ironic. Because the first job I applied for when I got to Bombay, in 1969, was with AIR. They offered me three hundred rupees a month to produce a programme. That's how much I was paying for my accommodation. So, in early 1969, I joined National Advertising as a copywriter. I was hesitant about accepting the job. National wasn't the most glamourous agency. Plus, most copywriters spent their early years correcting grammar and being enthusiastic about ideas they hated. I couldn't bear it – these guys in wide ties and wide trousers. I thought they were idiots. Selling soap and writing copy. And I was starting from scratch – I had no prior experience. My life with Dilip, in Bombay, had rendered the past four years of my career redundant. But I had to pay my share of the expenses.

Like everyone else, big, chaotic events have bookmarked my emotional life – political upheaval, war, riots. And the people whose paths crossed mine at those times became, inevitably, important to me in some way.

On the 8th of February 1969, Dilip and I were headed to Bakhtawar on Nepean Sea Road. We'd been invited to lunch at Babli and Titu Bhagats' – Mala Sen's mother and stepfather. I remember the date clearly because the Shiv Sena had declared the first-ever Bombay Bandh. We had no idea what the hell a 'bandh' was. We also had no idea who the Shiv Sena were. We loitered around the bus stop until someone explained the situation to us. No 'bandh' was going to get in the way of civil liberties. Or free lunch at a Brigadier's. If we didn't have public transport, we'd hitch a ride.

The first car that came along was a little Hillman, piloted by a handsome woman in her seventies. There was a young man sitting next to her, up front, maybe seven years old and a real charmer.

'Where are you going?' she asked.

'Malabar Hill,' we said, in chorus.

'Well, I'm going to New Marine Lines,' she said. 'My son lives there, and I can give you a ride to his place.'

It was better than waiting around. Plus, we were getting hungry. So, we jumped in.

'What do you do?' the lady asked me, as we pulled away.

'I'm looking for a job in advertising,' I said. Advertising seemed to be where all the interesting people congregated. They travelled the world, they haggled over aesthetics, and they listened to jazz and argued about film.

'Oh,' she said. 'My sons are in advertising.'

'The only one I know in advertising is Gerson da Cunha,' I said. I'd even been to see Gerson at Lintas when I moved to Bombay. Just to let him know that I was here and that I was looking for a job. He obviously hadn't been impressed – no offer was forthcoming.

'That's my son! That's where I'm going.'

We'd just met Mrs da Cunha, mother of Gerson and his brother Sylvester. The little man was a young Rahul. Sylvie, and later Rahul, are significant writer-directors in the theatre. But their real claim to fame are the Amul hoardings that have tracked the mood of the city and the country for decades.

Gerson was getting married on the 26th of February. Because he was travelling, Mrs da Cunha was going over to supervise renovations.

'Oh,' I said, confident in my insider knowledge of high-flown circles. 'To Caroline.'

Mrs da Cunha let go of the steering wheel and turned, all the way, to face me. The car swerved wildly.

'Who's Caroline?'

I lied valiantly about a friend of Gerson's I'd met in London and made some (clearly) stupid assumptions about. I don't think she was convinced, but – if she knew her son at all – she couldn't have been surprised. Gerson had a catalogue of doomed romances. He was sharp, good-looking, kind, considerate, very funny, with a voice that made your skin tingle. But with a romantic mandate that was always tragic. Why? I do not know.

He was marrying an Uma Krupanidhi, whom I'd never heard of. But we trooped along to the bungalow and nodded wisely as Mrs da Cunha explained what she was doing and why.

~

Dilip and I decided to get married. Almost as if we were holding each other hostage. We settled on the 16th of May 1969 as the date of our wedding.

Work had begun to pick up. I'd only been at National Advertising a little while before Vimal Ahuja asked me to help him out on his film – *Five Past Five*, with Zul Vellani in the lead. I took a few weeks off work, and it was like diving headfirst into the rabbit hole. Sometimes I think some of us become workaholics *precisely* because work *isn't* real life. You can control it. Things make sense. Effort has its just reward.

I left the secure bosom of National Advertising for the more vicarious pleasures of being a model coordinator at S.H. Benson's, because of Frank Simoes. I knew Fred Simoes, Frank's brother, in London, and that's how I came to their attention. The job was an amalgam – finding the right people for the right jobs, and minding the talent during the execution of the shoot/campaign/project. Sort of like a primitive casting director, much before the term existed in this country. I enjoyed the work, but it *was* like being a bloody peon.

On the side, I compéred a few fashion shows. I moderated a couple of discussions. I didn't like doing the fashion shows much – but it seemed a logical progression. I did, however, enjoy being front and centre. I never angled for it, but it was always an added benefit. What I would've liked was to have been in broadcasting. In the meantime, I needed to make rent. I wasn't ambitious, and I was pleased with what I was getting.

AIR asked me to host their *Women's Hour Weekly*, so I was back on radio again. This was a show that talked about women's issues and also dispensed advice and tips about how to balance work and home, bring up children and still look good. That kind of thing. *Femina* ran a story. As a result, I was approached to compére another set of fashion shows. I was a freelancer now, good and proper.

My nascent copywriting career was over. Before it had begun. Sort of like my marriage.

Mummy and Pappa came down from Nakuru a month before the big day. Pappa wanted a grand party, regardless of the size of the wedding, regardless of what we wanted. And Mummy wanted to break us up.

Once, only days away from the ceremony, Dilip and I had a minor disagreement, and I burst into tears. My mother-in-law-to-be put her arms around me. She tried to be as much of a comfort as she could.

'Don't worry,' she said. 'We'll get you another man. We'll make sure of it.'

At least it was better than her constant assertion that I was fat because of my exclusively North Indian diet.

My wedding – the only one I've ever had, I'm afraid – had this surreal strain running smack through the middle of it, a crazy red or a virulent yellow. At some point, it had become performance art.

The day itself was a disaster. We had a simple ceremony, just the signing before the registrar, in the presence of some thirty friends and relatives. The wedding was followed by a large dinner at the Radio Club for Pappa's Brahma-Kshatriya relatives and friends. No one else wanted to be there.

And it ended with Dilip prancing around our bedroom, knee-deep in the drift of discarded wrapping paper and plastic bags that had held our gifts, tossing them about like he was a child playing with dead leaves in autumn.

'Here you go, bourgeois,' he kept saying. 'Here you go. This is why you wanted to get married. This …' toss, toss, toss and prance '… this is why. Here, bourgeois. Here.'

Mills & Boon, this wasn't. I did the only thing I could do: I sat down and wept.

~

At least I had my work. I'd never travelled for shoots before. Even going to the suburbs was a big deal. The work was mostly for print campaigns. I remember the *Vogue* campaign. My model was Shobha Rajyadhyaksha. We shot in the Rajasthan Suite at the Taj. Shobha wore my wedding saree. The jewellery belonged to Gita Simoes, Frank's wife. The two of us trundled off to the bank, pulled ornaments out of the safety locker and dressed Shobha. That photograph can still be seen in the lobby of the Taj.

Hindustan Ferodo was also our client at the time. They manufactured trucks. For one of their campaigns, we needed a big, hulking Sardar. At a loss for ideas, I hung around Peddar Road until I found a Sardar taxi driver. I flagged him down, started the meter and had a nice, long chat with him.

'Look,' I said. 'I need a big, hefty Sardar truck driver for a photo.'

Thank God Bombay was a great deal more innocent back then.

My taxi driver took me to Sion-Koliwada, and that was indeed a paradise for Sardar truck drivers. Word got around that a crazy lady was looking for a driver for a photo and they soon lined up. I was a little overwhelmed. A group of titanic Sardars came up and presented themselves like I was calling attendance in school. They were polite and very good-humoured. It was a real pleasure. I picked the one I thought worked and walked into the office with an-honest-to-goodness Sardar truck driver.

I did that for about six months. Being a model coordinator, not auditioning Sardar truck drivers, that is. I wanted to be an account executive. The closest I got at S.H. Benson's was handling the launch for the Cottage Industries Emporium. I was the PRO. Then Jack Hawthorne, the head at S.H. Benson's, left. Within a few short months, Sherry Mukherjee, Jack's successor, broke away to form his own company. With him went Arrau Sinha Roy, Julian Almeida, Adil Screwvala and myself. The new firm was called AIMS. It fizzled out in a matter of months.

In the '70s and '80s, advertising firms in Bombay were like restaurants. Every week brought a blizzard of launches and an equal number of flameouts.

~

Dilip and I had a six-month leave-and-licence agreement on an apartment in Nyan Jyot, Cuffe Parade. The landlord was a Parsi gentleman by the name of Sahir Palonji. He only agreed to lease the place when Dilip produced his British passport.

Initially, we lunched together every day at Samovar, God bless. This was the small restaurant attached to the Jehangir Art Gallery. I worked out of Steelcrete House, Dinshaw Watcha Road, while Dilip was at the High Court. Samovar was everything you could ask for: location, price, vibe. In December 1991, I would attend its twenty-fifth anniversary party, wondering where the time had gone because it still felt like yesterday. There was a lunch gang – Dilip, myself, a whole group of college friends, artists and painters who occupied the tables at Samovar's veranda. We often spotted Shobha there too.

But Dilip never picked me up from work, never dropped me off. Didn't matter where I was, what I was doing. All part of the Open Marriage Contract.

Shyam and Nira Benegal came over for a potluck dinner once and Dilip turned to me and said: 'I say, old fruit, you owe me seven paise.' He'd bought a box of matches.

Time after time, Dilip would open the door to welcome dinner guests: 'Come, come, come. Dolly's been on her knees all day, cleaning the floors. And she's even pulled out and polished the silver. Come on in.'

Silver? *Silver*? I didn't even have a maid.

Each time, the words landed like a blow. I died a little. Dozens of little deaths.

~

I still can't quite believe *how* schizophrenic that time was. On the one hand, I had a show on AIR. I had a handful of magazine covers. I was Dolly Thakore. People knew who I was. I had vanilla fame – not too hot, not too cold. I liked it.

But I didn't really want to go home anymore. Dilip went at me like a sculptor goes at a rock – it's not the hundredth blow, but the ninety-nine that went before it that shape the object.

Somehow, my marriage had become an examination of my moral fibre.

Dilip desperately wanted membership at the Bombay Gymkhana. He'd been blackballed twice, even though he played tennis there regularly. In the end, my boss, P.N. Sharma from Benson's, got him in. So, that was my fault too.

Every time I introduced Dilip as my husband, he'd retort, 'What husband, whose husband?' Every single time. Our maniacal splitting of costs was a standing joke amongst friends. Even if it was a sachet of salt, it had to be settled right away. *Then* and *there*.

If I put the cushions out in a triangle, he'd rearrange them as a square. It was that simple. It was that fundamental. It was that petty.

Dilip has had two more wives. That's two marriages more than I've had the courage for. His other wives tell me that he's stayed the same. Which is a relief of sorts – it wasn't just me then.

~

One morning, Dilip emerged from the shower. He paced around the house in his towel. Then he wandered into the kitchen. A fresh packet of milk had been delivered that morning, and I'd done the Bombay thing – the milk had gone straight into a gleaming steel vessel, and then boiled and simmered and was now cooling, ready to be used. Dilip dipped his fingers into the milk, fishing out bits of malai.

'Get a spoon, please,' I said. 'Don't – don't do that.'

'What?' Fingers in and out of the milk. Eyes on my face.

'Don't do that. It – you shouldn't. It's not right. Get a spoon. Please.'

Dilip looked at his fingers and then thrust them at me, under my nose.

'They're clean. I just showered.'

'I didn't say they were dirty,' I said. 'It just makes sense to use a spoon.'

'Is there a law?' He asked the question like he'd seen through to the heart of the dilemma in a vivid flash, like he'd cracked the case wide open. He was triumphant.

'What?'

'Where is it written in a book of law that I cannot use my fingers, my *clean* fingers in a bowl of milk in my house? Show me.'

And he paraded around the house in his towel, asking to be shown the law that stated he couldn't handle a bowl of milk with clean fingers. He looked like a man who'd lost his mind and now insisted that he was the emperor.

~

What to say about this boring little horror show that my marriage had become? Not big horror, mind you, just stupid and hurtful. What to say to a man who called me 'grinning jackanapes'? In public? To my face?

Jackanapes: definition: 1. a conceited or impudent person.

2. a monkey or an ape.

I smiled too much, apparently. I was too eager to please.

I don't know when I realized I was in an abusive relationship. Just because he didn't hit didn't mean he didn't hurt. And he hurt. He hurt daily, like a ritual. He made humiliation mundane.

Ritchie had left his scooter with Dilip when he departed for America on the merchant ship. We only used it for international film festivals at the Shanmukhananda Hall, because we went after work. We'd finish late and taking a cab back was an extravagance. The scooter was used infrequently and, without fail, would stall at traffic signals.

Dilip wasn't strong enough to kick-start the scooter on his own. And in front of all those men on Mohammed Ali Road, he'd ask me to kick-start the scooter, while he berated me.

'Why? Why are *you* inferior? Why can't you kick the scooter?'

Maybe it was because I was poor. Ritchie had left a 'dud' scooter. And I'd never save any money. Dilip was convinced of this.

We were walking down Warden Road once. His parents were with us, visiting from Kenya. I ran into a kirana store to buy a bottle of Sunsilk – I'd forgotten to pick up shampoo all week. It cost three rupees twenty-five paise in those days.

A little further down the road, Dilip piped up. 'I say, old fruit. Did you find out how much the shampoo was in the shop next door?'

I hadn't, I confessed. But the difference would have been a few paise, if anything at all.

Dilip shook his head. He looked grave, and a little troubled. 'See, that's why you Christians have no money.'

We limped along, too stupid and too scared to sit down and call a spade a spade, tied to each other by nostalgia for our lives in England.

I will give him this: when we got along, we got along well. And Dilip really showed me the world. Film, books, theatre, music, art, sport – these were all things that Dilip brought into my life. Until then, my only interest in the 'arts' had to do with getting on stage.

Dilip pushed, prodded and cajoled, and changed forever the way I looked at culture. But we weren't equals. It was inevitable we'd drift apart.

By the end of that year, I was pregnant. Dilip wouldn't bring a child into this world. He said it would have been irresponsible of us. I had an abortion. Another little death.

The six-month lease in Cuffe Parade ran out. We found a place just off Pedder Road. S.H. Benson's signed the eleven-month leave-and-licence agreement, and Dilip paid the deposit – twenty-one hundred rupees. And in January of 1970, we moved again.

I've never moved house since. Others have come and gone. I've been here fifty-one years.

~

A telephone – and by this, I mean a landline, an artefact comprising Bakelite, fuelled by hope, prayer and certain swear words – was a luxury. There were maybe three in any given building. You made friends with the people who had telephones. And they tolerated random calls from strangers at random hours for people who lived in other apartments. People almost always called in an emergency, and only then. Those were the rules and we played by them.

A few weeks after we'd moved to Pedder Road, I received a message from my neighbours on the first floor – Shyam and Nira Benegal. There was a phone call for me. I went downstairs with some trepidation. I hoped it wasn't bad news.

'Is that Dolly?' a nasal, commanding voice asked.

'Yes.'

'This is Alyque. Alyque Padamsee.'

'Hi, Alyque,' I said.

'I hear you know bathrooms,' he said. 'And I'm looking for some bathrooms.'

Right. Backstory:

I'd just coordinated a shoot for a Johnson's ad. Wilas Bhende had been the photographer on that shoot, and we'd done an extensive recce of some very good-looking bathrooms. Now, Wilas was a very big deal – he shot all the major campaigns. He was working for Lintas next, and they were shooting the film and then the print ads for Maharani Soap, with Farida Darashah. Wilas had gone to a meeting, listened to the brief, put his teacup down and said: 'You have to call Dolly Thakore. She knows all the bathrooms. She knows the best bathrooms in Bombay.'

So Alyque called. And then turned up a half hour later and drove me to the handful of bathrooms I had shortlisted for the Johnson's ad. Alyque picked the one at Woodlands, on Pedder Road. The apartment (and the bathroom) belonged to Harshad Kumari of Limdi – better known as Jija. Jija was Sat's sister, and she lived in some style. That bathroom was like a palace.

Job done, Alyque asked if I'd like to be there for the shoot. I agreed straight away. I'd never been on an ad film set before. M.S. Sathyu was the cameraman.

~

M.S. Sathyu was awarded the Thespo for Lifetime Achievement in 2016. Thespo is a youth theatre festival. My son and his friend Christopher Samuel dreamt it up in 1999, and it was born on the carpet in my living room. It is now in its 23rd year.

I was there for the function in 2016. The first part of the evening was an extended Q&A with Sathyu, a genuine legend of the Indian stage, a director and designer for stage and screen, across generations, languages, milieu, the man who'd made *Garam Hawa*. As he warmed up, the Q&A became a free-wheeling conversation.

Sathyu suddenly brought up the first ad shoot *he'd* ever done. For Alyque, and for Maharani Soap. Sathyu recounted how they'd run out of the gel they used to create the foam that looked so enticing on camera. Because it was a Sunday, and the stores were closed, he and his associates had to rush around the neighbourhood to find a solution. They came back with armfuls of Surf – a washing powder whose legendary campaigns Alyque had helmed – and basically doused Farida in piles of detergent.

Alyque presented Sathyu with the award that evening. As Sathyu told this story, Alyque leant forward in his seat and looked across to me. 'We were there, Doll,' he mouthed.

We were. We had been. He was right. I hadn't thought about that shoot in years. And all I could do was smile and nod.

~

I was asked to join the Lunch Committee of the Advertising Club of Bombay. Most of the heads of Bombay's leading advertising agencies met to discuss standards and practices, but it was also a forum to bitch and moan and gossip, and occasionally steal a march. I wasn't quite sure I belonged, but when had that ever stopped me?

Alyque often gave me a lift to these meetings and often dropped me off after. It became quasi-routine. He'd be on his way from a meeting or heading to a recording. I was glad for the gesture and for the company. Bombay wasn't my city. Not then, at any rate.

Almost naturally, these extended to casual cups of coffee, and then that became the norm. We frequented the Hill Top Hotel in Worli, which was almost always secluded. I enjoyed the attention, but it was never awkward and neither was I embarrassed. Dilip and I had a very healthy outlook on these things – a legacy of time spent out of the country. Alyque was a male friend. That was it.

We talked about the theatre, and my life in England. The more time we spent together, the more we got to know each other. Alyque confided in me. So I confided in him. About Dilip. About my insecurities. About the good days, the occasional burst of sunshine followed by long passages of grey.

There was a thrill to this new friendship – I was talking about things I didn't discuss with anyone else. But then, sometimes, it's easiest to confide in a stranger.

~

I left S.H. Benson's for LPE Aiyar's and made the jump from model coordinator to account executive, a step-up. I was handling clients now. I was still doing *Woman's World* for All India Radio. I made eighteen rupees every Sunday. I'd take the bus to Mantralaya, walk down half the block to the dingy little office across from the MLA hostel and record my show.

The trickle of compéring jobs had become a steady stream. In my time, they were called 'commentaries'. There was a lady, Rooprani, who'd set up fashion shows. She was the first event manager I recall. The scripts weren't very good. I rewrote them as part of my job and then hosted the shows. That led to another show, then another, then another. Miss India – a much smaller enterprise back then – came calling. Then *Femina* Miss India, then Miss India *Eve's Weekly*.

Rewriting commentaries got me Films Division work. I started doing a lot of their voice-overs, the Indian News Reviews that went all over the country. A good ten minutes was about fifteen pages of single-spaced text. I had to enunciate clearly and find a turn of phrase that would transmit an idea or image succinctly, and be charming. I feel like it's a bit of a diminishing skill in today's world. I had to be reserved, but not bore people. When I watch the news today, it's mostly yelling.

The first documentary commentary I did was for Shyam Benegal's film on the Bastar tribe. That taught me how to edit copy. Which, ironically, was my first job with the British Information Services. Every 't' had to be crossed, every 'i' dotted. If you didn't get it right, it wasn't anyone else's fault.

Professionally, I had found the spirit of my London years. I was learning and growing every single day.

~

The Asian Advertising Congress was to be held in Delhi in November 1970. Agencies sent their top talent – men (and usually they *were* men) who were in decision-making positions. By July, I had realized that it would be great to attend – but only to gain experience. And if that was the case, why should my agency pay for it?

If I went on my own, delegate fees were three hundred rupees a head. That was my monthly salary. However, if you had a sponsor, if someone vouched for you ('yes, I think her being there will help her, and help the congress and help the advertising universe in general'), then you only had to pay half.

That was a worthwhile investment. What I needed, I explained to Alyque as he dropped me home after a cup of coffee, was a sponsor.

I wasn't angling for anything. I was just wondering out loud, sitting next to a friend.

I was a bit startled when a set of signed sponsorship forms from Mr Padamsee's office arrived the next day. I applied as a delegate and was duly accepted.

Come November, the big boys flew to Delhi and checked into five-star hotels. I booked my seat on the Deluxe Chair Car. I'd be living with my parents at Lajpat Nagar.

12

WHAT'S THAT BIT in *Jerry Maguire*? You know, when the girl and her son peer into business class on the plane and she says, 'It used to be a better meal. Now it's a better life'?

The Asian Advertising Congress was like that.

I showed up at the Oberoi on the first morning. The place was buzzing, full of beautiful people who manufactured beauty. It was exhilarating – an instant hit of adrenaline.

Alyque was waiting for me. He ushered me to the registration desk. The paperwork was taken care of before I had a chance to read the forms. And then Alyque did something really sweet, something I never forgot. He made sure I was invited to all the functions –

the dinners and the lunches and the cocktails, and not just the seminars. I had access to the rarefied Congress, the place where the real meetings happened, the seminar *within* the seminar. I could walk into any of the functions as an invited guest, even if Alyque wasn't there.

Who were the people I spent all my time with? Bal Mundkur of Ulka Advertising, Frank and Gita Simoes, and Alyque Padamsee and Gerson da Cunha, both of Lintas. They were legends by then, all these people, all twelve, fourteen years older than me, in their element. I was twenty-eight and I'd accomplished nothing, and I was on their playground. Alyque didn't leave my side for a minute. He was a complete gentleman, nothing untoward, no advances – sexual or romantic. Just really nice.

The big debate that first morning was about where to lunch. The others in the party were bored of luxury hotels and fancy restaurants. I suggested the University Café. So off we went, and we spent the afternoon trying to outdo each other with tall tales (some of them true, I'm sure) from our college-going days.

I watched some presentations I still remember. Barry Day of McCann did one. Gerson, Alyque and Bal Mundkur worked on *Bombay is Dying* – seemed like science fiction back then and reads like dollar-store prophecy now. Shai Holsaert, one of Bombay's leading models, performed an exquisite movement piece as an accompaniment to the presentation.

But these boys and girls played hard too. People were falling in love, sleeping with each other or drinking Delhi dry. One wintry November evening, the hotel staff panicked. Water continued to seep out from under the door of one of the rooms and they couldn't get anyone inside to respond. They rang the bell. No answer. They pounded on the door. No answer. They called the room from the reception. Nothing. Alarmed, they broke down the door. Gerson da Cunha, diplomat, poet, man of letters, was fast asleep in the bathtub full of warm, comforting water, while the tap ran.

Presentations would segue into drinks and then to the nightclubs. One evening, the party upped and shifted to the discotheque at the Maiden's Hotel. The next night it was the Tabela at the Oberoi.

On the last night, we attended a dance recital by Yamini Krishnamurthy on the lawns of the Ashoka Hotel. As it finished, Alyque turned to me. 'Let's get out of here. I'm bored of the same places and the same faces. We should head out, the two of us, and get dinner.'

He said he had to drop off some reels of film in the room he was sharing with Roger Pereira of Shilpi Advertising. Roger was also a Theatre Group regular. The Theatre Group was one of Bombay's oldest theatre companies, founded by Alyque's brother Sultan, better known as Bobby, in 1941.

Alyque thought we should deposit the reels before dinner. And, as it turned out, he was living right there, at the Ashoka. I should just come up to the room with him.

I demurred. I was fine in the lobby. Besides, we were heading out right away, weren't we?

He grunted a reply and was back down in no time at all. I'd stalled that move quite successfully, I thought.

We ended up in the Mughal Room at the Oberoi after dinner. We danced to 'Strangers in the Night'. We danced to 'Raindrops Keep Fallin' on My Head'. We danced all evening. Staying out wasn't a problem, because Alyque had a car at his disposal, and it had been at my beck and call right through the trip.

He dropped me home that night, all the way to Lajpat Nagar. When we got there, we stood in the street and chatted. I was a little reluctant to say goodbye. I felt like I was coming to the end of a really good dream, one that I wished would never end. My life had been on hold while we argued about creativity, and ate and danced and laughed. There were no packets of milk, no belligerent husbands, no jobs, and homes and budgets. But, like it did for

Cinderella, the clock was about to strike midnight and I had to go back to scrubbing the hearth.

Alyque was on the 7 a.m. flight the next morning. I would spend two days with my parents and then take the train back.

He said 'goodnight' and hugged me. He let himself back into the car, a tall man, a little hunched, even then. I watched him leave; the tail-lights winked once and the car turned out of the lane. I shook my head and let myself into the house.

I went to the bathroom to change and take off my make-up and brush my teeth. I stared at my reflection for a moment. It had been … *nice*. There was no other way to put it. Not romantic. But special. The way it is in school, when someone wants to carry your books for you.

I called myself a sentimental fool and went to sleep.

~

The doorbell rang at 9 the next morning. I'd just about woken up and I answered it. And there he was.

'What are you doing here?' I asked. No 'hello', 'how are you?', 'come in, have some tea'. I was elated and suspicious, but I wasn't really surprised. Not deep down. Something about this felt familiar, like I'd expected to see Alyque much sooner than I thought I would.

He began to grin.

'I sent Madhu on my ticket.' This was Madhu Gadkari, art director at Lintas. 'I sent Madhu on my ticket,' Alyque continued 'because I took his ticket in exchange. So, when I fly back this evening, I'll be Madhu Gadkari. Now, I've got us a packed lunch. Let's go to Tuglaqabad.'

I don't know if I've ever dressed quicker.

We only had a few hours. We chose the quiet of Surajkund instead. We sat on the ancient steps and looked out over the water. And, for the first time, we held hands. Our relationship had changed.

It was now something different. Or maybe it had just become better defined.

He dropped me home and left for the airport. I felt uneasy, a small creeping fear. It wasn't about what we'd shared at Surajkund, but what that meant. We were half a step away from a mess.

~

The next morning brought a telegram from Alyque. If he'd shown up again, I think I'd have fainted, then regained consciousness and punched him in the face.

Alyque was scheduled to return to Delhi in a few days for a radio convention.

'Please change travel plans,' read the telegram. 'Stop. Stay on in Delhi. Stop. Your presence essential.' I knew it was hogwash. I had Dilip and my job waiting for me in Bombay. I didn't change my plans and I didn't reply to the telegram. I spent some time with my parents and boarded the train the next day.

I pulled into Bombay Central station at about 8 in the evening. The train was three hours late. As I disembarked, my gaze fell on the outline of a familiar figure. A tall man, hunched.

I couldn't believe my eyes. Alyque quickly walked over and grabbed my bags. He wanted to surprise me when I got off the train. He'd been waiting for three hours. And in an effort to look like he wasn't just loitering, every time he thought he saw a face he knew, he'd had his shoes polished.

He was wearing a pair of very shiny shoes.

I was touched. All this so he could drive me from Bombay Central Station to Pedder Road, offload my bags and drive away. I thought about him, and I thought about Dilip waiting upstairs. Dilip, who would have thought it so very bourgeois to receive his wife at the station.

Alyque flew to Delhi the next day for the radio convention, which – despite the absence of my 'essential' self – took place as scheduled.

~

That weekend, my in-laws visited us. We were having our evening tea, sitting on the carpet, when the doorbell rang. I got up to answer it. Alyque stood on the landing, in the gloaming. Magic hour, they call it.

'We went to see a movie,' he whispered. 'At Regal. Pearl is buying tickets. And I said I'll park the car.' He paused and looked at me. 'But I had to see your face. I have to go now. Pearl will be waiting. I only came to see your face.'

And he was gone.

Who does that? Drive from Colaba to Pedder Road to see your face for an instant and then drive back to his wife?

That was the moment I fell in love with him. There was no line left to cross – I was his, body and soul. I returned to my in-laws and my husband and took my place on the carpet. I was calm, not too nervous. I hoped my face didn't give me away.

Inside, I was smiling. I was euphoric. I have never forgotten that feeling.

I was on a two-month sabbatical from work. Shivendra Sinha, my friend from London, was making a film and I was helping him, which meant my days were all my own. Dilip only returned home after 7 p.m.

The very next afternoon, the doorbell rang again. Alyque stood there. He'd stolen away on his lunch break. I let him into the flat. It was the 30th of November 1970.

Surely he can hear my heart, I thought. It's much too loud.

We faced each other. We didn't say much. Talking was done.

I remember him. I remember his touch.

We made love. For the first time. This was not sex, I remember thinking. Nothing that made me feel this way, whatever *this was*, something that made me feel *this* special, so good and so right, simultaneously brand-new and familiar, all at once – the term sex couldn't contain this. He was gentle and kind. Calm and considerate and absolute.

It was the sensation of an endless fall, with no fear of what waited after. I was now an adulterer and a mistress, and I could have died there, in his arms, no questions asked.

~

For a while, we fooled everyone. Including – of course – ourselves.

Once I was back at work, the Open Marriage Contract between Dilip and myself was in my favour for a change. We had no rights over each other, Dilip and I.

I began to have a lot of 'recordings' at 7 in the morning. Alyque would pick me up across the road and, we'd drive to a shack in Juhu for breakfast, at the Palm Beach Hotel (which is now the Ramada Inn). I'd be at work by 9.30.

I don't think we'd have made it in this day and age, Alyque and myself. Traffic wouldn't have allowed it. Had he tried the parking stunt now, it would've taken him an hour and a half.

The clandestine breakfasts must've really cost Alyque. He was never a morning person.

I started to spend a lot of my weekends 'with Esmie', in 'Bandra'. Alyque would pick me up, and we'd drive to the picnic cottages in Versova. Sometimes, we checked into a room at the seedy Hotel Ajanta in Santa Cruz. We were lucky. This was a time before television and no one recognized us.

Our trysts were rushed and sordid and necessary. They were blissful.

The world, now soft-focus, passed by me in a blur. Even Dilip, reliably caustic, had receded to middle-ground. I was a secret society of one, and I was in love. People have survived on less.

We stumbled on, in a daze of lust and guilt and joy, for about eight months.

~

In mid-1971, Alyque was invited to design the Indian Pavilion for the Conference on Atomic Energy in Geneva. We discussed ideas all the time. Alyque squeezed my hand tight – it would be wonderful if I could go with him. A scale model went up at the Atomic Energy Building, opposite the Yacht Club. I went to see it often. I looked at plans and layouts. I helped where I could. It felt like 'our' project, it had been given to 'us'.

With Alyque, things always came unannounced. Shocks and surprises, both. Trips to Surajkund. Pickups at Bombay Central. The need to see my face.

One afternoon, at the Ajanta, he turned to me.

'We'll be leaving for Geneva soon.' His tone was matter-of-fact. But there was a particular stress on the 'we'. He waited for me to challenge the statement. For me to show him where it was written that he could not take his wife to Geneva with him.

I think he tried to ask me what I wanted from Geneva. I think he tried to make me feel better. I think he tried to tell me that, actually, I was the one he wanted to take but just *couldn't*. But for the first time in our relationship, I cried. I cried because I had no claim over him. I cried because I was the dirty little secret.

I got a stream of letters from Geneva. 'Sitting on a park bench, stealing moments to be able to write to you'. Telegrams that only I could decipher: 'The Dalda Tin is Empty'.

He was away for six weeks. Our relationship changed in that time – it curdled ever so slightly.

Alyque wrote saying he wanted to see me on his return. He'd meet me under the tree at Lotus Court, where we held our ad club meetings. I didn't want to see him. I saw him waiting and held off as long as I could. But conditioning kicked in. I didn't want anyone else to spot him. I ran downstairs and into the car.

He'd got me a Swiss music box. It played 'Raindrops Keep Fallin' on My Head' – the first song we'd ever danced to. And he was clearly lovesick.

This was the start of a pattern that would define our time together. Alyque could be calm, gentle, generous in a way that I'd never known. That's why it hurt when he was cold or callous or unfeeling. That's the delirium that love engenders – this push and pull. And Alyque knew the effect he had on me.

We did this dance for a long time. The euphoria followed by the crash followed by the euphoria. Up, down, round and round.

We inched towards an anniversary, of sorts. Dilip was at the High Court until 7 in the evening. He and I had settled into a strange mixture of contempt and concern. Strangely, things between us were less volatile than even a year ago. Mostly, we ignored each other, especially if we were out. Every conversation revolved around separation and divorce. We had drifted so far away from each other that it didn't matter.

One evening, in late 1971, Alyque told me he'd been living out of a suitcase at Kulsum Terrace, the family home in Colaba, for weeks. Sylvester da Cunha had seen the two of us together, and Alyque had been given an ultimatum. He'd decided to move out. But the onus was on me.

It didn't take a lot for me to agree to Dilip's proposal for a separation. On the 1st of December 1971, two-and-a-half years after we'd got married, he moved to Buckley Court. I helped him pack, and I drove him to his temporary digs.

I called Dilip's father before we made the final decision. I wanted his blessing. I wished to keep 'Thakore' as my last name. It was my professional name in Bombay now. And it seemed safer, more Indian, less Christian. It made absolute sense, and I hated myself a little.

Pappa said 'yes'.

For a week, it was paradise. Dilip and I, freed of our burden, suddenly enjoyed each other's company again. We met for dinner every night. Alyque would come home at 10 and stay until midnight. Then he'd return to Colaba.

The Bangladesh War broke out on the 7th of December 1971. Dilip, bless him, thought I'd be terrified. There were blackouts and air-raid sirens going off at random hours. He moved back in, for my sake. Inadvertently, he messed up a system that had taken over a year to perfect. I was less than patient with him because my secret life had been curtailed again. Our relationship returned to its former glory in rapid order. Meanwhile, Alyque moaned about the lack of our time together. I don't think many people in Bombay were as relieved as I was when the seven-day war ended. Dilip moved out again. This time, for good. And Alyque began to stay later and later, and then overnight, until he moved in on a permanent basis.

~

Frank Simoes formed his own agency and after two years at LPE Aiyar's, I left to join him. I was an account executive by now. Our main clients were the Taj, Siemens, Raymond and Blue Star. I looked after Blue Star.

The advertising manager at Blue Star was a man by the name of Hari Mathur. He 'cured' me of advertising. I dreaded meetings with him. Advertising, at the best of times, is a pretty soul-crushing experience. But if you manage to find someone who can take that and make it even more joyless … well, you're lucky. Because it means you're done with advertising for life. I spent all my time going back and forth between client and agency. Hari quibbled and moaned and micromanaged. Minute, unnecessary changes. Over and over. It was catatonia by a thousand small cuts.

I was with Frank Simoes until around 1974. My advertising career lasted about six years, all told.

The only really interesting experience was something called *Advent*. The Advertising Club of Bombay put together a programme at the Taj. It was the first time I worked on a multi-media presentation. The script blended audio-visual and live elements, and it was a massive undertaking. We started work the day before the event, stayed the night at the Taj, slept on the carpet in the banquet hall for a couple of hours, woke up the next day and did the thing. Turned it into a play, basically. It was a terrific success.

~

On the 19th of November 1970, Indira Gandhi flew in to inaugurate the Children's Complex in Bandra on her birthday. Ali Yavar Jang was the Governor at the time, and Begum Ali Yavar Jang had put together the function. I went as Alyque's guest.

During the ceremony, a tiny woman next to me struck up a conversation.

'What do you do?' she asked.

'I am on the radio,' I answered, 'and in advertising. What about you?'

'Oh, I'm a social worker.'

She had my undivided attention. I always wanted to be a social worker, but I had no idea what that entailed. Something halfway between my earliest efforts in education at Chakeri and the protests in London? Maybe?

'I've always wanted to do social work,' I said.

'Really? Are you serious?'

'Yes,' I said.

'Do you have a telephone?'

I gave her Shyam and Nira's number. The function ended and I forgot about it. Three days later, I was summoned downstairs.

'Dolly ...' always drawn out, like a greeting, or the start of a song. 'Dolllleeeeee.'

'Hullo,' I said.

'Dolly. Are you really interested?'

Yes, I said. Absolutely. And that's how Dr Zulie Nakhooda came into my life. That's how I became involved with the India Sponsorship Committee.

~

Once upon a time, there was a tiny woman called Zulie Nakhooda. She went to the Tata Institute of Social Sciences and became Dr Zulie Nakhooda. As part of her graduation project, Zulie found herself in charge of ten orphans from underprivileged backgrounds. She lived in Usha Sadan, in Colaba. Which is a strange little cooperative housing society, a bit like Chelsea Hotel. Very many rich people live in tiny two hundred and three hundred square foot apartments, jumbled together in no discernible order. Be that as it may, it wasn't somewhere you could house ten kids.

Once again, this is how things happen. Through the kindness of strangers.

A Mrs Bhave said to Zulie: 'Why don't you bring the kids to Khandala?'

Mrs Bhave had a large bungalow, right opposite the Khandala Public school, owned by Mr Khandalawala. The kids could use the large balcony as a living space during the day, while Zulie figured out what to do.

So off she went to Khandala, kids in tow.

The same Mr Khandalawala took a walk every day. And, every day, he'd pass Mrs Bhave's house. He saw these kids, eating, bathing, living there. After about ten days, he stopped to ask Mrs Bhave about the kids. So Mrs Bhave told him.

'These are ten orphaned children that my friend Zulie is trying to look after and I'm housing them while she figures out just what she can do for them.'

Mr Khandalawala frowned and nodded. He thought for a while. 'Look,' he said. 'I've got ten acres by the Bushi dam. It's yours if you want it.'

Out of nowhere, Zulie had ten acres of land in Lonavala. True, it was ten barren acres, nothing on it, not even a hut. But she had land. She approached Begum Ali Yavar Jang, who agreed to be president of the project. She, in turn, put Zulie in touch with Laurie Baker, the well-known architect who spent most of his life working on the twin problems of low-cost housing and keeping Indian building traditions alive. He had completed a similar project in Ethiopia.

Laurie told Zulie he'd be happy to design the campus. He would use local material and he would make it as affordable as possible, but he wouldn't come to Bombay.

Zulie appointed a local contractor. Work had begun on the single (and at that point, only) cottage when I met Zulie, and she asked if I'd come on board. I said yes, so off we went to Lonavala.

A space like that is a monument to endless possibility. That's what I felt when I saw those ten barren acres for the first time. And the single cottage, like a beacon, the point where we'd shaped the horizon.

The monsoon of '72 hit. For no apparent reason, the cottage flooded. We had to deduce backwards, from the finished cottage to the plans. The contractor had done a great job, but he'd read the schematic back to front. Next to a dam, on a hilltop, in the western monsoon, the results were resoundingly wet.

'What do we do, Dolly?' asked Zulie.

I thought about it. 'Well, I've got a friend who's an architect,' I said. Technically, he was a civil engineer. Technically, he wasn't even my friend back then. But when have little things like that ever stopped me? So, I went to see Anil Dharker.

Imtiaz and Anil had moved to Bombay from Glasgow. They lived above Premila Lal – Kiki Watsa to us – she of the cookbooks. Anil would go on to become one of Bombay's conscience-keepers – journalist, editor, author, defender of liberty and common-sense. And of course, the beating heart of Tata Literature Live! It was such a blow to lose him in March 2021. One more in the year that took so many.

Anil put me in touch with Lalita and Yashwant Das, who were both architects from MIT and had just started a town-planning consultancy in Bombay. I enlisted the two of them, and we went back to Lonavala.

They fell in love with the place and the idea, 'tsked tsked' over the construction work and took over. They began by building troughs and then started to deal with problems as they cropped up, one by one.

We started with one functional building. Once the euphoria subsided, we realized it was just that – an empty shell. No facilities, no furniture, nothing.

'What do we do now, Dolly?'

We had no money. We had plenty of goodwill. And we knew lots of people. What kind of establishment would give away things that our kids might be able to use? What kind of place had a high turnover of everyday articles? What kind of an institution needed things to look new or almost new?

I started to gently bully the Taj and the Oberoi. Give me all the cutlery and linen you have rejected or retired. Give them to me and you help a bunch of kids.

That's how the India Sponsorship Committee's Antar Bharti Balgram began.

The endeavour had Alyque's wholehearted approval. If I was going up to Lonavala, I never had to ask twice for the car. He also sponsored a child. And that is one of the things that I always appreciated about him, even after our relationship had ended. He never hesitated to attach his name to causes that he believed in. Like Anil, he became one of the city's conscience-keepers – a liberal secularist who would die for your right to question him. As long as you extended him the same courtesy.

Those ten acres in Lonavala are now home to a full-fledged campus that supports a hundred and fifty kids. We have seven cottages and a workshop for vocational training.

It's a place I used to take the boys – my nephew, Zhya; and then my son, Quasar.

It's still a place where the possibilities are endless.

~

Lalita and Yashwant, eventual saviours, became a part of my life, and Lalita and I became close friends.

When their daughter, Pulka, went abroad to study, Yashwant and Lalita separated. The divorce caught a lot of us by surprise, but the two of them were so sanguine that it made me wonder how well we ever really know anyone. This was doubly true of Lalita herself.

She was a brilliant architect – and she was just lovely: smart, funny, warm. She built schools for Prime Minister Chandra

Shekhar. She lived very close to Prithvi Theatre and every time I went to Juhu, either to watch a show or perform, we'd meet. Often, I'd spend the night at her place.

Around 2013, she got very busy. We barely spoke on the phone. She kept talking about some big project. I hadn't seen her in six months. Out of the blue, she called one day.

'Dolly, I'm going out of the country.'

'How wonderful,' I said. 'Where?'

'I've suddenly got this huge project, this massive estate somewhere in the Middle East. But it's an American project, so I'm going to America first.'

She wanted to appoint me her literary executor. She sent me a whole lot of books with instructions about where they were to go. And she sent me a power of attorney because I'd helped her get a book deal with Niyogi Books.

'You do what makes sense to you,' she said, 'as far as the book is concerned. That's why I'm sending you the POA. And there are two more manuscripts.'

'Lalita, when does one see you?' I asked.

'I'm sorry, Dolly. I'm very busy.'

I received the books and the manuscripts and the power of attorney. The next time I heard from her, she was at the airport.

'Dolly, I'm on my way to America, I'm at the airport, I'm leaving. I'll be back in three years.'

And then she was gone. Not a trace of that formidable presence, of a life lived amongst friends and peers. Nothing. Lalita Das didn't exist.

A few months passed. I heard nothing. I started making some enquiries. I called her friends. Then I called friends that might be better placed – a female DIG, an Air India pilot. Nothing. I wanted to see if her flat was available for one of my sister's friends to rent and discovered she'd sold the flat. I rang her lawyer, and they said she'd left no forwarding address. I rang her landlord, and he said he had no contact details. She'd sold her car, disconnected her phone, gotten on a flight and vanished into thin air.

End 2016, I received a strange message – odd news from an odd source, and that makes me believe the information. This person went to see a lawyer and overheard that Lalita was dead. So, they rang me up and asked: 'Isn't she a friend of yours? What's this about Lalita being dead?'

This was almost exactly three years after I'd last spoken to Lalita. I had no idea, so I rang her husband. He had no idea. I rang her daughter, who's in America, and she hadn't heard anything either.

It's a bizarre little sidestep. I don't know what to believe. But it left me feeling empty. And a little uneasy.

I hope she's okay, wherever she is.

~

Here's an interesting thing about the times we lived in, back then, so very different from the more enlightened times we live in now. In the initial few months after Alyque and I went public, I was shunned. But Alyque wasn't.

I wonder if gender had something to do with it.

Surely not?

A fabled union had unravelled. At its heart was a storied romance. Alyque had been in love with Pearl since college. And had waited almost a decade to marry her.

I'd broken up a family. There were kids. And I had a husband. Well, sort of. I was the 'other woman'.

~

I'd never expected to win any popularity contests. I was in love. I put my head down because I had my man by my side and, in the light of day, it was enough.

But I would not settle for being the 'mistress'. I wasn't going to let the world around me – the arbitrary standards of 'propriety' – do that to me. I'd been burned once – I should perhaps never have married Dilip in the first place, if I hadn't worried so much about form and convention.

So I did the best I could. I insisted that all my mail, and all the invitations I received, still be addressed to 'Dolly Thakore', and not 'Mrs Padamsee'. I obsessed – to an unhealthy degree – about paying my share. We split costs down the middle, a legacy of the Dilip years but at *my* insistence this time.

Math was the only way to stave off my guilt. Self-loathing came and went like the tide. All I *could* do was keep accounts like a maniac. My share was seventeen hundred and fifty rupees a month. I eked it out. I lived well, but I had to count every paisa. Even though Lintas had begun to pay for a number of things – newspapers, the telephone and Alyque's expense account, I couldn't afford extravagances.

People wouldn't talk to me. They talked to Alyque. He visited his family. His friends were still his friends. His circle was still his circle. But the same standards didn't apply to me. The world had, for the moment, decided that I was contagious. So I wore a smile like a mask, kept my chin up and my back straight.

I wonder if gender had something to do with it. Surely not?

It's the little things. Being a woman is also being a minority.

13

BY APRIL 1972, some of Alyque's Theatre Group circle began to treat us like an ordinary couple: Farrokh and Vijaya Mehta, and Homi and Kamal Mulla. And Kersey and Usha Katrak, who I've always had a particular fondness for.

Kersey was a genius. He'd spent a year in England, mostly drinking in pubs and writing poetry. He'd worked at National Advertising and LPE Aiyar's, just like me. Then he launched MCM –

Mass Communication and Marketing – a company that completely altered the landscape of advertising in this country. He catalyzed an atmosphere of creativity – everyone *wanted* to work at MCM, even though the pay on offer was just about average.

Usha was no slouch herself. A fine actor, she ran her own firm at one point. She was also one of the four people who created the Amul Girl – the cherubic little cipher who has graced the famous Amul hoardings for over fifty years. Together, they were an astonishingly creative couple.

Kersey understood, intuitively, how to build brands and how to capture attention in a relatively innocent market. Young talent thronged to him – almost all of Indian advertising's present heavyweights had an early association with him. Unsurprisingly, he wasn't a businessman. MCM floundered and then shut down. Usha and he left Bombay to live in an ashram in Mirtola, near Almora, then in UP. It was a place that eventually combined Bhakti philosophy with Gurdjieff and Theosophy into a humanist outlook.

Alyque would coax Kersey back to Lintas in the '80s. His mind was still as sharp, his instincts as keen. Only the young interns were confused by this seemingly vague man who had the best ideas.

~

Poor Gerson walked a tightrope. He was Alyque's boss and a theatre heavyweight. He also knew me from 'Before Alyque'. He had to balance his social interactions between camps.

For the rest of the general circle of common friends, I was still Dolly Non Grata, but we refused to be shamed.

For a year, maybe, life was bliss. Alyque and I didn't spend an evening apart. From work, we'd go to rehearsal. We had an appetite for each other. I felt like I had started to blossom as a result of this relationship.

~

Three men changed the way I thought about the world. They were Kris Srinivasan, Dilip Thakore and Alyque. But Alyque was the only one I worked with.

The first play Alyque directed me in was *Mira*. Written by Gurcharan Das, it was about the Bhakti saint Mirabai. Zafar Hai, the documentary filmmaker, was in it. So were Dina Pathak and Homi Daruwala. I played Udabai, the Rana's sister. Indira Kohli played Mira. And when Indira got married and then pregnant, Nirmala Mathan took over.

Alyque turned it into a multimedia production. We performed with a screen as a backdrop. Throughout the show, different images were projected onto the screen. The musicians sat on a platform above the screen. It sounds a bit simplistic now, but bear in mind this was '71 or '72.

As a director, Alyque was detailed, meticulous, exacting. Some might have called him overbearing. I, for one, loved it. He told an actor when to sit, how to sit, how to stand, how to move, how to cross their legs. He wanted cigarettes lit on a certain line, in a certain way. He'd tell you when to flick the ash. He didn't want a page to turn or a leaf to flutter onstage without choreographing it, and without having rehearsed it.

We were functionaries in his vision. Because the vision wasn't collaborative he had no need to share it. You showed up and got told what to do.

In contrast, I acted in a play called *Suddenly Last Summer*, directed by Adi Marzban. Adi was a genuine polymath – a career newsman (it ran in the family), a writer and director; a titan of Parsi theatre. He played several instruments and he was a keen ventriloquist and magician – a man who wove a unique spell. He also worked across companies and cliques and genres and languages.

And no one brought in the audiences the way he did.

We used to rehearse at Adi's house on Altamont Road. On the first day of rehearsal, we read the play. Adi listened carefully. Then he addressed us in that deep, nasal twang.

'Okay, tomorrow rehearsal at 6. Everybody learn your lines and come.'

I froze. With Alyque, we'd read the play over and over, the whole cast. We'd discuss the script. When we got on the floor, we'd still have our scripts in hand. Every move went into the script, a tiny note in pencil, in the margins. Alyque would also tell an actor he wanted a line in a particular way, whether he wanted the tone to drop, to rise, where he needed a whisper, where he needed anger. All faithfully recorded on the script.

Woe betide if you forgot. Alyque's temper was legendary. No one seemed to mind; although I'm not sure if it was actually received with as much equanimity as I remember. At that time, he was the emperor of all he surveyed.

On the second day, Adi mapped out a vague floor plan in the space. Mostly, he just pointed at corners. No chalk or tape or anything. Alyque would've had it looking like a crime scene.

'Imagine there is a bench here and a sofa here, a window here and a door there. And you come in from here …'

And that was it. There were no further instructions. Where to look, how to use hands, when and how to sit, when to stand. It was up to us.

I went home and cried. I couldn't do it, I told Alyque. I was disoriented. I felt scared and isolated. *Left completely to my own devices.*

Some schools of theatrical thought believe that *this* is what casting actually is: find someone you think can play a role and leave them to their own devices. Here, the director is a watchful eye, the first audience member. He is not the autocrat.

This is why Adi Marzban productions were as vivid as they were. Because he had a roomful of fantastic actors who'd been liberated. And because they were free agents, they paid very close attention to what was happening on stage. Their co-actors were likely to do something that would take them by surprise during a show. When it worked, it was utterly magical. And it worked more often than not. A play would start as one thing and, by the end of the rehearsal process, become something else entirely.

Mind you, he had some *fantastic* actors. Bomi and Pilloo Dotivala, Bomi and Viloo Kapadia, Hosi Vasunia, Scherazade Modi, Ruby Patel. They all worked with Adi extensively and were plugged into his particular brand of chaos.

It's not for me to say who was better. I think there is merit in both approaches. Adi's method of working made people want to come back again and again, and that was something that you felt when you watched those productions.

Alyque, on the other hand, played to a larger cross-section of audiences. He also worked across a bewildering range of genres and scale – man with a lifelong theatrical itch who experimented ceaselessly. He understood spectacle like few others and yet got tagged as someone with a very intellectual approach to the theatre. That gulf, the masses and the classes, and work that caters to everything in between, still exists. But it is narrower now than it has been at any other time in my life. Back then, everyone looked down on everyone else. It helped, a little, that people worked across cliques. Ronnie Screwvala worked with both Adi and Alyque. Likewise, Sabira Merchant and Hosi.

~

Whatever I was, in the scheme of Alyque's life, I had become part of the landscape. His family brought me into the fold. I even introduced Alyque's mother to my parents in 1972 when they came to watch *The Birthday Party*, and then looked on with bated breath. Mama could be unpredictable and she promptly shocked my parents by acknowledging the slightly, ahem, unorthodox nature of my relationship with her son, and also her feelings about that relationship: I was welcome. For the moment. While we were unmarried.

My parents didn't know what to think. I didn't know where to look.

~

That summer, Alyque took me to Kashmir. We lived on a houseboat. And, yes, it *was* 'Paradise on Earth'.

We visited the Hazratbal Shrine. Security was tight, a legacy of the theft of the Hair of the Prophet. Alyque and I took a shikara to the foot of the mosque. We disembarked to the sound of the evening azaan. We asked for directions to the minaret where the relic was kept. We were told that it was private – access was restricted. But the tone of the exchange indicated that access could be negotiated. We asked nicely and made a donation, and we were ushered up a winding staircase.

We were from the city, and we thought we knew crowds. We were caught by surprise. As shikarawallas responded to the call, Alyque and I were slowly propelled towards the inside of the building. And then it became apparent that we were seconds away from having any say in the matter – the crowd grew and grew and grew, a surge of men, headed to offer evening namaaz.

But then, handkerchiefs were offered to us. My hair was shorter than Alyque's and I was wearing a pair of trousers and a blue reefer jacket. I didn't look much like a woman. I didn't know whether to be relieved or insulted.

Alarm bells started to go off in my head. We needed to leave immediately. Very slowly, agonizingly, we fought against the tide of people. I grew more and more frightened every passing minute – we weren't supposed to be here, it wasn't right. Finally, we made it back outside. I didn't breathe freely until we were back on the shikara and the shrine had receded into the distance.

~

We were atop a hill in Gulmarg one morning when we saw a couple waving at us. On closer inspection, we spotted Romola and her husband, Chikki Ranganathan, good friends of Dilip and mine. For no real reason ('what *will* people think'), Alyque and I lied. We were on a recce, we said, with an Italian television crew. Romola and Chikki nodded. They didn't believe a word of it. We were living together, but we were still a badly kept secret.

~

We stumbled along for the next two years. Delirious in each other's company. Inconvenient in public, like an affliction one doesn't mention in polite society. The theatre continued. So did the radio jobs and the compéring.

We'd been together three years. They went by in the blink of an eye.

Alyque surprised me with a trip to London in 1974. He'd booked our tickets and made all the arrangements. It was a wonderful gift. I was thrilled. I hadn't been back to London since '69, but it was still my city. I had people, and places, to see. We lived with Chotu, Alyque's brother. He was an architect and he had a flat at Golder's Green.

Alyque had work. I helped as much as I could. I made him breakfast. And I was also in charge of sourcing tickets for the theatre. This meant standing in queues, waiting for the discounted tickets that are the secret currency of every theatregoing habit. It doesn't matter if you can afford it or not – if you can watch a runaway smash for twelve pounds, it's a better show. Trust me.

Being a tourist had its challenges back then. Mostly because forex was rarer than gold. Because Alyque was at the office, Lintas would at least sort out his lunch. I'd exist on chocolates and cheese, and on cigarettes.

Being a smoker wasn't easy either. I didn't mix brands. Some part of my livelihood depended on the timbre of my voice; all the commentaries and the radio shows. I smoked Chinar and poor Esmie kept me supplied when I was away from India.

I became a smoker when my mother came to visit me in London, all those years ago. I know. It's as stupid as it sounds. My mother was a smoker. Kents, if I remember right. I felt like she'd take me seriously if she saw me smoke too.

I smoked for almost twenty years. The story of how I quit is also a milestone, but that will come in its own time.

Meanwhile, back in Bombay, I was a little bemused when Alyque complained about how much he hated to travel. He'd had it with living out of suitcases, he said. He didn't know how Gerson did it, this constant globetrotting. All he needed, Alyque decided, was to travel every two years or so, to recharge his theatre batteries.

I can't say that the trip was an epiphany. I could admit, to myself, every once in a while that our relationship wasn't perfect. But I was in awe of him. I was the ingénue, and Alyque curated my view of the world. I was the perfect mid-career partner for a grandee. I revelled in the attention it brought me. I revelled in the exposure it afforded me.

On the 13th of September 1974, we were scheduled to perform a reading of *The Duchess of Malfi* at the St. Xavier's College auditorium. Nisha da Cunha directed Alyque, Gerson, James Hardcastle and Partap Sharma. Alyque wanted me to handle front of house. On my way to St. Xavier's, I stopped off at Kulsum Terrace in Colaba. Alyque's brother, Bubbles, was there. He was by far the sweetest of the Padamsees.

'Hey, Doll. I'm going to Khandala.' He had a real American twang. Made it sound like 'Hey, Dawl. Ahm goan to Can-da-la.'

He'd borrowed Alyque's car for the trip, the little green Herald, which Alyque could spare because he used the office car most of the time. He was taking Purveen, his wife, and their two little kids, Zaheesha and Zavid, up to Farrokh and Vijaya's place. He said bye at about 1 p.m. in the afternoon and drifted away, like a languid hurricane. His energy was infectious, but he moved at his own pace. It was part of his charm.

I got to St. Xavier's at about five in the evening.

'Oh, Doll,' said Alyque when I saw him. 'Bubbles called. There's been some sort of accident. Just find out, would you?'

The only phone on campus was at the reception. I stood there, trying to call Mama, Alyque's mother. Back then, a successful phone call was like winning the lottery. You needed a large slice of luck. I was still there, half an hour later, when Alyque's nephew Renan Jeffereis showed up. He was so agitated that he ran right past me. Then he registered who it was and backtracked.

'We have to move, Doll,' he said. 'Bubbles has gone.'

'What?'

We'd imagined an innocuous accident – a little scratch, maybe a dent. How could Bubbles be dead when *he'd* made the call? And then, with rising dread – what about the kids?

'Mama has already gone on ahead,' said Renan. 'You bring Alyque. I'm taking my Ma to the hospital.'

Inside the auditorium, the performance had already begun. Amal Allana and Ayesha (better known as Pooh) Sayani, Alyque's nieces, were in the audience. I was supposed to be with them. I didn't know how to break the news to Alyque during a performance. And Nisha was always highly strung. Every choice seemed like a bad one. I waited until interval and dragged Nisha upstairs to the terrace. I explained what had happened.

'What are we going to do?' Nisha thought she'd asked the question at normal volume, but she was screaming. It was awful.

We went back downstairs. I took one look at Gerson and knew that he knew. Alyque still had no idea. I made a snap decision. I wasn't going to tell him here. It wasn't right. Instead, I told him that Bubbles had indeed been in an accident and we had to go to the hospital.

Alyque took off his make-up. James made an announcement that he would take Alyque's place for the rest of the reading. Amal,

Pooh, Alyque and I got into Alyque's Ambassador and drove to Sion Hospital.

'But Bubbles called himself, so everything must be okay,' said Alyque. He repeated it over and over, like a litany.

The three of us in the car with him tried hard not to cry. Things were very far from okay.

Bubbles was dead. His daughter was dead. One ayah was dead.

Purveen had been driving. Somewhere near Panvel, a truck had come down the wrong lane and hit them head-on. Purveen and the other ayah survived. Eighteen-month-old Zavid was listed critical.

We parked outside Sion Hospital. While Alyque checked the doors, Pooh and Amal hurried in. I put my hand on Alyque's arm. He felt the tug and turned to me.

'Al, I have something to say to you,' I said. 'Bubbles is gone.'

Alyque just looked at me. He looked through me. He turned away. He leant his head against the gate. He stayed that way for a while. I kept my hand on his arm. He felt so slight. Like he would drift away if I let him.

'Where's Mama?' he asked finally.

'She's inside.'

Purveen was in one wing and Zavid in another. We drifted through the corridors like ghosts. People began to arrive. Bubbles was popular and the news had spread like wildfire. They'd announced it after the reading.

It was Alyque who took the decision to transfer Purveen and Zavid to Jaslok, so that they'd be next door to us. Gerson drove the ambulance because we didn't trust the driver. Nira Benegal drove Gerson's car.

Mama had lost her second adult son, and at least one grandchild. The family was shattered.

Purveen was in hospital for eight days. They released her after some tests, once she cleared the concussion protocol. She had a few scratches. That was all. That was it for physical injuries.

Zavid spent six weeks in ICU. His eyes would flutter. We were convinced that it was only a matter of time before he got better. I was in charge of the nurses and the doctors, blood donors and visiting hours – the hospital stay in general. I'd go down at 2 or 3 in the morning, in my night clothes, if that was what was required.

Alyque went back to work on Monday morning. I was at Frank Simoes by then, and it was easier for me to juggle my schedule.

A few days later, the doorbell rang at 10 in the morning while we were both trying to get ready for the day. It was the police. They'd come to inspect the car, the smashed-up little green Herald that had been towed to our building and was parked downstairs.

Alyque was in a hurry to leave, and I don't think any of us had properly processed the events of the weekend.

'Doll, just go down and see what these people want,' he said.

'Al, I can't go down dressed like this …' I was still in my night clothes.

'Well, get changed, go down and see what they want.'

'But what do I say to them?'

'I don't know. I'm late for work.'

'But –'

The fight erupted before I saw it for what it was. Within seconds, it had turned nasty, while the cops waited downstairs, while two people were still in hospital, days after multiple funerals.

I've always understood *why* we fought. I never understood how it unravelled.

At one moment, Alyque whirled towards me. He took a step in my direction.

Something snapped in my head. I cowered, like a bad dog.

Alyque stared at me. For an eternity. Then he got dressed and left.

He must have attended to the police then. Because they never came up. That's all I know. I never thought about it.

Sitting on the floor in my kitchen, I started to cry.

That step towards me. It struck so deep I wanted to die.

There's a knife I still have to this day. It's the largest one I own. I picked it up. I held it against my wrist. I moaned for hours. Because I didn't have words, not that day. I cried and I howled, like he'd ripped my tongue out. I locked myself in. I lay on the gadda in our bedroom. I didn't answer the phone.

People banged on the door. They could hear me. But I wouldn't open up. First, the neighbours. Then friends. Then Alyque's family. It didn't matter.

I lost hours, just lying there on the gadda, huddled next to the door, knife against my wrist. Sometime that afternoon, there was a soft knock on the door.

'Dolly?'

I didn't answer.

'Dolly, it's Purveen.'

She had got out of bed and made her way here. Minus her husband, minus her little girl, her son in the ICU. She'd come to help, because she could. Through my exhaustion, I saw someone extend a hand. A gesture I couldn't refuse.

I opened the door.

~

Did we talk about it? Alyque and I?

Not really.

I'm sure there were flowers that night. I'm sure we made love. I'm sure we talked about how passionate we were, how that set us apart.

I'm not sure we actually talked about it.

How prosaic, then. How like everyone else, when we thought we were special.

Love can be the most awful thing in the world. It brings out the best in you. And, sometimes, to preserve that illusion, we don't say the things we should. We were both guilty of it.

We just didn't know it then.

~

Bubbles and Purveen had a complex relationship with his mother.

Mama always was a little suspicious of the women in her sons' lives. Perhaps all mothers are. But not too many have to deal with that kind of loss – two adult sons, grandchildren, hope wrecked on a two-lane highway on the outskirts of Bombay.

After Zavid died, Mama's relationship with Purveen cooled. Maybe it was grief – every time she saw Purveen, she was reminded of things lost, things taken away. Maybe she blamed Purveen in some indirect way. She'd been driving. She'd survived.

I don't know. I don't think anyone knows. What I do know is that Mama asked Purveen to return the furniture that Bubbles had taken from Shiraz, Mama's furniture showroom, along with other things she'd given the family.

It all seemed so unnecessary, but maybe it was her way of coping.

~

The gloom lifted a little in October of 1975. Teddy Omar came to town. He was a childhood friend of Alyque's. He took the whole family out to dinner. We went to a restaurant called Coronation, on the first floor of the Prarthana Samaj building. Alyque and I were late and we walked onto the terrace to find the whole family seated at a long table. There was an empty chair next to Alyque's mother and she beckoned him over. And for the first time in our relationship, Alyque waved back and indicated that he'd sit with me instead.

After dinner, as we clambered down the stairs to the street, Mama admonished me. She told me I wasn't family. I'm not sure how serious she was. But that little remark, along with what had transpired with Purveen, got me thinking.

Over the course of the three years that Alyque and I had shared a flat, he'd brought in a box divan, an American bed, a cupboard, a lamp and a cabinet from Shiraz. Three days after dinner at Coronation, I told Alyque that I was going to return all of Mama's furniture. I didn't want to deal with her demands when we separated. *If* we separated.

At 6 in the morning, I emptied out the cupboard, the half-mirror dressing table, put all the furniture in a truck and sent it back with a note.

'Dear Mama, these are all the things Alyque brought from Shiraz. Kindly acknowledge.'

The grand gesture was all fine. Alyque woke up and looked around. The place looked like a hurricane had hit. All our clothes were strewn about the bedroom.

'If there's no cupboard by the time I'm back this evening, I'm never walking into this house again.'

Well, *that* put another perspective on things.

I went through the listings. There was a cupboard for sale at Kemp's Corner. It belonged to film actor Nigar Sultana, although I didn't know that when I read the ad. I called and went over. I paid six hundred rupees for the cupboard, put it on a thela and walked home behind it. Once I had it upstairs, I put all of Alyque's things into the cupboard.

He returned from work and strolled about.

'Nice cupboard,' he mumbled.

I received a bouquet of flowers the next day. 'For her determination and guts', it said. As far as combat pay goes, it's better than nothing I suppose.

~

Did we ever become 'normal'? In the eyes of the world?

I don't know. Not completely. That would be my guess. I don't know why – some hint of scandal titillates, I suppose. Even though we were trying our best to get on with our lives.

Alyque's life had been bifurcated, with surgical precision. There were two families. They never, ever, mixed. Occasionally, he'd inform me of a party or a show that I wouldn't be able to attend. This usually meant that Pearl would be in attendance and I'd stay home or find another engagement that evening.

Was I as sanguine about this as I projected to the world? I wish I could say 'yes'. In truth, it gnawed at me. I didn't want to thrust myself into Alyque's life and family. But the always-persistent feeling of being unwanted, of being unloved, one of the true legacies of my childhood, haunted me. I felt like a split personality. A public persona. And someone scared and occasionally alone, a victim of her own insecurities.

All of which came to a head one single evening. When Ronnie Screwvala got engaged to Manju Nanavati, we reached the venue on Marine Drive to discover Pearl had already arrived.

I was happy to leave. Alyque, perhaps having perceived my sense of isolation, insisted that he would walk in with me, or not at all.

Pearl shifted to a room adjacent to the hall. Alyque and I entered the party. And most of the guests eyeballed us like we were the evening's entertainment. I felt like they'd dimmed the lights and put a spotlight on us. It's one of the few moments in my life that I wished I wasn't the centre of attention.

Ten minutes later, Pearl left via a side entrance.

So, three people trying to do what they thought was for the best. And all three ended the evening feeling unhappy and hollow.

Still, we remained sport for so many people around us. I lost count of the phone calls I received from friends: 'Sorry, Doll, Pearl's coming.' And then they'd promptly invite Alyque to dinner.

~

In 1975, I spent a lot of time at the Asiatic Society. Alyque wanted to perform *Marat/Sade* in Hindi. The production was eventually called *Paagalkhana*, and starred Karan Razdan, Kavita Chowdhary (who would later play 'Lalitaji' in Alyque's famous Surf commercials) and a very young Satish Kaushik. I did a lot of research, trying to transform the French Revolution into something that would resonate with Indian audiences.

Alyque and I would meet every day at Horniman Circle and lunch, sitting on the grass, going over the progress I'd made that day. Then he'd go back to Lintas and I'd return to the library.

We could be wonderful together. We frequently were.

And I recently discovered six of my notebooks from that time – full of notes in a tiny hand, ink faded to almost sepia now, a wealth of research from almost fifty years ago.

~

I also recorded audiobooks with Talking Book Studios for the members of the National Association for the Blind to listen to. *Freedom At Midnight* was one of the many titles we put on tape. I had a long association with the NAB from that point on, trying to help them raise money and awareness.

The actor Dilip Kumar, incidentally, was NAB's grand patron. We once landed up at his house in Pali Hill because we needed him to deliver a byte to the camera. He suddenly asked for a script. I was stumped for a moment. Then I jotted down something from my childhood and helped him with the recitation.

'O what is this thing called light, that I might never enjoy,' it went. 'What are the blessings of the sight, O tell a poor blind boy …'

At least all that elocution amounted to something!

~

Alyque also directed *Vultures*, perhaps one of the first of Vijay Tendulkar's plays to grapple with violence and moral decay in minute, granular detail. Violence would become Tendulkar's beat, the mirror he held up to society. I badly wanted to play Manik, the scheming sister in the titular family of vultures who drive their father out of the house, but Alyque wouldn't cast me. I played the part much later, when I had to step in for someone else.

~

I also started to get requests from educational institutes, aside from invitations to give lectures or be a chief guest or judge.

The women's college Nirmala Niketan got in touch with me. Inaugurated in 1955, they initially offered a degree in just home science. Over the years, they had increased their ambit to include a three-year BSc and two MSc courses. They wanted me to direct a radio play for them. Given the work they were doing, they didn't have to ask twice. We performed Premchand's *Sawa Ser Genhoo*, a classic short story about how a rich man uses the loan of just over a kilo of wheat to bind a poor farmer into a lifetime of servitude.

Out of the blue, I got a phone call from the principal of St. Xavier's School after the radio play had been broadcast. He wanted permission to be able to include the performance in the school's social studies curriculum. I was happy to provide it.

In 1976, along with Dalip Tahil, I directed *The Emperor's New Clothes* with the kids from the Spastic Society. Even then, relatively early on, I knew that this combination – theatre and a social cause – made me happier than almost anything else.

~

One Sunday, in the April of '75, we were at lunch at Jerry's. She was Alyque's sister, and Pooh Sayani's mother. Pooh emerged from her room and made a beeline for Alyque.

'Alyque! What's this I hear?' she asked. 'You're taking Raell abroad?'

Alyque looked sheepish.

'Yeah,' he said. He wouldn't quite look me in the eye.

I waited until we were home. Surely a trip abroad was too big for him to have forgotten to mention? After our trip to London, Alyque had stressed, over and over, how much he hated travel …

Alyque was patient and gentle. He brought on the full force of his charm. He explained that he wanted to take Raell abroad. He wanted to bridge the gap between Raell and himself. And, in time, this might help Raell and myself.

Mollified, I asked how long he'd be going for. And when?

'For two months,' he said. 'In two weeks' time.'

I cried. I couldn't understand why he wouldn't tell me. Did I not deserve to know? Did he think I'd oppose it? Or didn't it matter?

He cajoled and teased and charmed. We made up.

On the day he was scheduled to leave, I emerged from the bedroom in my favourite skirt, a brown pinafore, worn with a gold top, and asked if that was okay to wear for the evening. When Alyque travelled, it was expected that I would drop him off at the airport and wait until the flight was airborne, in case there was a delay, and to fetch him when he returned.

But we'd also made it such a practice to keep the families separate. I should have perhaps thought about it twice. I didn't because I was already upset – we hadn't been apart for any length of time in years.

Alyque looked puzzled.

'Where are you going?' he asked.

'To the airport,' I said. He still looked unsure. 'To see you off.'

He grunted. 'You can't sit in the same car as my daughter.' He sounded honestly confused, as if he couldn't understand how I failed to see that, and his tone implied I should know better.

I cried. Again. I wish I could say it didn't hurt. But it did. It still does.

Alyque called Gerson and requested that his car ferry the kids to the airport. The two of us would take a taxi.

By the time we arrived at the airport, Alyque was cold and distant. He would write to me from America about how sorry he was, but that was weeks away. At that moment, he tossed a perfunctory 'goodbye' over his shoulder and disappeared into the terminal.

Then, things happened quickly. Pearl's son, Ranjit, left in Gerson's car. I didn't have enough money to take a taxi home. It was two in the morning. I hovered around the parking lot like a refugee, upset and at a loss. Leslie D'Souza, Alyque's travel agent, was heading home and offered me a lift to Mahim. From there, I caught the No. 4 All-Night that got me to Haji Ali. So, at about half past three in the morning, I walked up the hill from Haji Ali to our home.

I cried. Of course. I felt hollow and scared.

The next morning, I was struck by a strange sense of grief. We'd turned a corner. Alyque existed in the present – he'd fight, he'd make up, he'd get angry, he'd turn me on. But he wouldn't – or couldn't – take the long view. And we were in trouble. We were circling the same ground, over and over. And I missed him, like I was in the grip of a fever.

I drifted for a few days. Art galleries, plays, meals with friends. I was in mourning and I didn't even know it.

I passed through Lintas one morning during that grey phase. I stopped to say 'hullo' to Gool Mistry, an old friend and senior secretary to Gerson da Cunha.

14

GOOL ANNOUNCED THAT Gerson wanted to see me. I didn't know what about. I was always a little bit in awe of Gerson. He was a renaissance man, maybe the only one I knew well.

Gerson invited me to a party at Brahm Vasudev's place on Carmichael Road that night. It was the 16th of May. That date. That damned date. It would continue to haunt me – in good ways and bad. I remember it well because Devika and Suresh Bhojwani got married that day. I was scheduled to attend the wedding at the Taj. Gerson offered to pick me up after. He was insistent, in his charming way, enough for me to feel a kind of timorous excitement. I was being singled out. But there was surely nothing there – Gerson was Alyque's boss, his friend of thirty years, a schoolmate and a theatre colleague.

I was very conscious of his presence that night. If Alyque made the world about himself, Gerson made it about you. He was chivalrous, a real gentleman. When he married Uma, in 1969, their union didn't make much sense. She was as aloof as he was gregarious. She was small, and he was the most attractive man in town. She spent all her time in Calcutta, while Gerson stepped out with some of India's most beautiful and talented women. His list of regular dates was a chorus line of startling beauties: Gita Patnaik, Vilma Varghese, Shai Holsaert and Shobha Rajadhyaksha. Uma and Gerson have sustained, and they are a wonderful couple today. But they seemed mismatched back then.

I pondered over these things as I leant out of the Vasudev's window after dinner. I became aware of Gerson's presence, next to me, like he'd been there for years. It was effortlessly comfortable. I was pleased when he decided we should head home. In spite of his solidity, there was something delicious about the moment – it was all so new. It's why people stray, that *newness*.

I lived five hundred yards down the road. I asked him in for coffee, as one does. And I was thrilled when he accepted.

~

It's difficult to explain *what* happened with Gerson. It was never physical. We held hands. And that was it. Typical of Gerson.

But those two months were the most euphoric I've ever experienced in any relationship.

I've never fallen in love with anyone the way I did with Gerson.

~

My sister Pam married Hartley Anderson on the 31st of May. With Alyque in the US, Gerson became de-facto man of the house. He took charge, and he did it with grace and good humour. He played host at the ceremony.

We spent time together – parties, dinners, films.

The relationship with Dilip had been an adolescent one – petty, silly, doomed from the start. With Alyque, it was global warming: extreme weather, all around. One minute, we couldn't keep our hands off each other; the next, we were arguing.

With Gerson?

What is that Margaret Atwood poem? 'Variation on the Word Sleep'? Is that it?

'I would like to be the air that inhabits you for a moment only. I would like to be that unnoticed and that necessary.'

It was like that. With Gerson.

Letters and missives continued to arrive from the US. Many outpourings of love. I did not reply.

Two months passed. As if in a dream.

~

The latest telex from the US, via Lintas, announced the date and time of Alyque's arrival. It was accompanied by the details for the car that would drive me to the airport.

I went. To this day, I'm not sure why. Maybe I felt guilty. But I was sure that I would tell Alyque we were done. We'd hit a rough patch before he left, and I had discovered another kind of relationship was possible in the time he'd been away.

The flight was delayed. Outside the terminal building, I paced non-stop. I was unsure of how I wanted to break the news to Alyque.

He emerged all smiles and pent-up affection. On the way home, he was all hands. I felt limp, distracted, diminished somehow. 'I'll wait until I get home,' I thought.

I'll say it again: In my mind, we were done. The relationship was over.

Another part of me knew that this was the Dilip scenario all over again. And I backed away, an inch at a time, because I was afraid of the fallout, I was afraid of having to explain things the next morning. Better to leave it? Just the way it was?

At home, Alyque opened up his bags like a magician performing a complicated trick. Amongst the profusion of gifts, to make up for the note we'd parted on, he'd bought me twenty-eight sets of lingerie – very sexy, very expensive, Folies Bergere.

We made love. My heart wasn't in it. I went through the motions.

And all the while, running through my head: 'What are we going to do?'

We did nothing, Gerson and I.

Those two months slipped away from us, a bubble of time with no record of it ever having occurred.

Gerson would often visit just before I had to go to Television Centre, the building that later became Doordarshan Kendra, in Worli. I loved his presence. No man has ever made me feel so safe.

But that's where we remained.

Alyque and I muddled on. Gerson drifted in and out of my life. Soon, he moved on to UNICEF and then postings in Latin America and New York. What I felt for him remained – it has never gone away. Time took the rest.

Television came to Bombay in 1974.

Kunwar Sinha, my friend from London, was made producer for the English News because he'd worked with the BBC. He was the one who reached out to me.

I remember the auditions being very strict. We were given scripts to read. Pronunciation had to be correct, we had to sound good, and we had to get the names of people and places right. We also needed to be able to pick up the information off our cue cards and make it look natural. These were the days before teleprompters. It wasn't too tough, because of the experience that I'd had. As always, the question of my credentials had never crossed my mind before the opportunity arose.

I remember that Gerson auditioned. As did Siddharth Kak (who would later host *Surabhi* on Doordarshan) and the actor Vijay Crishna, an old friend from Delhi.

I was an established actress, but I was also a broadcaster and a compère and had international experience. I'd been doing a lot of voiceovers for commercials with Partap Sharma. By then, I was also doing a lot of the Films Division *Indian News Reviews*.

I thought it was a good career move, the right one at the right time. But it was also television, darling! It would be *something* to be one of the first newscasters in Bombay. And I was thrilled when I was contracted to read the news in English.

Television was still a nascent medium – one (state) channel, in black and white. Across neighbourhoods, dozens of people huddled around a single set. Programmes became fixtures in daily schedules. A group of readers and hosts became epochal personas – not because we were very good (that's a separate conversation), but because we were the first people on TV. People still come up to me at airports, and I haven't been a newscaster in about thirty-five years.

We were paid a princely sum of fifty rupees per broadcast. By 1982, when news became nationalized and the Bombay newsreaders went off-air, that amount had risen to a hundred rupees a turn. We'd also been restricted to a maximum of two turns a week because of union rules.

For a little while, I enjoyed being a minor celebrity. I was a 'face'. People asked me for autographs, shopkeepers offered discounts and free drinks, rickshaw and taxi drivers refused to accept fares, and I inevitably got shunted to the head of any queue I was in.

Let me be clear: I didn't mind any of this in the least.

The big red bindi became my trademark. As did the string of pearls I wore on air. Parents told me that they woke up their eight-year-olds at 10 p.m. to hear me read the news. That was flattering and alarming at the same time.

It was like the first cigarette you truly enjoy, and I dragged deep. There's a rush and the chemicals swirl in your brain and that's the real addiction.

At parties, I was noticed in my backless string cholis, my leather pants and my one-shoulder gowns. I was one half of a media power couple, and I was in a live-in relationship with an advertising legend and theatre maverick.

Alyque and I once went to watch IPTA's *Azhar Ka Khwaab* (Shaw's *Pygmalion*) at Rang Mandir, in Bandra. During the interval, the crowd spotted Shashi Kapoor. A very civilized murmur of recognition went up. When Alyque and I made our way from our seats, a few rows behind Shashi, a similar, but much quieter, murmur went up.

Alyque looked around with a raised eyebrow.

'You're well-known amongst the riff-raff,' he said. He grinned, 'I'm known amongst the intelligentsia.'

~

Of all things, the Emergency had a bearing on my life as a newsreader.

We knew we were living through a complicated time. Resistance, as it were, also needed to be discreet. But by the time elections had been declared, things had changed a little.

I canvassed for Ram Jethmalani and attended all his meetings. I even helped Dilip, who ran as an independent candidate and lost his deposit.

Thirteen years earlier, I'd marched in a Republic Day parade. In less than a decade and a half, being patriotic meant something else entirely. All that remained to be seen was whether or not the rest of the country felt that way.

On the eve of the election results, Alyque, Kersey Katrak and I drove from Express Towers in Nariman Point to the offices of the *Times of India* to follow the latest results on their tickers. Sanjay Gandhi had already lost, and we were all aware that we were witnessing something truly historic.

I was scheduled to deliver the 6.30 a.m. news bulletin. I dashed home to change into a saree and then went to the studio. I was the one who announced that Mrs Gandhi had been defeated. Apparently, I smiled as I said this.

As a consequence, I was blacklisted from TV for a while.

~

I can't claim to have been a career newsperson. I wasn't a journalist, not in that sense. But I was forced into having a slightly different perspective on newsworthy events; it came with the territory.

Years later, on 2 June 1988, we received word that Raj Kapoor had died. I accompanied the actress Nadira to the funeral in Chembur. But when I got there, the Films Division unit spotted me and prevailed upon me to do the live commentary for the funeral.

~

In 1976, Vimla Patil, the editor of *Femina*, asked me to compère the Miss India show to be held across ten cities. The tour travelled through Surat, Baroda, Ahmedabad, Amritsar, Delhi, Lucknow, Bangalore, Madras, Calcutta and finished in Bombay with the finals.

We travelled in an air-conditioned vestibule that linked up to trains as the route required. We had butlers and train staff on call twenty-four hours of the day.

The models who travelled with us were Salome Aaron (now Roy Kapur), Valerie Pereira (later Agha, and even later, Bee), Kalpana Iyer, Malti Swaminathan, Benjamin Gilani and Protima Bedi. Vimla's assistant, Shanti Chopra, brought her children along for the six-week trip: twelve-year-old Sangeeta and ten-year-old Sumeet. Sangeeta, of course, went on to become a highly regarded fashion designer, while Sumeet made his name as a fashion photographer before moving on to real estate a few years ago.

~

If I had to nominate a soul sister, it would be Protima Bedi. I was the film negative to her Technicolor 3D; a pale imitation. She was the original. She stuffed every second of her life full of living, something that is very hard to do.

We knew each other, of course. But I had always been Kabir's friend. It was on this *Femina* tour that we became close, and would remain so. I'd never known anyone like her. I loved her honesty and her daring. She never cared about what anyone else thought of her.

I *wish* I could've been like her. Because I had nothing on that woman. I was living with a man, out of wedlock. People spoke about me behind my back. And it gnawed at me. I needed acceptance, above everything else. Not Protima.

Here's the thing: Protima didn't judge. She didn't judge me. She didn't judge anyone. She never gossiped. She lived and let live. She looked you in the eye and took you at face value. She did this for everything and everyone in her life. That's how she was. And that, I think, allowed her to not judge herself.

How she got there, I do not know. She came from a very conservative family. And she was an absolute and total wild child. That leads me to believe that she was a force of nature – not created, just unleashed.

Some of it was the times, the 'freedom' we enjoyed in the '70s. When I met her, she was courting Kabir. She was daring with the clothes she wore. But it was really her spirit. The outfits were an accessory. The attitude was all her. She was free – just free. Completely and utterly. Her own person. I've never met anyone who was more generous – with her time, her talent, her money, her regard. She never said 'no'. She lived in the moment, always spontaneous. Nothing was beyond her. She trafficked in joy and youth. Those were the things that drew her. And those were the qualities she responded to.

Does it sound like hero-worship? Heroine-worship?

That's because it is.

Valerie was the same, but the polar opposite. Gentle, sweet, soft-spoken. She was made of the same steel as Protima but manifested it differently.

We first met Val at Jalal Agha's birthday party. And Jalal introduced Alyque and me to this pretty, simple girl, saying she was his fiancé. We nodded, turned around and rolled our eyes because all these exotic women were in and out of Jalal's life all the time.

But the quiet one belled the cat. Valerie married Jalal in 1975. They were both in *Death of a Salesman*, and they had both become close friends. We often left Quasar at their house with Saleem and Vanessa, their kids.

We shared so much.

Val would later divorce Jalal and marry again and move to Florida, where she works as a realtor and interior designer. She always did have a wonderful eye.

But I'm getting ahead of myself. I met two of the most important women in my life on this *Femina* trip. By the end of it, we'd become close friends.

I don't know why they were drawn to me. They found my life interesting, maybe. And we did some fascinating, exhilarating things together. We had independent lives. We didn't cling to our men. We kicked down the door and ran out.

They were such extraordinary women. Not perfect, but, my God, they were memorable.

~

That first tour really was a rolling circus. Each of our ten stops had a Miss Femina *insert name of location* Competition. I'd be introduced to a new set of contestants in every city. I'd interview the girls, write the commentary and compère the show. We'd run a segment with the contestants. Then our models would take over. They'd showcase clothes or fabrics of whoever the local sponsor was. This was a separate interlude, unconnected to the competition. It allowed the contestants a chance to change costume while points were tallied and an unfortunate few were eliminated. Then another segment, followed by another interlude. And so on, until we had a winner. All the regional winners then gathered in Bombay. We groomed them for a few weeks, and then held the national Miss India Contest. The whole process – the ten cities, culminating in the finals – took a couple of months. We did it every year. *Eve's Weekly* had its own Miss India contest too. Most of the people involved were the same, except Gulshan Ewing was the editor. Different day, same suspects.

We were not short of incident on the tour. Protima was usually the centre of attention. This time around, she had extra motivation. Kabir had just deserted her for Parveen Babi.

Protima collected admirers wherever she went, as a matter of course. But she was on a mission this time. She pirouetted at the end of the runway, in a full-length flared lehenga, sans underwear, *every* show. We watched ministers and VIPs lose their minds in real-time. We saw the little flick of the eyes, the rake down and up, back to the face, to the breasts, to the – 'wait one minute, does she really have no –'

She didn't even pretend that it was an oversight, a quick change gone wrong. She scandalized poor Debu Dutta, our technical director, by continually asking whether he could see her pubes under the floodlights, whether he could see that she was freshly shaved?

If she wasn't causing mayhem during the shows, she'd disappear like she did in Bangalore, with a Swiss 'friend' who had 'followed' her from Bombay.

In Surat, we were escorted, four-to-a-car, by the representatives of Modi Enterprises, the sponsors on this leg of the tour. Our escorts all wore uniformly ill-fitting Safari suits. Within minutes, Protima started to call out whether our hosts were dressed to the right or the left – 'where the will blows' and so on. The girls tried to suppress their giggles and muffle their laughter, with little success. Being the senior-most, I felt it incumbent upon myself to apologize for the behaviour of – ostensibly – my wards.

We were surprised by the aplomb with which the suits waved the apology away.

'Bombay girls only talk,' they said. 'Surat girls do.'

Later, over tea and dhoklas at a senior dealer's haveli, the collected wives enthralled us with gossip. Most Bombay gynaecologists, they whispered, got rich on Surat money. How? Because they ran a profitable market in abortions, and demand in Surat was high. In joint families, things sometimes got a little intimate. Cousins and uncles and aunts. People were randy and they wouldn't stop. Pregnancies had to be terminated. Out of sight.

After the very vegetarian cities of Surat, Baroda and Ahmedabad, the train pulled into Lucknow. We'd dreamt of kebabs the entire trip. I was the designated 'local'. My know-how might have been from fifteen years ago, but cities didn't change quite so rapidly back then. I took Valerie and Protima down to our popular watering hole in Hazrat Gunj. Many of the Romeos from my university days now owned some of the better stores there.

The Kashmir Fruit Mart was a particular favourite. Vashu Bhatia was the Romeo concerned. I remembered him on his scooter as he zoomed past the gates of Loreto College, resplendent in his legendary black-and-yellow attire. When we visited the shop as a gaggle of teenage girls, the elders would shoo us away. That evening, when I asked about Vashu I was told he had taken his six-year-old son to the doctor and would return shortly. We waited for him, perched on sacks of walnuts and pecans.

Vashu's stock rose that evening, as he 'Ganjed' with Bombay's leading models, all these stunning girls in hipster sarees and backless cholis. He took us to the best kebab place, known only to residents, housed in a garage.

Back in the car, Protima became philosophical. '*Kebab to kha liye, ab Nawab ki zaroorat hai.*'

Vashu was not to be outdone. '*Roz is naali mein pade rehtein hai, bas aaj nahin hai.*'

I asked about Nargis Hussain. When I was a student in Lucknow, she was the most beautiful woman in the city. In Lucknow, that's saying something. So, Vashu drove us straight to her place. The whisky flowed as we attempted to make up for a decade and a half. We also met Akbar and Tony Ahmed, sons of Sir Iqbal Ahmed and brothers of Zeenath Ahmed who had been the head girl at Loreto during my time there. Akbar was a recent recruit into Sanjay Gandhi's Congress and Tony was a practising advocate.

With parents and siblings, 1955

In 195

Ritchie, Esmie, Dolly and Pam, 1951

St. Anne's English High School with teache
Dolly Aranha. Dolly Thakore is second fro
left in the second row from below, 195

With Denaz Khory in *Money Makes a Difference* at Cawnpore Club, 1957

In *Pied Piper of Hamelin Town*, 1956

The Mikado, St. Mary's Convent, Kanpur. Dolly (third from right) played Pitti Sing, 1958

With Pandit Jawaharlal Nehru. Dolly is seated fourth from right, 1961

With Nandini Narain, 1962-63

With Kenneth Maharaj Singh in the play, *Rape of the Belt*, Miranda House, 1962

Patrick amd Rahael Solomon, Lovey and Moon Jackson, Rani Solomon, David and Dora Rawson, Suzie and Samuel Solomon, 1965

With Dilip Thakore, London, 1966

With Farrukh Dhondy and Farshid Bharucha, London, 1966

With Dilip at a flat party in London, 1966

The four Rawson siblings at Dolly's wedding, 1969

With Rosemary and Anna Panknin, Berlin, 1967

With Kris Srinivasan in Beirut, 1968

In London, 1967

With Dilip, 1969

With Zohra Segal during a BBC recording in London, 1966

Working as a model, 197

With Dina Pathak in *Mira*, 1972

Reading news on television

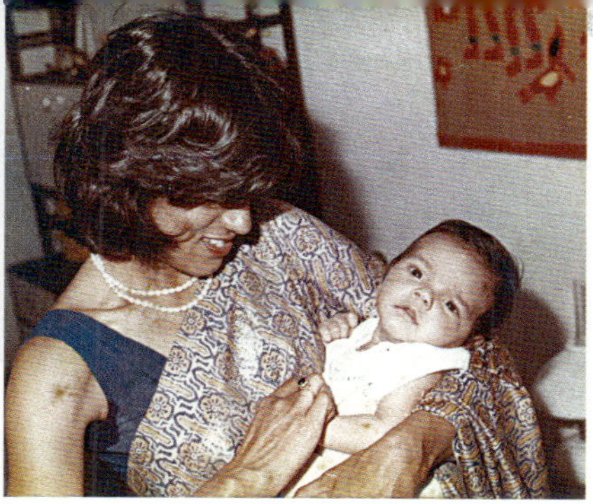

With her nephew, Zhya Jacobs, 1974

In *A Streetcar Named Desire* with Dalip Tahil, 1976

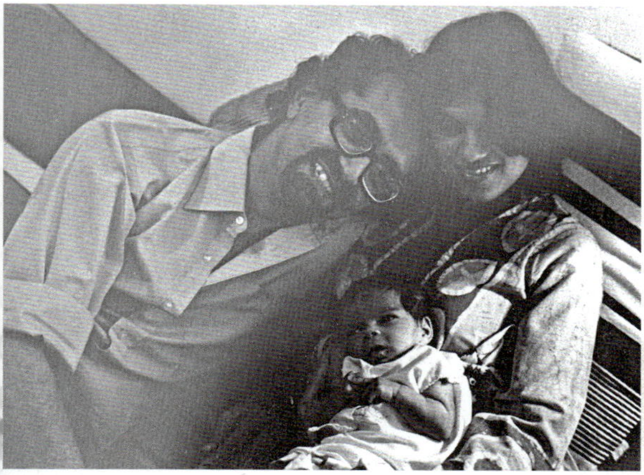

With Alyque and Quasar, 1978

With Alyque, 1979

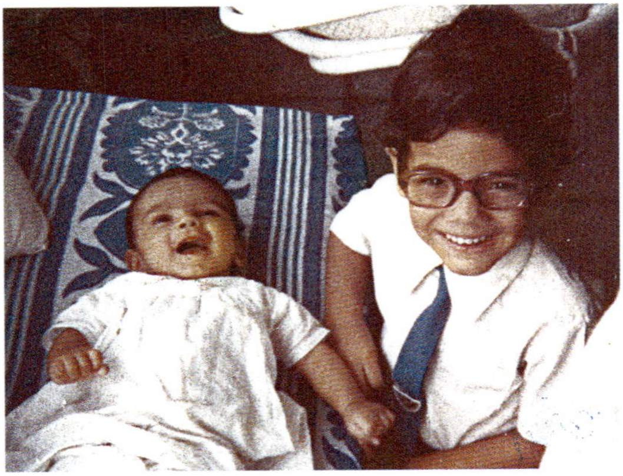

Zhya with baby Quasar, 1978

With Alyque in *Death of a Salesman,* 1981

During the filming of *Gandhi*, with Simon Kaye, Michael Stewart, Rani Dubey, Ben Kingsley, Rohini Hattangadi, Saeed Jaffrey, Richard Attenborough, Billy WIlliams, November 1980

At Rishi Valley, 1988

With Dennis, Esmie, Ritchie, Alyque, Quasar, Sanjna, David, Dora, Pammie, Zhya and Jai, 1993

With Vijay Kichlu and Protima Bedi, Bangalore, 1989

In *Tum Kya Jaano Preet,* with Kishore Bhatt as Pandit Deen Dayal and Dinesh Thakur as Azhar, 1994

With Protima, Pooja and Valerie, 1991

With Zhya and Quasar

Interviewing Hema Malini in *Hello DD* for Doordarshan in the 1990s

Compèring at the Art of Giving Event for the Richard Gere Foundation with Pritish Nandy and Sanjay Dutt, 1998

Compèring a dance programme for Sitara Devi, 2002

The original five from the *Vagina Monologues* – Sonali Sachdev, Avantika Akerkar, Mahabano Mody-Kotwal, Dolly Thakore, Jayati Bhatia, 2003

In the film, *Mitta Vs Mittal*, 2007

In Kohat at the St. Augustine Church where Dolly was christened, 2004

With (from left) Rahael, Jai, Pam, Jason, Sanjna, Ritchie, Esmie, Dennis, Hartley, Quasar and Mary, Australia, 2009

Being 'Bindi Nani' with Ellis, Milla and Sanjna, 2020

With Rani Aunty, 2018

With Alyque and Quasar, 2016

Quasar, Shazahn, Alyque, Raell and Sharon with Dolly at her seventy-fifth birthday, 2018

History is inescapable in Lucknow. Like Delhi, they have big chunks of it lying around. But, unlike Delhi, almost all of Lucknow lives with its history – shoulder to shoulder, jostling for sunlight. There's no 'old' and 'new'. It all *is*.

Our talk turned to Nawabs. The Ahmeds and Vashu decided to take us to Jimmy of Jehangirabad's place. On the drive there, they regaled us with legends of murder. Someone had been killed in one of the minarets on Jimmy's property. It was fun while we were in the car. Once we got to the estate, our laughter died away. The long and winding driveway was dark, and we felt like we were in a maze, being propelled towards … *something*. Without warning, as we rounded the final bend, the building loomed over us, dull, dirty, yellow, like an abandoned house. One by one, the girls gasped. We could see a figure, wrapped in a pale saree, under a single naked, crooked bulb that dangled from the high ceiling. It was an eerie, desolate sight.

Who was she? Was it a prank? Did we see an apparition? No one ever explained.

Through long, dusty rooms that hadn't been aired in decades, we were led to Jimmy's modern apartment, housed inside that old relic. Thousands of old books marked our passage, the titles indecipherable under cobwebs.

You could see the whole city from the minaret, Jimmy claimed. Were any of us interested? By then, talk of murders and ghosts had done its work. None of us wanted to go to the minaret. Except, of course, for one person.

So off went Protima. The longer she was gone, the more worried we got. Eventually, she reappeared some forty minutes after she'd left. By then, our collective nerve had been shattered, and we returned to the hotel.

The Nawab of Pataudi, 'Tiger', was at the same hotel. He had also been, until recently, the captain of the Indian cricket team, a position that – depending on the state of a series or tournament – might very well be the most important job in the country. Tiger was a legitimate icon, a proper celebrity. He was royalty, he'd been to university in England, and he was married to a film star. He was also a sportsman of rare distinction – one of India's finest batsmen and a supreme fielder. Vimla Patil pulled me aside and asked if I would approach him to be our chief guest. I've never really been *that* kind of shy, so I went. He was charming and obliged right away. The show in Lucknow was a tremendous success.

Back at the hotel, Protima changed into one of the long diaphanous Lucknow chikan kurtas we'd bought in bulk. No underwear of course; it wasn't even a question. But when she started to pencil in her eyebrows, we all got excited.

As a teenager, Protima had Protima-d herself. Someone told her that if she shaved off her eyebrows, they'd grow back thick, luscious and irresistible. She did, and they never grew back. So, Protima pencilled them in every single day.

More importantly, she would never let a stranger see her without her eyebrows.

All of which meant only one thing: she had a date, at this hour. The choice of outfit suggested the date was at this very hotel. Not even Protima was going to head out into Lucknow late at night without a bra.

A betting pool formed in seconds. Who was the lucky – or unfortunate, depending on your point of view – gentleman? Valerie and I had our money on the Nawab of Pataudi. He was at the *same* hotel. He was a charmer. And he was married. Protima liked a challenge. We wanted to tail her, and then interrupt the liaison at the most inopportune moment. But Protima was a veteran at shenanigans, and she gave us the slip. A few minutes later she called to say that, in many ways, she'd rather have been with us. We were having much more fun than she was. She didn't return, though, and we went to bed.

At about six in the morning, Val and I woke to frantic pounding at our door. We leapt out of bed to find Protima there, trembling.

We led her inside, gave her some water. She sat down between our beds and told us what had happened.

She'd been with a friend. In contrast to our hopes and dreams, they had spent the whole night chatting, sitting on separate beds in a twin-sharing room. At some point, a group of goons affiliated to a political party barged into the room. They accused Protima's friend of sullying the reputation of the city. There was some yelling and finger-pointing. And because the defenders of culture were so agitated, Protima managed to get away without any of the men noticing, before the situation turned violent.

There was no further incident. But the three of us didn't feel completely safe until we were in our train saloon. We'd had our fill of Lucknow.

Back in Bombay, I was the only one who had someone waiting to receive me at the platform when we pulled in. Alyque, with a huge bouquet of flowers. The other lovelies had beaus. Val and Salome would be married soon, but Alyque was always good at the grand gesture.

Once we were home, he insisted I shut the bedroom door. On the back of the door were the following lines; well at least the ones I can commit to print. Some are too private. Here are the rest:

'Things I miss about her' –
That class on the TV screen
That style and swing on the dance floor
Her clean cleanliness
Her satin smooth skin
Her adorable bottom
That strong jaw line
Her dress sense
The way she huddles under a blanket even in hot weather
The first time she cried
The first time we danced
Lazy Sundays in bed

A home a man can be proud to bring friends to
The fact she's not too jealous
Her help during crisis
AND HER COMPERING OF MISS INDIA SHOWS
THAT MAKE ME MISS HER!

– 7 June 1976

15

IN FEBRUARY OF 1976, Protima asked me to compère a dance recital of hers, at the Airport Centaur. It was a really small gathering – fifteen or twenty people. But it was a significant milestone because it was something that would become a huge part of our lives.

The previous year, Protima had an epiphany at the age of twenty-six, when she was a well-established model and a mother. She had thought there was a fashion show at the Bhulabhai Desai auditorium, but she wandered into an Odissi recital and was completely mesmerized. She had to meet the source of this beauty, the point from whence it flowed – Kelucharan Mohapatra.

She found him backstage, this tiny, bare-chested genius who had been playing pakhavaj for his students.

'I want to learn to dance,' she told him.

He looked her up and down, this most urbane of women, smoking furiously.

'*Aap kya karegi, ma*?' he asked.

But he didn't know Protima at all. She pestered him relentlessly.

'All right,' he said. 'We're leaving for Cuttack on the 10 p.m. train. If you can make that train, then I'll take you on.'

Protima was a little rattled by this. 'I have two children,' she said.

Guruji must have smiled and nodded, sure that he'd never see her again. But he gave her a lifeline.

'It takes two nights to get to Cuttack,' he said.

Protima didn't hesitate. 'I live in Juhu. I'm going to go home and make arrangements. I'll be at your door in Cuttack before you are.'

Protima went home. She borrowed money, and left instructions with her help – Anthony and Mary. They would look after the kids. She bought a plane ticket to Kolkata, and then took a train to Cuttack. She arrived at Guruji's door before he did, stretched out a dari and lay down. She stayed with him for three months.

Crazy and awe-inspiring, all at once. *That* was my girl.

She'd had an awakening the likes of which she had never experienced before. Dance became her life, and she threw herself into this new discipline, at a relatively advanced age, training for twelve, sometimes fourteen hours a day.

Later, she would give performances as fundraisers for the dream of a school. The plan was to teach seven Indian classical dance forms, six days a week, eight hours a day, for seven years. As Surupa Sen, the once-in-a-generation choreographer and soloist (and current Artistic Director of Nrityagram) put it: 'Don't tell someone how many years you've spent in dance school. Tell them how many hours.'

I compèred very many of those performances. The performance at the Centaur was the first. We would travel together. Protima, as always, was generous to a fault. If she'd been given a plane ticket, she'd use the money for two train tickets. If the organizers put her up in the Windsor Manor, in Bangalore, as often happened, I'd share the room with her.

~

In June of 1976, I received a telegram from the Ministry of Information and Broadcasting. They invited me to be on the selection jury for the National Film Festival in Delhi. I was chuffed. This was a different kind of affirmation.

I spent two weeks viewing films at Sapru House. We worked 9 to 9, watching five, maybe six films a day. I sat across from Amita Malik, who was *the* enfant terrible of Indian film critics. Also present were Rajinder Singh Bedi, the poet Aksh, Ashapurna Devi (who'd worked with Satyajit Ray), Balwant Gargi, Bachchan Srivastav and Anil Saari (the reviewer from *Screen*, who startled me by asking if I was Dolly Rawson from Christ Church College, Kanpur?). G.D. Khosla was the chairman of the jury.

It was a real education. The people on that panel were able to look at the work in front of them, and have immediate and visceral reactions, and yet draw on history and philosophy. They knew each film furthered and referred back to a medium that sought to redefine itself at every screening, an ever-growing pool of meaning-making. The experience of those two weeks was an immense help in my career as a critic in the 1980s and '90s.

~

I had a rotating set of employers on radio. AIR was state-sponsored, and a bit like the BBC. You could only broadcast non-commercial programmes. The others were more fun. I did programmes with Radiowani. And I was the voice of Radio Gem – all of their announcements and advertisements. I was even a member of the Radio Advertisers Producers' Association (RAPA). It was a serious business back then, as it is now. But Radio was also the primary source of news, information and entertainment for a long, long time, in a way that is difficult to contextualize for generations that have grown up with television, cable and the internet. Radio was the most widespread, most accessible medium well into the '80s and '90s. I believe it remains a missed opportunity, even today, because so much of the country still doesn't have access to television. The insidious assault of the mobile phone, however, will ultimately render that statistic defunct.

~

In 1976, Alyque was invited to the Advertising Film Festival in Cannes. He bought me an air ticket, and we made a long trip out of it. Even though he was the Creative Head of Lintas, we had to make do with a tiny room in a modest hotel. The walls were thin enough for us to hear the unmistakable sounds of orgasm next door.

France, baby!

Christian Dior straight silhouettes down to the ankles, but *clingy*, were 'in' that year. And blunt haircuts. I had to do the best I could with my colourful silks. With my knotted cholis, my bindis and my silver, I was exotic deluxe. I didn't care. It got me enough attention for the few days we were there.

At the Opening Ball, Creative Heads from Lintases around the world had the centre table. Tony Perone, the Head of Lintas Rome and a bit of a hunk, sat with us. As did the Creative Head of Lintas Austria. His date was a tall, Twiggy-slim stunner who *was* in the latest Dior.

All the men at our table lined up to dance with her. So much for the bindi and the backless. I was a bit disappointed that Tony Perone didn't ask me for a dance.

Over dinner, Twiggy and I bonded. Her name was Alexandra. I should have known then. People don't normally withhold their second names, even if they're, y' know, *French*. She was ever so nice. She had a conjurer's touch with compliments. I was the first Indian she'd ever met … I looked like a princess. She invited us to dinner in the Latin Quarter the next night, and we accepted.

The following evening, Alexandra did the ordering, and the food and the wine were both exquisite. We exchanged stories. She was intrigued by India, so I showed her some photographs of Goa. Our handsome young French waiter glanced at the photos and let out a strangled yelp.

'Calangute,' he said, pointing at the photograph. He looked overjoyed. Then he noticed my look of surprise.

'Six months I work in Cannes,' he said. 'And six months I am in Goa.'

I know a bunch of people from Bombay who now follow the same migratory pattern.

During our conversation, Alexandra expressed a desire to try on a saree. I was having the time of my life, so I offered her one of mine for the closing ball. 'Come to the hotel a half hour early that evening,' I told her, 'and I'll drape it for you.'

All in all, it was an excellent evening. We finished the last of the wine and sat back. The bill arrived. Alexandra was all business. She fished about in her handbag and then disappeared into the tiny kitchen. After a little while, she reappeared. She looked despondent. In her excitement, she explained, she had forgotten to put her wallet into her evening bag. And now the restaurant wouldn't allow her any credit. She felt *terrible*, given we were guests, foreign guests and everything … but.

Alyque's face fell. He realized, a little too late, that he'd been scammed. He was an advertising legend, after all. He pulled out his wallet and counted out all the Francs he had.

We wandered back towards the hotel, deflated. We'd been played good and proper, but we were too polite to raise a fuss. We window-shopped in glum silence. I eyed the black bikini I'd coveted earlier that day. Alyque, ever the lead prophet of telling it like it was, glared at me.

'You've just eaten your bikini,' he muttered in Hindi.

Alexandra picked up the undercurrent of tension. 'What's going on?' she asked. And she wouldn't allow us to change the subject until I explained that our meal had put a dent in my potential swimwear purchase.

She was at great pains to put us at ease.

'Don't worry,' she said. 'I work here, and I get 50 per cent off. I'll make *sure* you leave Cannes with this bikini.'

By now, both Alyque and I recognized her MO. We bid her a hasty good night and beat a hasty retreat. Too much Alexandra wasn't good for our health. We'd also figured out what she was actually after. Invites to the Awards Ceremony and the Closing Ball were a precious commodity. We'd cracked it, we thought. We were from Bombay, and you couldn't fool us. All it had cost us was a black bikini and where in India was I going to wear it, really?

The day of the Ball arrived. We'd decided to leave the hotel an *hour* ahead of schedule, just so that we could avoid our intrepid French escort. We'd underestimated the competition. Alexandra turned up *two* hours ahead of the agreed-upon time, and I found that I couldn't back out of my offer.

Because I wore (and still wear) knotted cholis, the blouse fit her perfectly. But she was taller than I was, by a good eight inches or so. I tied the petticoat very low, revealing a shapely midriff. She might have been a freeloader, but she was going to look outrageously sexy. Even Alyque was slightly dazed by the sight of her. She looked stunning. 'To the saree born'.

All she needed was a few tips about walking with one leg in front of the other. She looked so good that I felt compelled to volunteer my silver pendant and a red bindi to complete the picture.

Alexandra was the cynosure of all eyes as we made our way to the ceremony. Pleased with the flood of compliments, she ducked into a bar to show off her makeover. And Alyque decided it was the perfect moment to slip away.

The queue was endless. It was a proper black-tie event. Bouncers patrolled the velvet rope and men in tuxes checked off invitations with great concentration, like we were trying to get into a maximum-security prison. Lo and behold, Alexandra rushed up to us, breathless and flustered.

'Ooh la la,' she said. I promise she said it. And then: 'I'm so sorry, I 'ave left my invitation at 'ome.'

Alyque wasn't having any of it. He ignored Alexandra, ensured she couldn't engage me in conversation, and shoved me into the event before we could get suckered again.

At the Lintas table, the two of us were plagued with the same question: 'What is she doing in a saree?'

We saw Alexandra inside the venue a few minutes later. She'd bamboozled someone else into letting her attend. But try as she might, the Lintas table – perhaps the group of people she'd profited from the most – had closed ranks.

Dinner and dancing followed the function, and most people began to wander to the casino. In a short while, the action shifted to the tables. Alyque and I followed the general migration, but we kept an eye on Alexandra. There was the small matter of reclaiming my saree and my pendant.

And then she disappeared. Thinking that she'd be considerate enough to return borrowed clothes, even after five days of Olympic-level freeloading, we joined the mass exodus for the Minerva. She knew that we were leaving for Nice at 6.30 the next morning, en route to Athens. We were sure she'd find us. After all, she knew where to look.

When we returned to our room, there was still no sign of her. I thought I'd give her until the morning. But, a few hours later, when I enquired with the concierge if anyone had left a package for me, I drew a blank. All I could do was leave my forwarding address, with Alexandra's name on the envelope, in the hope that she'd send the clothes on.

The concierge looked at the envelope and blinked.

'Excuse me, Madame?'

I turned back.

'Mademoiselle Alexandra?'

I nodded.

'But Madame,' he said, looking ever-so-slightly-French and bemused. 'She is not a woman. She is a man.'

We left Cannes minus a saree, but with a story we have dined on for many years.

~

From France, we went to Athens and Copenhagen. And then onto America – my first time ever. We drove, all the way across the country, because that was what some of our heroes had done – the Beats, Kerouac, on the fabled Route 66. The United States can be mythic. Sometimes, like a Wim Wenders film, the only way to experience it is a road-trip. Hours and days, and miles and miles.

I remember the Grand Canyon. I remember the Petrified Forest in Arizona. I remember thinking of how small we were, in the scale of things. How tiny, how *new*.

Maybe that was the best of us – Alyque and myself. Away from home, on the road, free from the pressures of living our lives day-to-day.

I remember driving all the way to Santa Monica to meet Robert Lee, one half of the duo (the other being Jerome Lawrence) who wrote *Inherit the Wind*, perhaps the most widely performed play of the twentieth century. Alyque and I were keen to meet him because we'd done the play ourselves. It was a lovely, warm encounter.

We parted company in San Francisco. Alyque would head home. I was going to see my sister Pam in Australia. I flew direct to Sydney – the 'other', shorter way.

I didn't know it, but I'd carried serendipity with me in my cabin baggage.

I was living with Pam and her husband, Hartley Anderson. Hartley's mother mentioned to me that Caroline Jones of the Australian Broadcasting Corporation wanted to do an interview with me. Hartley's brother, Doug, was also on the radio, and that's how she had reached out. I was game. So, on the appointed day in early September of 1976, a chauffeur-driven car – and a pretty swish one at that – was dispatched to fetch me. Suitably impressed, I hopped in and was driven to the studio.

Once we got to the compound, the driver had to go through a series of checks before he could deposit me at the designated point. At every one of these, he rolled down the window and leant out.

'I have a VIP,' he said. Every time. Needless to add, this was all rather enjoyable.

We stopped at the foot of a set of stairs, a lot like the Town Hall steps in Bombay. Before I could lift a hand, a good-looking young man in a corduroy jacket ran down and held the door open for me. He was my chaperone.

In the elevator, I looked at him closely. I couldn't shake the feeling that he looked familiar. He was cute too.

He smiled. 'I used to know a Dolly Rawson in London,' he offered.

I identified myself and submitted that I was, in fact, the same person.

'We've actually met,' he said. 'My name is Michael Mortan Evans.'

Of course! He'd been a young journalist at the *Evening Standard* when I'd been in England, and here we were all these years later. I hugged him, and we walked into the offices chatting like old friends. Michael told Caroline about how we knew each other. The ice had been well and truly broken. A twenty-minute chat became a forty-five-minute interview, and the two of us went off for a drink together after.

But, more importantly, I introduced Michael to Pam and Hartley and they remain friends to this day.

~

I never quite lost the habit of running into old friends in the most unexpected places.

In February 1989, the French President Francoise Mitterand travelled to Bombay to inaugurate the Festival of France. Rajiv Gandhi officially welcomed him at the Tata Theatre. I anchored the live telecast.

I like to believe I have a thing with the Gandhis, some kind of special bond, all the way back from catching Panditji's garland as a schoolgirl. Or maybe my life and work just allowed me to be around them more than most people.

Security was tight. The Tata Theatre was in lockdown and everyone, including the prime minister of India, had to be there before time. He arrived at 5.15 for a 6 p.m. event. And because the prime minister was already there, so was everyone else.

I spent forty minutes ad-libbing senselessly. Who was in attendance, and why, the importance of the occasion, the design of the theatre and why it was an arc, celebrities and what they were wearing, and how impactful their jewellery was in person … As I droned on, I sensed silence behind me, as if that little pocket of the Tata had somehow been separated from its surroundings. Our own little bubble, as it were. Someone put a hand on my shoulder. I looked up from the monitor, a little puzzled. A full head of tousled, curly grey hair framed a smile I knew. This was Aftab Seth, an old friend from Delhi University. Aftab placed his visiting card in front of me. He was now joint secretary and official spokesperson for the PM, Rajiv Gandhi. Aftab nodded, ever so slightly. I turned around. Rajiv Gandhi stood there. He shrugged, as if to say, 'They brought me here.' He went back to gazing at the monitor with the fierce concentration of a television producer. My jaw dropped. My prattle died out, like someone had hit mute, or like there had been a problem with the audio feed. The prime minister just grinned. He was bored, and this was currently the best seat in the house. The rest was my problem. He lurked behind me a little while longer. He seemed to be enjoying himself. I have no idea what I talked about. It was totally unnerving. And you couldn't really object. I mean, the prime minister!

Ten minutes later, the security detail arrived to escort the Reluctant Prince to his engagement. And I thought, how odd it must have been for him, the one man who wanted none of this. For himself or his family.

~

On the 7th of July 1974, Esmie and Dennis were blessed with a little boy. Zhya Jacobs was my favourite member of the family, without question. I took the bus from Pedder Road to Bandra every morning to go and see him at Dr Ganatra's hospital. I must've really annoyed the little kid. All I did was hug him for a half hour and then rush back for my afternoon speech and voice class at the Hill Grange High School.

Let's make no mistake about this. I was the cool aunt. Pam was in Australia, and I was Dolly Massi who let Zhya get away with almost anything he wanted. Esmie and Dennis travelled a lot, and they both worked irregular hours. I was the designated babysitter. Zhya went wherever I went.

I took him to the India Sponsorship Committee's Antar Bharti Balgram, which I visited once a month. I took him to rehearsals from the moment he could walk. He was a charming young man and fit in anywhere. Even Alyque, never a fan of young children, adored him.

I have a vivid memory of Zhya's imitation of Noel Godin in his prime.

'I am I, Don Quixote,' he would sing, clutching an aluminium dekchi, 'the man of La Mancha. My destiny calls and I go.'

The dekchi would then become his golden helmet and he'd sprint up and down the aisles of the Bhulabhai Desai Auditorium in Churchgate.

Sometimes I remember him running pell-mell up and down dusty carpets, that grin plastered across his face, and I can barely breathe.

The world is not what it was. Every day, I'm reminded of this.

~

On the 16th of March 1977, Imtiaz and Anil Dharker had Ayesha. We went to see them after they'd come home from the hospital. Sitting there, with Ayesha on my lap, and Zhya in my life, I decided I wanted a child.

I'd been on the pill for a decade when Dr Nergish Motashaw, my gynaecologist, decided we'd fooled my hormones long enough.

She advised an IUD. Two years later, she wanted to get rid of that as well. New research indicated long-term risk.

Although I sometimes wonder why I was the only one who took on the responsibility of birth control in all my relationships. If sex is fun for everyone involved, then the prevention of pregnancy should perhaps be a shared thing as well.

This desire to have a child was a new development. Alyque and I had been together eight years. I was thirty-four years old. I only had a couple of years before pregnancy became a medical risk.

I thought it would complete the experience of being a woman. I'd done everything else.

I had the IUD taken out in 1977. By January 1978, I was pregnant. Much to Alyque's consternation, we were expecting our first child in September.

~

We argued. A lot. I wasn't doing it to get him to marry me, I told Alyque. The baby would be my responsibility, because it was *my* choice. I was strong enough to bring up a child on my own. I was also stupid enough, back then, to believe that it would be easy.

But Alyque remained unconvinced. To this day, I'm not sure why. Did he think that it would cramp his style, the life he enjoyed with his girlfriend? That he would cease to be the centre of attention?

Was he worried about extra responsibility? That he would feel compelled to take on?

All of these things?

I don't know. I will never know.

I was as healthy as a horse. There were no scares, no precautions, no restrictions. I took to pregnancy like a duck to water. I think that infuriated Alyque at some level. Not only had this happened without his approval, but I was enjoying myself too much for his liking.

He was never a patient man. But he was on tenterhooks for those nine months. Over and over, we talked about whether I was sure, whether I was ready. From start to finish.

In May of 1978, we had another argument. One of those arguments that had become more and more regular. This one got so bad that I locked myself in our bedroom and called Denaz and Cyrus Tata. I begged them to come home and intervene.

Relationships are always on a slippery slope. Unless you're vigilant, you *will* find your lowest point. Like water, down the path of least resistance. Because standards must be maintained. They are never absolute.

Love keeps you coming back. It's the hope that kills you.

Denaz came. Cyrus came. They sat Alyque down. They tried to defuse the situation.

We went to sleep. The next morning, we were lovers again. The earth still circled the sun.

~

Between 1977 and 1979, I hosted a pan-India radio show called *Glaxo Bonny Baby Time* for Radiowani. Leading paediatricians from the city I was in that week presented a paper on the show. Usually, the subjects were various aspects of pregnancy and birth, and the potential problems a child might face in the first three years of his or her life.

This segment lasted between five and seven minutes. Then five sets of parents from that city were asked three questions based on the talk they'd just heard. The winners would win a (limited) supply of free baby food.

The show was broadcast every Sunday for two years and it was very popular. I criss-crossed the country: Cochin, Trivandrum, Madras, Hyderabad, Bangalore, Lucknow, Calcutta, Delhi and Bombay. Each of those cities still had those names.

During the seventh month of my pregnancy, I decided to create a bank of programmes. I was due in September, and I knew I wouldn't be able to travel from August. My producers at Radiowani were amenable to the idea, if I could generate the content.

So, for a while, this is what my schedule looked like:

I'd travel to the other cities Monday to Thursday. On Friday, I'd return to Bombay. That night and the following night, I'd present the news on television. While in Bombay, I'd have a series of tasks to accomplish. I still lived like I had done in England – no domestic help at all. We could've, and perhaps should've, employed a caretaker. But that would have driven up costs. And I was maniacal about splitting everything down the middle. Especially now, since I'd made the decision to have a child. I couldn't afford that, and I would brook no discussion about it.

Maybe I had inherited some of my mother's mania about money, and about looking after the house. I'd clean an apartment that hadn't been swept or dusted in four days. I'd wash and iron the clothes. And I'd cook for the days I wasn't in Bombay, because Alyque loved my cooking, and I wanted to do it for him. Even if I was traveling, I wanted him to feel like I was looking after him. He lived in my house. It was important to me. I still needed to be loved and valued, still had to be everything to everyone.

Monday morning, I'd leave again.

Lather, rinse, repeat.

By the eighth month, I was permanently exhausted. But I was locked in. I'd made these choices and there was no end in sight, not until the baby arrived. One of the days I was in Bombay, Alyque picked me up after I was done with the news at ten. I asked if we could go somewhere to eat because I couldn't bear to think about cooking.

He took me to Shetty's for chaat. I should mention that Alyque loved chaat. It was a fixture when he went out, and when he threw one of his parties – 'Beer and Bhel' would become standard fare.

Also, for a man as practical as he was, he had a peculiar lack of understanding of proportion. It wasn't intentional. He just didn't get it. There were countless cast parties where he thought a single traybake would suffice for dozens of people. And he'd watch, bemused, as someone got on the phone, placing distress-biryani-calls.

I was too tired to remember how oblivious he could be. And I can't stand chaat, at the best of times. I asked Alyque if we could go somewhere else. All I wanted was soup and a sandwich. The only place you could get a decent soup and sandwich at that hour was Shamiana, at the Taj.

He'd misjudged my mood completely. It's possible that he just didn't know how hungry and tired I was by then, how far down a fox-hole. And I hadn't told him, not really, because it had become a point of pride. It was *my* decision to have the child.

'I'll pay for your soup,' said Alyque. 'And you can pay for your sandwich.'

Well, I *had* insisted on splitting costs. Down the middle. So this was my mandate, really.

I had the soup and asked for the cheque. Hungry or not, I couldn't afford the sandwich. And I was now angry.

On our way home, conversation turned to office politics at Lintas. Alyque was scheduled to take over as managing director because Gerson was going to Brazil. I gave him as patient a hearing as I could.

'I think I'll ask Stanley to come over from Calcutta,' he said, suddenly. We were on Pedder Road by then. Stanley Pinto was Manager, Lintas Calcutta.

'And ask Keith Stevenson to join me.'

'Al, Stanley has said to me that he will never come back to Bombay,' I said. I paused. 'And Keith doesn't want to work with you.'

The car sped up. Alyque *hated* being contradicted. I was only trying to help. He drove to the Haji Ali roundabout (which existed back then) at breakneck speed and swung the car around. The tires squealed. He slammed on the brakes and the car screeched to a halt. He leant over and shoved open the passenger door.

We sat in silence for a while.

Dinner, *and* a show, I thought. What a bonanza.

Then we came home.

~

We must've had good times, no? We *must* have.

It's just that the bad stuff sticks. And it sticks because it still has the power to sting, even after all these years. I'm surprised that I remember every detail of my life with Alyque. I just wish he'd been a little more considerate. But more than that, I wish I'd been a little more considerate with myself.

We *did* have good times. We filled our lives with laughter and work and friendships, and yes, sometimes it was messy.

But we stuffed every second with *doing*. And how many people can you share that with? Day after day? For over a decade? Unless there is something profound at the heart of it?

I wanted my child to be Alyque's. That was important to me. Him, more than anyone else.

~

I was three weeks pregnant when I read the word 'Qasa' in an issue of *India Today*. It was attributed to Zulfikar Ali Bhutto, the former president of Pakistan. He was in prison, on death row. The word itself was Persian.

'Qasa' – the righting of all wrongs.

One evening in late January, I asked Alyque what he thought of 'Qasa' as a name. Alyque mulled over the word as we sat on the parapet wall overlooking the sea at Bandra Bandstand. We were going to spend the night at Esmie's.

'People will say "Casa",' he said. 'Like Kasa Pepino. Or Casa Bambino.'

That was probably true. But he wasn't done.

'If we add a "u" after the "Q", it becomes harder to mispronounce.'

That was it. We said it out loud, tasting the word. It felt … *right*. We agreed. If we had a daughter, we would call her 'Quasa'. And if we had a boy, we would add an 'r' and he would be 'Quasar'.

The next morning, we tried the name on the family. And Dennis immediately said, 'Hang on, that's an imploding galaxy.' We pulled out the encyclopaedia and looked up a word we thought we'd invented the night before.

Quasars were amongst the most luminous and powerful objects in the known universe. Their light had just begun to reach earth after millions of years in transit.

After that, the child growing inside of me was never referred to anything else but Quasar.

~

In the eighth month of my pregnancy, I returned from Trivandrum after another *Bonny Baby* excursion. It was a Saturday. Lalit Bijlani of Blitz screened private shows of foreign films for special guests at his mini auditorium just off Colaba Causeway, opposite Metro Shoes. I remember this distinctly because bandicoots had chewed through my high heels in Trivandrum, and I hobbled back to Bombay. After the Blitz screening, I dropped off my shoes at Metro for repairs.

Alyque and I often had potluck dinners with Shandana and Pradeep Khaitan, who lived on the second floor in the same building. We returned from the film around 9 in the evening and rang their doorbell to see if they were still game for dinner. They were. We went upstairs to fetch the food. I thought I'd use the loo before I went downstairs. Pregnancy makes you pee like you're surviving on a diet of beer. And I felt *something*.

Alyque insisted we walk to Jaslok right away. I argued with him all the way down the hill and around the corner. I thought he was being paranoid. I wasn't due for another three weeks.

My water broke in the elevator. I walked in through the lobby and went straight to the maternity ward. Labour pains came, as advertised, on cue, like clockwork.

Alyque called Denaz. Her father was at the same hospital, undergoing treatment for cancer. She sat by my side for the rest of that night and into the next morning.

At 4.55 a.m. on the 20th of August 1978, my son Quasar was born.

The moment they wheeled me out post-delivery, I turned to Alyque and said I was ready for the next one. The experience of giving birth to the little man had been exhilarating. I felt a wave of love so strong that the discomfort of the final month, and the eight hours of labour, felt insignificant.

Deryck Jeffereis, Alyque's brother-in-law, sent me a card which said: 'Welcome Quasar – a very small star-like cosmic source of light and radio waves.'

And I have to say: the kid never let me down. We had each other's frequency absolutely right.

~

I was up and about within hours of delivery. I went to the attached bathroom by myself. I took a shower without any assistance. And when I was allowed visitors that afternoon, I sat up in bed and beamed at everyone. Titoo Ahluwalia said that I looked like I'd delivered a child a week ago.

The next day, doctors discovered too much bilirubin in Quasar's blood. He had mild jaundice. Nowadays it's something that most babies simply shrug off after a few days in hospital but, back then, it was cause for concern. The doctors muttered words like 'blood transfusion' and looked worried. I began to panic. Quasar had arrived early and Alyque left for a scheduled trip to Jaipur after I'd given birth. Shyam Benegal was filming *Junoon*, and Alyque was very keen to see how battle sequences were staged. He wanted to make *Tuglaq* into a film. It was an obsession on par with Terry Gilliam's for *The Man of La Mancha*.

So, while we debated whether a day-old infant should, in fact, have a blood transfusion, I was surrounded by a group of fiercely protective women: Vimla Patil, Valerie Agha and Protima. They closed ranks, kept me sane, kept me laughing, and sent doctors and nurses running for cover.

Quasar spent a few extra days in the hospital before he was cleared to go home. He didn't require a transfusion. On the day we were discharged, we spent three hours waiting for Alyque. He showed up at noon. We'd been ready since 9 a.m. It took another forty-five minutes to clear bills. We were tired and hungry. My visions of a postcard memory – Alyque, Dolly and Quasar paused at the threshold of their apartment – were just that: idealized fiction. I consigned that mind-movie to the rubbish heap. I had other things to worry about. Because Quasar was three weeks early, I wasn't prepared. No cot, no nappies, no clothes.

We got home close to one in the afternoon. I'd last been here ten days ago. Nothing had changed. And yet everything had. I put Quasar on the floor and wrapped him up tight in a sheet. 'You're home,' I told him.

The doorbell rang. I answered to find Gurcharan Das standing there. He was a good friend, then the managing director of Richardson Hindustan Ltd., and later Proctor & Gamble. He was also the playwright of *Mira*, the first play Alyque cast me in. Alyque, in all his wisdom, had invited him for lunch. It was a measure of how unprepared we were, of how little we knew about what we'd got ourselves into. We'd expected to be home in the morning, with everything under control, before Gurcharan arrived. Motherhood was going to be more complicated than that.

I left Quasar there on the mattress and started cooking. Gurcharan is a vegetarian and that was lucky. Otherwise, we'd have eaten around 4 in the afternoon.

Through it all, Gurcharan kept apologizing. I demurred and cooked. Quasar cried. And Alyque tried to smooth things over.

'No, no. It's fine,' he kept saying. To whom, I'm not quite sure.

Later that evening, Valerie arrived with reinforcements. Her son, Saleem, had outgrown his bassinet, so Quasar had a cot. And she had brought with her every item on the new-born-baby-shopping-list: pillows, blankets, bottles, sheets, clothes, diapers, everything.

~

A few weeks later, I was invited to compère the White Cane Open Air Ball in Pune. My one condition was a tent where I could breastfeed Quasar. I put him in a carry-cot, and we travelled for the first time.

I wonder if Zeenat Aman remembers helping me change his diaper in the washroom at Santacruz Airport?

By October 1978, I resumed my duties on *Glaxo Bonny Baby Time*. Quasar graduated from the carry-cot to a sling around my neck. In Hyderabad, we lived at the Ritz. The room was festooned with diapers drying on every available surface. Disposable diapers were yet to become easily available. Hyderabad was also where Quasar had his first camel ride.

Alyque didn't have much time for a mewling and puking little child. If he was in a script meeting or a reading at home, he'd often ask that I take Quasar downstairs. I didn't have full-time help for months, so I started to take him along to a lot of my assignments.

At every step along the way, angels stepped in, lent a hand, held my kid, even if it was for a single minute.

The village raised my son, and he's better for it.

Shama Zaidi and Javed Siddiqui were his babysitters every time I had a newscast and they were at home for production meetings on *Tughlaq*.

Quasar came to every play I reviewed at Prithvi. There were times when Shabana Azmi would take him to the loo.

In 1982, when we went to Delhi for a fashion show with Shanti Chopra, we all travelled by train. And Juhi Chawla, one of our models and soon-to-be Miss India, cheerfully took him to the bathroom.

Quasar spent a lot of time in TV studios, sometimes perched on the platform under my news table during broadcasts. He spent a lot of time in the wings and green rooms. He had an excellent, intuitive understanding of backstage etiquette.

Poor guy never had a chance. He was always going to end up in the theatre.

IV

Concussion Protocol

16

IN MARCH 1979, I was in Madras to record an episode of *Bonny Baby Time*. We were staying at the Taj Coromandel, thanks to Glaxo. We finished at about half past 12 in the morning, and I asked my producer if I could try and make the late flight back to Bombay. I had a ticket for the next morning. It had just turned the 10th, my first birthday as a mother, and I wanted to try and make it back to Quasar as soon as I could.

I was welcome to try, said my producer. If it didn't pan out, I always had the ticket for the next day.

The next step was to go downstairs and talk to the reception. I couldn't give up my room completely – what if I didn't get a seat? The Taj were reliably excellent. 'Go,' they said. And come back if you can't make the flight. Also checking out at the same time was a gorgeous German man, a young Kabir Bedi look-alike in a denim suit.

I took a cab to the airport. And while I was waiting at the Indian Airlines desk, I saw the same young man being ushered into the duty officer's room. He was flanked and trailed by a small mob of Indians. Clearly, I wasn't the only one who'd been taken in by his beauty. I leant across the desk.

'If he gets a seat before I do,' I said to the man behind the desk, eyeballing him like I was a tough cop, 'I'm going to raise a hell of a stink.'

The young German fellow emerged after a while and came and stood beside me at the counter. I figured it was best to get to know my enemy, so I bummed a cigarette off him. Contact made, I discreetly enquired what flight he was trying to get aboard and what number he was on the waitlist.

He was going to Bombay, all right. He was waitlisted thirteen. I was twelve. I turned back to the man behind the desk – trying to express some combination of triumph and implied threat. But the desk jockey had the last laugh. A busload of tourists had just arrived from Tirupati, and neither of us was going to get on the flight.

I asked the young man whether he was heading back to the Taj. He was a little startled. I explained that I'd seen him check out. He said he could, but he didn't know if he'd get his room back. Let's give it a shot, I said. And we hailed a taxi together.

His name was Michael Kohler, and he was twenty-three years old. I asked what he was doing in India and he said he was visiting family.

'Oh, so your mother's Indian,' I said, thinking that his bronze skin and the link to Kabir (whose mother was also Caucasian) made sense. After all, his surname was German.

'No,' he said. 'My father.'

I was intrigued, so he told me his story on the car ride back to the hotel.

As a child, Michael had been the victim of bullying in school for that same bronze skin. The world wasn't as accommodating back then, and certainly not in Germany where they were grappling with their national identity. He'd become a hothead, someone who got into fights.

Later, this is something I'd see in my son.

At the age of fourteen, Michael beat up another kid in school, and as punishment, his grandparents banished him to the loft. This only stoked his rage. He spent his detention trying to destroy everything he could see, pulling down trunks and suitcases, flinging them around.

In one of these suitcases, he discovered his parents' marriage certificate, dated a full year after Michael's birth.

Something clicked in his head. The colour of his skin, his parents' reticence, his grandparents' silence.

He picked up the certificate and went to talk to his mother, Helga.

It didn't take much for the truth to come tumbling out. Helga had been a student at Princeton. Michael had been conceived there, the result of a single encounter with a fellow student, an Indian with a fairly distinctive name.

Suddenly, Michael had a mission. He waited until he graduated and found work as a journalist. He made some enquiries in Germany. They found two men in India with the same name. One was a politician in Karnataka. The other a vice-chancellor of a university in a small town in south India.

So, at the age of twenty-three, Michael came to India to find his father. He travelled from Delhi to Bangalore. He established that the politician hadn't been in Princeton at the same time as Helga. That left the vice-chancellor.

Michael made his way to this small town, not too far from Bangalore, and called the gentleman in question, posing as a journalist from Germany. The vice-chancellor politely told him that he was scheduled to retire in six months' time, and that Michael would be better served speaking to his incumbent. Then he hung up.

Michael mulled over his options. And decided that he'd come too far from being a fourteen-year-old getting into fights because of the colour of his skin, to settle for not knowing. He walked onto the campus, made his way to the office building, pushed through those giant bat-wing doors, like saloons in Westerns, strode up to a gigantic desk and looked this mild-mannered man straight in the eye.

He asked if the name matched. It did.

He asked if the vice-chancellor had ever been a student at Princeton. He had.

He asked if he'd known a German student called Helga. The man hemmed and hawed, but admitted it.

'I'm her son,' said Michael. 'I'm your son.'

I assume it took the vice-chancellor a while to respond. Even today, it sounds surreal.

It wasn't a happy ending, though. At least, not then.

The man admitted that Michael could very well be his son. But he was a married man. His wife was in the village, trying to build a house for their retirement. They had remained childless, in spite of wanting children. He could not, *would* not, introduce Michael to the world as his son.

I imagine the encounter was enough for Michael. He'd looked his father in the face, and he'd unravelled one of the mysteries of his childhood. And that was enough. He didn't want or need anything else. He allowed the vice-chancellor to give him a lift to Bangalore, and they parted ways.

We'd just about returned to the hotel. I'd listened to his story, agog. But something occurred to me.

'What are you doing in Madras?'

Michael grinned. This was the other side to my impetuous new friend. He'd fallen in love with one of the cabin crew on the flight from Delhi to Bangalore. She told him that she was scheduled to fly Madras-Bombay on the 10th of March, which is why he'd been trying to make it aboard the flight tonight.

I didn't know what to make of him, apart from the fact that I liked him a great deal.

The Taj gave me my room back, and I talked them into letting Michael have his old room back. He was on the same flight as I was, the next morning. And even though he had a room in a hotel in Juhu, he came home and met Alyque and Quasar. We've been friends since.

I've lived with him every time I've been to Stuttgart. He worked as an editor for an interior design magazine back home, and he and his girlfriend would pass through Bombay at regular intervals, en route to Bangkok. Their first trip was in 1986, and they've stayed with me every time they visited. I gave my wedding saree to his then-fiancé Erica, and she has it to this day. Decades later, about four years ago, I introduced them to Gerson and Uma, who often travel to Germany for film festivals, and they have, in turn, become friends.

When Quasar was touring the UK with *A Midsummer Night's Dream*, around 2007, Michael and Erica flew to London specially to watch the show.

I was just trying to bum a smoke off a white man so that he wouldn't take my seat on a flight. Chance is a subtle *and* glorious thing sometimes.

~

In July 1979, Rani Dube passed through Bombay. She'd brought Richard Attenborough with her. Richard's long-cherished dream project, *Gandhi*, was close to realization. Rani was the co-producer, and she had brokered a meeting between Richard and Indira Gandhi. Mrs Gandhi had given the project her blessing and introduced the two of them to the National Film Development Corporation of India (NFDC). Richard was on a follow-up visit. Of course, it was Rani, so Richard was madly in love with her.

On the 25th of July, Rani brought Richard over to my apartment at around 3 in the afternoon. I was breastfeeding Quasar. We chatted for a while. The walls of our home, as ever, were covered with photographs from plays Alyque had directed. Talk turned to the theatre, to the BBC, to children and life. At half five, I rang Alyque to say, 'Ahem, *Richard Attenborough* is here, and would you come home and we can all have dinner, because, you know, *Richard Attenborough*?'

I remember we went to Copper Chimney and had Kakori kebabs. But the moment Alyque walked in through the door, Richard turned to me and said, 'That's my Jinnah.'

Two days later, he rang me up.

'Dolly, it's Richard,' he began. 'We're starting work on *Gandhi*, as you know. And I was wondering if you'd like to be the casting director?'

It was on the strength of the photographs and the long chat we had that day, about my years in the theatre and my work as a model coordinator and as a host. But mostly, I suspect, it was just a hunch.

I jumped at it. Although no one I knew really knew what 'casting' entailed. So, it was just like every other job I ever had.

By November of 1979, Quasar and I moved to the Ashoka Hotel in Delhi. We lived there for the next six months. I was casting director for *Gandhi*, but I was also the unit publicist and PR liaison.

Richard had already decided on his Gandhi: Ben Kingsley. He was going to cast all the white parts from Britain (and in the case of Martin Sheen and Candice Bergen, the US). I had to find all the Indian actors.

I also worked as a theatre critic at the time, and I watched almost every play on the boards, across the city. I spotted Rohini Hattangadi and called Richard in Delhi.

'There's a young actress I want you to see,' I said.

'Kasturba?' he asked.

'Kasturba,' I agreed.

Richard was leaving Delhi for London that night. But he would stop in Bombay if he could meet this actress. Would I be able to take a room at the Airport Centaur? He'd nip out, see her and then go back across the street for his flight to London. International flights operated from the same terminal.

Rohini had a show that night. It was past 11.30 before she made it to the Centaur. Richard and I were sitting on the couch, and the moment Rohini walked in through the door, he clutched my thigh.

'This is it, Doll!' he whispered.

Richard had seen something intangible – a quality, an essence. He had a hunch about Rohini. She'd fit into his vision and further it. He could see her *on screen*. That was what casting was about. That was what one half of filmmaking was.

At the time, Rohini wasn't confident about her English. This is something that a lot of people overlook when casting Indian actors – the language they *think* in. Rohini was comfortable with Marathi and Gujarati, and Hindi. Richard spent some time talking to her and, eventually, she left. He turned to me.

'If she can lose about eleven kilos, that's my Kasturba.'

This, then, was the other half of filmmaking: the journey from casting to the shoot. I rang Rohini the next day. Together, we went to see a Dr Vishnu Khakkar at Kemp's Corner. He was a dietician. I was impressed that Bombay even had a dietician in 1979, but I suppose that was to be expected of a city with an interest in fashion and a booming film industry. Vishnu had a tiny office, but it consisted of two rooms. He examined Rohini, heard the brief and then told her that she could eat two chapattis and a bowl of dal for lunch *and* dinner, and nothing in between. And she had to walk for an hour and a half every day.

Rohini lived in Wadala at the time. Right or wrong, I was convinced that she *might* follow the dal-roti diet but, left to her own devices, there was no way she was going to take a walk every day. So she'd come to mine, we'd go to Vishnu's office and lock ourselves into the second room. I'd sit in the chair and she'd walk around the table for an hour and a half. We did this every day for three weeks. She lost five kilos, and I called Richard with a progress report.

'Send her,' he said.

The delegation to London comprised Rohini, Smita Patil, Bhakti Barve and Naseeruddin Shah.

Smita Patil was very much the trendy pick. She was quite a big star by then. She was critically acclaimed and shared, in particular, a wonderful creative relationship with Shyam Benegal. But she wasn't right for the role. She was too sultry, too aware, had too much spark for *that* version of *that* story. It would've been bad casting.

My pick – so much water under the bridge now – was actually Bhakti Barve. She was a fine actress. And I felt that she looked like Kasturba. That was enough to seal the deal in my mind.

Naseer's trip was a political move. He'd made it clear that he was only interested in playing Gandhi. And Richard was set on Ben. But Naseer was a star, a name in the Bombay film industry, and Richard wanted to pitch a host of other parts to him – Nehru, in particular. Which shows how well he knew Naseer. Because *that* was never going to happen.

Money wasn't a problem. We put this group of actors on a flight to London to shoot some tests. In fact *Gandhi*, as my first film, was a bit of a ruinous experience. The producers allowed – 'empowered', I think, is the right word – me to take decisions and paid for them *without asking any questions*. In other words, they trusted me to do the job they'd hired me to do. They delegated and left it at that; if I screwed up, that was completely my responsibility. No other job has come close.

Richard said 'no' to Naseer playing Gandhi. Naseer, in turn, said 'no' to Nehru. He wasn't part of the film which – to this day – feels odd, given that I cast four hundred and ninety-eight Indian actors. A lot of people remember him being in the film! They've ghosted him in, because it feels logical that he would've been there. Naseer would have to wait about two decades to play Gandhi in Feroze Khan's stage production.

Richard called from London to say that Rohini was his Kasturba. He loved her simplicity and naivety – things that are difficult to fake on screen.

The next step was to better her English. I got Kusum Haider to be her teacher in Delhi. I suppose that would be her 'dialect coach' in this day and age. Rohini was a model pupil. She maintained her diet and her exercise routine, and she was serious about her English lessons and the spinning class she took with Ben.

Wait. What I mean is that both Rohini and Ben learnt how to weave cotton. They weren't on exercise bikes, peddling madly.

One of the major criticisms at the time was that Ben Kingsley was too 'muscular' to play Gandhi. Ben did all he could to remedy that. He was on a strict diet, and he did a lot of yoga. When he arrived in India, we removed all the furniture from his hotel room so he had to sit and sleep on the floor. The walls were covered with pictures of the Mahatma.

The backlash to the casting decision was inevitable. We were always going to have to confront the question: How could a foreigner play Gandhi? Bizarrely, the makers of 'parallel cinema' were the only ones who raised the issue. They showed up on the first day of shoot, waving black flags. I spotted my friend Shama Zaidi amongst the picketers. On our side of the fence was Govind Nihalani, one of the leading lights of the parallel movement but also our second unit cameraman. The protests were orderly. No one ran around breaking things; there were a number of write-ups and opinion pieces. Richard was polite, but firm – Ben Kingsley was his Gandhi. All said and done, Ben was of Indian stock. His grandfather had migrated from India. I mean, we were *really* straining the boundaries of credibility with his Indian ancestry, and everyone knew it. But we had Mrs Gandhi's backing. Doors opened for us, trains ran on time and locations were a cinch. Gandhiji's contemporaries, Ramkrishna Bajaj and Bharat Ram, were closely involved. The NFDC had given us nine crores.

The protests made it to the newspapers and were duly praised; the film rumbled on.

At the pre-shoot party for the Indo-British unit, Roy Button turned to Kamal Swaroop, both third ADs, and asked for a glass of water. Kamal replied, 'The Raj went a long time ago.' That was about it for on-set strife.

Would we get to make it the same way again? Today? With a British director and a British lead? I don't know. That's dinnertime conversation. Would they get to make *Apocalypse Now* the same way?

We rolled on the 26th of November 1979. And it really was an army on the move. It had taken Richard decades to get to that moment, and you could see how much it meant to him, because *every single minute* on that production had been accounted for. People knew exactly what they were supposed to be doing.

Amal and Nissar Allana worked as set decorators. Their universe ranged from trains to cars to jewellery, costumes, shoes. Every detail had a separate team, and all roads led back to Richard – casting meetings, production meetings, lighting meetings, script meetings. And somewhere within that maelstrom, Richard found time to concentrate on the performances, to create a work of great integrity and beauty that has stood the test of time.

We shot in Porbandar, Bombay, Pune. Never Ahmedabad. The scenes set in South Africa were shot in Okhla. The shot of Gandhi silently giving a poor woman his safa by letting it drift across to her in the river was shot in Udaipur.

I went to one location during the recces. This was for the sequence where Gandhi and the protestors in South Africa were attacked by security forces on horseback. I was too busy to travel after that. In a strange way, I became the doorkeeper for the production. The outside world had to get through me before they got to the film, for anything. The requests ranged from the routine to the ridiculous. Everyone wanted a slice of the pie: producers, hangers-on, friends, politicians. People wanted to visit the set. People wanted to meet the actors. People wanted a say on the screenplay.

We were lucky that Richard had been dealing directly with Mrs Gandhi. That meant we could be firm. Sometimes, we just had to buy peace. Ben occasionally wanted a beer at the end of a day's work, and we had to ensure he wasn't seen by the press. We'd already had one headline: 'Ben Kingsley, Gandhi, drinking beer.' He was also an attractive man in the middle of a career-defining performance, so we had to shield him from the ladies. If he did stop to speak to someone, the press couldn't get wind of it. For a while, I was his minder in the modern sense – the advance party, the bodyguard, the person pulling strings, just out of shot.

It was an exhilarating time, but it was bloody hard work. Luckily, Richard and I had found our wavelength early with Kasturba, and I had a strong sense of what he was looking for.

My old friend Roshan Seth played Nehru. We'd tested Victor Banerjee as well but Roshan had the sophistication of Nehru and won hands down.

Anupam Kher, in his one-man show *Kuch Bhi Ho Sakta Hai*, tells a story about *Gandhi*. He believed that Nehru was *his* role, one that he was born to play. After all, he was Kashmiri and fair. On his way to Delhi, he had a vivid dream: the minute Richard Attenborough spotted Anupam, he would stop and say, 'This is my Nehru.' The dream was so real he saw his name up in lights, 'Anupam Kher as Nehru'.

We had shifted to the Ashoka by then. Our living quarters were upstairs and our offices were downstairs.

In his show, Anupam recounts how he saw Richard and me walking down a corridor.

'Dollyji,' he apparently called out. We glanced at him, and I asked him to go and sit in my office. And that was that.

We never did cast Anupam, not even in a bit part, although he ultimately dubbed for the Hindi version.

Richard cast Saeed Jaffrey as Sardar Patel. I didn't agree with that call. I still don't. He just wasn't right for the role. Harsh Nayyar played Godse. He was another Indian actor from the West (America or England, I forget) who wrote to Richard and won the part.

I had a hand in everything else. From Supriya Pathak to Neena Gupta, and Om Puri (God rest his soul, that brilliant, brilliant man) to Shekhar Chatterjee, who played Suhrawardy and whom I'd spotted in Calcutta. I mostly cast actors from the theatre. I mentioned Bhanu Athaiya to Richard, and she went on to win the Academy Award for costume design. She was a very well-established designer before *Gandhi*. What I loved, though, was her mumbled complaint at one point, 'All I'm making is kurta pyjamas.' But then, that's all the Congress leaders wore at that time, with the sole exception of Jinnah, who had some rather excellent suits. Alyque was hopeful that he'd get to keep his clothes from the shoot and was most disappointed when they were on the next flight to England.

Of course, when Bhanu won the Oscar, it was all '... yes, Jodhpuri pyjamas but, you know, I had to cut them in a very specific way.' Ah, show-business.

During post-production, I worked on the dub for the Hindi version and helped with the music. The film was scored by George Fenton and Pandit Ravi Shankar (ironically, looking after the 'English' and 'Indian' versions). George came down to Bombay in November of 1981. He stayed at the Taj. Ravi Shankar was staying with some friends near Pedder Road. Every day, I'd pick him up and we'd go to the Taj. Richard sent us the film on video cassettes. So, I got a player and a monitor from Western Outdoor and set them up in George's room. For three weeks, George and Panditji would watch the film bit by bit, talk about the score and make notations. Once they had the score on paper, they would record in London. Panditji told me who he wanted, and I coordinated travel with the production office in London. The musicians who travelled were Panditji himself, Shiv Kumar Sharma and Ustad Alla Rakha. I went to the airport to see them off because the instruments needed to be booked as excess baggage, but had to be handled with great care.

Vipula Kadri of PRIDE India would ask me to compère Indian classical music concerts over the next decade, most of which were fundraisers. I already knew Panditji and Ustad Allah Rakha from *Gandhi*. I got to know the Ustad's sons as well, and Fazal and Taufiq never fail to remind me that I once taught them elocution at Hill Grange High School. Much later, in 1989, I also had the privilege of compèring the Zubin Mehta concert at the Brabourne Stadium.

Around the same time as the work on the *Gandhi* score, Pandit Ravi Shankar performed at the Ravindra Natya Mandir, and I was very keen that Zhya attend. He was seven years old and had been admitted to Jaslok Hospital for an eye operation. I prevailed upon the doctor to allow me to take Zhya out for just an hour, and he agreed. We didn't even make it past the alaap, but it's a memory I'll always cherish.

I was still recovering from my accident when we dubbed for the Hindi version of the film. Richard was kind enough to sanction a room next to the recording studio, purpose-built in the Sea Rock Hotel. There was a bed next to the control booth, and I could lie down between takes if I needed to. Vinod Sharma translated the dialogue. Anupam Kher dubbed for Sir John Mills, who'd played one of the Viceroys. Pankaj Kapur dubbed for Gandhi, although he'd played Pyarelal in the English version.

The Indian premier was at Regal. I can confirm that Indira Gandhi did not, in fact, attend. At the time, I thought it the most exhilarating moment of my life, the crowning glory. With the passage of years, I've gained a little perspective. But that film taught me so much and gave me a set of memories I'll never forget, some of them the proudest of my career. I met and worked with Nigel Hawthorne and Sir John Mills. I met Suresh Jindal, the associate producer. He's still a vital, treasured part of my life. We shot at Teen Murti Bhavan in Delhi, and the Municipal Commissioner's Bungalow on Carmichael Road (standing in for Jinnah's house) and the residence of the General Manager of Western Railways. And that funeral scene – one of the greatest ever filmed.

It went to the Oscars and won so many awards. But, by then, it was a British film, Richard's film, and seemed very far away indeed.

Richard and I remained friends until his death in 2014. Ben Kingsley visited India again in 1990, and I had everyone over for a meal at my house. It was lovely. He's now a Knight of the Realm. And I hear he prefers to be called 'Sir Ben'.

I'm glad I was there; I'm glad I was part of it.

17

WHILE I WAS on television, I started to branch out into interviews. I didn't have a weekly or monthly show or anything, just the occasional chat with someone, usually a feature, never on spec. It was an extension of writing commentaries, of hosting shows, except that I was now a 'face'.

My first great interview wasn't even an interview.

In September 1979, I was on a flight from Hyderabad to Bombay. We only had Indian Airlines back then, and it was all economy. As

I boarded, I noticed a familiar silhouette at the head of the aircraft, first row. Very familiar. I was startled to realize that I had just walked past Indira Gandhi.

I knew her social and personal secretaries, Ami Crishna and Usha Bhagat. I asked the stewardess if either of them was on board. She had no idea. Some things about Indian Airlines never change. I asked the stewardess if she'd deliver a note for me. She said 'yes'. Today, she'd get fired.

I scribbled hurriedly on a piece of paper. I think my note said: 'Dear Mrs G, I would love to come and chat with you. However, if you are busy, I will understand.'

Moments later, a gentleman materialized next to my seat. I suspect he was Mrs Gandhi's personal secretary, R.K. Dhawan. I'm not sure, because he never introduced himself but he looked familiar. He asked if I wanted to meet Mrs Gandhi. When I said 'yes', he asked me to follow him. I gathered up my papers and leapt to my feet. We made our way back up the aisle.

Mrs Gandhi turned from the window. She looked me up and down. She noted the papers.

'If you're a journalist, I will not speak to you,' she said.

I told her that I wasn't a political journalist or a commentator. She nodded and, to my amazement, indicated the seat next to her. I sat down.

She wasn't the prime minister then, of course. She was travelling as a politician, a member of the Opposition, which is why she was on a regular flight. We spoke for seventy-five minutes, pretty much the whole time the seat-belt signs were off. The chat was frank and funnier than I'd expected. We talked about the student unrest in Kashmir. We talked about her trip to Bombay. She was to make her first election speech at August Kranti Marg. I stayed away from the Emergency and Sanjay Gandhi's Turkman Gate incident. I had to remind myself that I wasn't a journalist. And that she had set the terms of this encounter. Apart from that, I could have been speaking with a favourite aunt.

I was wearing a Kerala mundu. She noticed that. She asked me who tailored my cholis. We talked clothes for a bit. When we landed in Bombay, Mrs Gandhi turned to me. 'Dolly, do me a favour, please,' she said. 'I'm going straight to the rally from the airport. See if my saree is okay from the back?'

So, just before the doors opened, I took a moment to fix her saree.

~

She won, of course. By a landslide.

And when Indira Gandhi regained power, she played a small part in one of the more interesting radio jobs I ever had.

In August 1981, I covered the demonstration of the APPLE Satellite's capabilities for AIR. This was the first Indian communications satellite that the Indian Space Research Organisation had launched. The demonstration itself, as well as the live relay, were *both* technological marvels.

At the Space Application Centre in Ahmedabad, ISRO demonstrated to the country the use of India's first experimental satellite. The APPLE was already in synchronous orbit, having been launched in June, positioned just above Nagpur. For an hour, transmission switched between AES (Ahmedabad Earth Station) and DES (Delhi Earth Station) a total of four times, to demonstrate to the Indian public that their country had now entered the Space Age. There was always a lag of a few seconds as the transmission switched, and all of us waited with our hearts in our mouths. APPLE only had one operating transponder and it made for an anxious interval.

Then news arrived that the satellite was tilting off balance. I didn't understand the technicalities. But Dr U.R. Rao, Chairman at ISRO, very patiently explained the phenomenon to me. He likened it to Jatayu flying, but with one wing cut off. Having watched Protima perform *Ram Charitra Manas* as part of her repertoire more than once, I understood the reference and was able to relay that to my listeners, one of whom was Prime Minister Indira Gandhi. It was nerve-wracking, but that made a successful broadcast all the sweeter.

Radio wasn't what you'd call a dynamic medium. But I still got to have a handful of memorable experiences.

Another one of these was a visit to Sagar Samrat, the first oil rig in India. That was an AIR assignment as well. I had to conduct a series of interviews on board, just off the coast of Bombay. The interviews were standard – how and why things worked the way they did, and the experience of being on a rig.

My recordist Harish Mirchandani and I flew by helicopter. I was the second woman, after the prime minister herself, to set foot on Sagar Samrat. I'd never flown in a helicopter either. The only condition we had to comply with was to be back ashore by 4 p.m. It was too risky for the helicopter to fly after that. The combination of fading light, wind patterns and the tide made it dangerous. If we didn't take off in time, we'd have to spend the night on the rig.

I spent the entire assignment hoping we were terribly behind schedule, because who doesn't want to spend a night on an oil rig? But they were too damned organized, the people on Sagar Samrat. They practically shoved us back onto the chopper at the appointed time.

They looked after us so well, though. They were patient and accommodating. The crew led us around like we were precocious children. And the food was extraordinary: everything on that rig was imported; that was a crew stipulation, I think. It was like a meal at a five-star hotel, for free. It's a pity we didn't have mobile phones and digital cameras back then. I would have loved photos of that trip.

Just a week after the trip, the same helicopter crashed moments after take-off. All fourteen people on board died.

I know I mention luck a great deal. It's not lip-service.

~

By 1981, we'd almost outgrown our first apartment. Especially with Quasar in tow.

'Doll, this house is too small,' Alyque kept saying. 'We've been here twelve years. I need a bigger place. I need to entertain.'

We identified three potential locations. Some building on Little Gibbs Road, Sagar Darshan on Warden Road, and a place called Christmas Eve, up the hill opposite Breach Candy Hospital.

Something about Christmas Eve was just right. We learnt about the place because Lintas owned it and B.C. Dutt, the head of HRD, lived there with his wife Anasuya. We went to see it last, at 10.30 at night, Quasar accompanying us in his kurta-pyjama because he hadn't fallen asleep.

I liked the place from the start. It was 2,200 square feet, three times larger than my little apartment. It was shabby but it had potential. I could see us growing old there, once we'd made it our own.

I turned to Alyque.

'This is it,' I whispered.

We had to be discreet. B.C. was due to retire in 1982. He'd been living there a long time, and his wife was a well-known divorce lawyer. We didn't want those kinds of complications. Alyque was confident we'd get the apartment, provided we kept a low profile. If Lintas was reluctant to part with it, then he'd just buy it off them. Alyque had that kind of money.

'It'll be in your name, Doll,' he said one day. We'd been talking about the décor, and this was an unexpected turn in the conversation because he'd never indicated anything of the sort before.

'We'll leave this flat and we'll take whatever pagdi we get – three lakhs, five lakhs. That'll go into your bank account as savings. And Christmas Eve will be in your name. Just don't tell anyone.'

I was very touched he thought of me in those terms. Even though we split everything down the middle and we weren't married, this was the first time he'd attempted to validate our relationship in that way. An apartment, in the city of Bombay, even back then, was a pretty firm commitment.

From 1981, every night we were home, Alyque and I talked about what we were going to do with the place. We talked about posters and art and spare bedrooms and plans for the mezzanine and how we'd entertain. And we didn't tell anyone except for the three people I *wanted* to tell.

I told Sir Richard Attenborough, who perched on the mattress in my living room during meetings and then went back to the Taj. 'The next time you come to Bombay, Richard,' I said, 'you'll be my guest.'

I told M.J. Akbar, who didn't live at the Taj and would occasionally spend nights at our place, sprawled out on the same mattress.

And I told Kersey Katrak. I wrote him a letter. Usha and he had moved to Mirtola and whenever either of them came to Bombay, in the winter or whatever, they'd stay at Gerson's like a bunch of backpackers. Kersey knew that things between Alyque and me had been strained. I'd taken Quasar with me to visit Kersey and Usha, and I'd shared some of my misgivings with him.

'Alyque and I have put our troubles behind us', I said in that letter. 'We have turned the corner. And you must come and live with us the next time you're in Bombay.'

Christmas Eve met my criteria too: It was close to a taxi stand and a bus stop, which was necessary because access to Alyque's car could be limited, and nearby I had a Sahakari Bhandar, a greengrocer's and a hospital.

~

In September of that year, I was compèring a show for Shanti Chopra when I received the news that Picky – Nandini Narain, my friend from Loreto – had passed away. It came as a real shock. We'd met just a few months before that. Alyque, Quasar and I had taken a trip to Simla and Manali in May of that year, and we'd met Picky in Delhi on our way back.

It was always good to see her. We were linked in so many ways – our childhoods, the fact that I took her job at the British Information

Services, triggering a chain of events that set the course of my life. I'd even been part of the gang trying to find a suitor for her.

That marriage had ended badly – messy, with a family torn apart. But when we met, she was doing well. She'd found love again. She was calm and hopeful, and I was glad because she was someone who deserved only the best.

And then this – a sneaky, sudden illness and gone. At the age of thirty-eight.

I didn't know it then, but it presaged a deepening of tone – the onset of grey, a more sombre outlook, that would define the next part of my life.

More than anything else, I missed her.

~

Alyque had done a film with Jyoti Thakur for 'Friends of Trees' to commemorate the start of the movement. Alyque wrote the script and was on set during the shoot. I helped with the edit. He was paid twenty-eight thousand rupees, and he surprised me when he received the cheque.

'I'm going to open an account and put it in your name,' he said.

And so, I was the proud owner of a Citibank account with a single deposit of twenty-eight thousand rupees. We'd done things for each other all through our relationship. He'd taken me out of the country with him. And I looked after him the best I could. But we'd always been very careful about our finances, at my insistence. I had a real fear of deprivation, and I made money in fits and starts, through a variety of jobs. This gesture was unprecedented. In November of 1981, Alyque surprised me.

'I've bought a property,' he said. And he asked me to give him the twenty-eight thousand rupees, to close the deal.

He'd purchased three-quarters of an acre in Awas, Alibaug, across the harbour from the Taj hotel. Alyque called it our paradise. Just for Quasar, him and me. It had a hundred and fifty-odd coconut trees, supari trees, and a handful of mango, banana and guava trees.

The property came with a borewell and a very basic hut with mud walls and floors. When we went, we slept on the veranda, under mosquito nets. We built a shed with a hole in the ground to serve as the toilet. 'Sanitation' was a bucket of fresh mud. It kept the flies away and it killed the smell. We hung a sheet to demarcate the shower area and the kitchen.

It was primitive and utterly beautiful.

Alyque didn't want to be bothered with what to build and how, and which trees to plant. I could do what I wanted but I wasn't to pester him.

I got in touch with Lalita and Yashwant Das and took them to Awas. Again, they came up with a scheme that was as simple as it was pretty. We envisaged a single-storeyed structure, open from all sides, where the rooms flowed into each other and the breeze had access from any direction. We hired carpenters and masons and subcontractors. I enlisted my parents, retired and living in Delhi, and stationed them in Awas to supervise the work. It was just about impossible to get the workers to do anything unless I was present. 'TV-wali Bai' seemed to be the only threat that worked. I'd show up, work would jump forward like a scalded cat. Then I'd leave and things would drift for days. It could've been a play by Beckett. *Waiting for Plinth*.

I was writing seven columns for an assortment of papers and magazines at the time. I had the radio shows in addition to being the aforementioned 'TV Bai'. I was also acting in two productions. I was in Adi Marzban's *Farroukh of Finchley*, originally *The Arabs Are Coming*. And I was playing Linda Loman in *Death of a Salesman*, opposite Alyque's Willy Loman, Vijay Crishna's Biff and Ronnie Screwvala's Happy.

William Greaves, of the Ford Foundation, watched the show and wanted me to apply for a scholarship and study drama in the US. That never panned out. But Greaves did conduct a workshop with Vijay Crishna and myself at Prithvi, titled 'Stage to Screen'. He got us to perform a scene from the play – first as if we were performing on stage, and then as if we were pitching for the camera.

~

One evening that May, Alyque stopped what he was doing.

'Isn't it amazing, Doll?' he asked. 'That we haven't had a day's boredom in thirteen years?'

It *was* amazing.

Alyque grinned. 'And you still turn me on,' he said.

I doodled on my pad for a bit. I wasn't thinking about the flat, or the next day, or the next twelve years. It was just a lovely thing to hear, between the two of us.

~

On the 16th of May 1982, we had two shows of *Death of a Salesman* at Prithvi theatre. That date again, like a bell tolling in the distance. We performed the 9 p.m. show, packed up and then fetched Quasar from Val and Jalal Agha's flat next door. We were home around 1 in the morning.

I had no shows the next week. I'd submitted my columns for the deadline on the 15th. And my next set of telecasts were on the 24th and 25th.

'I'll go to Awas tomorrow,' I said to Alyque. 'I'll have a week. I'll get some work done.'

I left on the morning of the 17th, at 7 a.m., with Quasar. The driver dropped us off. We were to return on the morning of the 24th. Quasar would spend a week with his grandparents. We'd work on the house, we'd eat simple home-cooked food that always tasted divine, and we'd look at the stars every night.

~

The driver picked us up on the 24th. We got home at about 10.30 in the morning. As we pulled in, I saw Alyque's car parked under the building.

'How nice,' I thought. 'Al's at home, and Quasar will get to see him.' I remember that distinctly: I was pleased because I thought Quasar would get to see his father.

As we stepped out of the lift, I noticed that the door to the apartment stood wide open. Two men were in the process of carrying out a huge trunk. I recognized them – Mervin and Peter from Lintas. For a split second, I was confused. Then I thought: we've got possession of Christmas Eve. We must have got it a year earlier than we expected, and this is Alyque's surprise for me. He's taking everything he can, and he's waiting for me to move the rest.

I walked into the apartment and the walls were bare. Stark, as if no one had lived in this house for thirteen years. Of course, I thought, he's taken the paintings, that's what's in the trunks, and he's taken what he can and he's going to say, 'Doll, you pack up the bedding.'

He'd taken the paintings. And my house had only had paintings and photographs. No fancy furniture. We had an Akbar Padamsee, and we had a Husain. We had an Anjali Ela Menon.

I walked into the bedroom. Alyque was there, wrapped in a towel, just out of his bath.

'What's happened, Al?' I asked.

'It's too late,' he said. 'I'm going. I'm not treated like God in this house.'

Those were his words.

It's too late. I'm going. I'm not treated like God in this house.

I collapsed onto the mattress. We didn't have a bed, just a mattress on the floor.

'Where are you going?' I asked.

'I'm going to Rajasthan. Surf is doing badly in Rajasthan. I've got to go and check it out.'

When does the MD of a company go to Rajasthan to find out why Surf is doing badly? I didn't realize I'd asked the question out loud.

'You don't know Hindustan Lever,' he said. 'They're very particular.'

And that was it. He left.

I stayed where I was. I wept. My three-and-a-half-year-old son watched his father walk out of the apartment. He sat by me. He held my hand. He tried to hug me.

'Don't worry, Mama,' said Quasar. 'I'll look after you.'

This is a promise he has kept.

~

Alyque was gone. He was never coming back.

He'd taken the paintings. They were all his, yes. He'd paid for them, yes. In a sense, he took back what he owned.

But how to explain to your child why the walls of his home were suddenly bare? That the signs of family could be expunged so easily?

We'd bought one cupboard, between the two of us. It held all the stationery. Alyque was a great one for bringing stuff back from hotels and from the office. We stashed it all in that cupboard.

The guys from Lintas had emptied it out. I didn't have a piece of paper to type on. Not a pen. Not a pin.

I remember having to step out of the house to buy six hundred rupees worth of stationery. That is the first thing I can remember, in the aftermath.

I remember I read the news that night, and the night after. I remember stepping out of the studio once the telecast was over and crying. The first night and the night after.

All through the following week, the driver would stop by, embarrassed. He picked up clothes, books, and last of all, the telephone. He was there to take back what wasn't mine.

~

I rang Brian Mascarenhas. His response was reliably male.

'Doll, you must have had a fight,' he said. 'You must have said something.'

Brian and Alyque were best friends. In a strange twist of fate, they'd both lost brothers. Brian had started his career as a salesman for *Reader's Digest*. After that, he worked for Nari Hira, and then went into business. He owned advertising hoardings all over Bombay. He was married to Sharon Prabhakar.

Brian was so concerned by this development, by Alyque's leaving, that he came to see me the next day.

'Where's Sharon?' I asked Brian, towards the tail-end of that conversation.

'She's gone to Nainital,' he said. 'She and her mother wanted to take this nostalgic trip, because her mother was a piano teacher in Nainital.'

~

I didn't have all the answers. Some of them, I don't have even today.

I know that I lived through a death. That is the only way I can explain what happened. The end of a life. It was that abrupt, and it left that much of a void.

Were things perfect?

No. I can't claim that.

Perhaps the relationship had deteriorated. Perhaps my insistence on a child had been the terminal blow.

In 1979, Alyque wanted me to talk to the landlord and get the apartment transferred in his name. I refused. Maybe that was a sign. Maybe it was the final straw.

Things weren't perfect.

And neither were we. Thirty-eight years later, going through my notes and diaries for this book, I discovered letters that Alyque sent me from the US, while on his trip with Raell. He apologised repeatedly for how he had left things between us. Reading them now, tiny handwriting that almost leaps off the page, I was overwhelmed. It was a window to the best of him: passionate, intense, loving.

I had missed the apology completely. It didn't register, because I was so hurt.

For just a moment, the gears slipped. And in spite of our best intentions, things were never the same.

I'd fallen in love with someone else. I drifted away and drifted back.

Maybe that had happened to him too. In that vacuum, he reached out to someone who paid attention. I don't know.

He felt stifled in his first marriage, he'd told me. Perhaps I went too far in the other direction. I left him so free from bonds that he felt uncared for. Perhaps being away on *Gandhi* for such a long time had had an impact. It's possible. Things had been uneven since that American trip – they never quite settled. I felt distant. And now I think he felt ignored, perhaps taken for granted. We were both aware of that, although we never discussed it.

To this day, and to my dying day, I will say this: I wasn't surprised by what happened. I was surprised by *how* it happened.

I really thought we'd made it through the choppy seas. That we'd found peace and companionship, and a deep, mutual affection that nothing could alter.

We'd drifted away, we'd come back, we had a child, we were getting a house together.

Not a day's boredom in thirteen years. And I still turned him on.

Apart from my child, this had been the most significant relationship of my life. An end should have cost him more. That's all.

~

And now conspiracy theories bloomed through my fevered brain. Some of these things happened. Some of them were things out of a nightmare – two and two adding up to seventeen.

Then, I couldn't put it all together. Now, I don't have all the pieces. And care less.

Stray events and incidents from years ago, seemingly unconnected, came back to haunt me. The memories arrived with agonizing slowness, landing like evenly spaced, perfectly weighted body-blows. I began to view things through a very specific filter. Everything was stained a particular hue.

~

The afternoon we were at the Sayani house, all those years ago, when I found out about Alyque's trip to America with Raell, Jerry had asked, 'Doll, who is this girl Alyque spends so much time with?'

'Which girl?' I asked.

'The one Alyque's always locked up in his bedroom with?'

Alyque had a spare bedroom at Kulsum Terrace. It was still referred to as 'Alyque's Room'. He rehearsed *La Mancha* at Kulsum Terrace and he came home late. I never thought about it. I was on television twice a week and I got home near twelve. What did it matter that Alyque was getting in at one?

But Mama Padamsee had asked Jerry and Jerry had asked me.

'That's Sharon,' I told Jerry. 'He's teaching her how to sing.'

Brian had hounded him into it. Sharon wanted to be a singer and Brian wanted Alyque to mentor her.

'I'm trying to help them,' Alyque would say. He'd roll his eyes. 'They're twits, Doll. They don't know anything. I'm trying to get her to be sophisticated.'

When Quasar and I were in Delhi, in pre-production for *Gandhi* in 1979, Alyque got Sharon an assignment to sing at the Oberoi. And when he came to visit, he spent all his time with her. I was too busy to notice. Too full of myself.

~

A few days after Alyque left, carpenters from Lintas rang the doorbell. They wanted to know where to attach the bolts on the door. They couldn't find Alyque, so they presumed I would know.

'Which door?' I asked.

The carpenters looked puzzled. One of them stepped forward.

'The door in the new house, madam,' he said.

I was about to ask 'which house?' when the whole thing started to make sense. Alyque *had* gotten possession of the apartment in Christmas Eve a whole twelve months before he was scheduled to. Or, twelve months before *I* thought we'd be getting possession.

The phone rang. It was the production manager on *Octopussy*. I was handling their overseas media. They were currently on location in Udaipur.

Alyque had been holed up in his suite at the Lake Palace, Udaipur, he said. With a Sharon Prabhakar.

~

I called Brian.

'It's Sharon,' I said. It was the first inkling either of us had had. I was bitter and serene and triumphant and utterly bereft.

The fun with phone calls didn't stop there.

My friend, Indu Sen, called a few days after. She sounded unhappy. 'Why didn't you tell me?' she asked.

'Tell you what?'

'That you people have moved in next door?'

'What?'

'Stop pretending, Dolly. I saw Alyque on the balcony this morning.'

'What balcony?'

'At Christmas Eve, Dolly. Why didn't you tell me that you were moving in?'

Indu lived at Somerset House, opposite Christmas Eve. That meant Alyque was back in Bombay and that he was living in the flat we'd found together.

It took another couple of days to confirm that he had, indeed, moved in with Sharon.

~

Here are these flashes, dancing across my mind's eye, like dust motes in the afternoon sun, some silent, miniscule, cosmic hailstorm.

These are the things that I agonized over; true, false, inconsequential. These were my nightmares:

The singing lessons. The girl in the bedroom that Alyque spent all his time with.

When had all this happened? When did the two of them start to regard each other as something more than friends?

I remembered being at the Oberoi Grand in Calcutta. We were travelling with *Death of a Salesman*. And Alyque had a strange conversation on the phone about 'the little hut'. He covered the mouthpiece at one point to explain to me that he was talking to Raell about a play she planned to do. That night, he made love to me three times, even though we had two shows the next day.

A few weeks after that, Quasar and I went to Lintas to visit Alyque. He was on the phone again, and he asked us to leave his office because it was a 'personal call' about a project. He mentioned 'the little hut' again. We waited outside while his secretary peeked at us out of the corner of her eye.

Was he talking to Sharon about Christmas Eve? *I'm* convinced he was.

Does it matter? Not anymore. But in those few months, I questioned everything. I suspected everyone. It was all pain.

That's what grief is. A constant exercise in 'what if'. And 'when'.

~

Sharon did to me what I had done to Pearl.

That's what I believed for a long time. Until I learnt to look at it another way.

Alyque had simply moved on. We'd run our course. Sure, he could have been a little more considerate with how he'd done it, but he ripped the Band-Aid off and walked out the door.

I lived in a deluge of guilt and grief. In a single moment, I was again the other one, the dark one, the ugly one.

When Alyque left, I couldn't sleep. I couldn't eat. Everything that went down came right back up. And every time I closed my eyes, I remembered what had happened.

He'd left. He was gone. He wasn't coming back. Someone had just upped and taken one of my limbs, just like that.

I thought we'd have another thirty, forty years of fighting and making up. Of never being bored of one another.

On the 30th of May, I went across to fetch my parents from Awas. I do not know what they made of everything that had transpired. I never asked. They were simple people and kept to themselves. If there were any tears or if they felt real alarm, they did it in private. I had enough to worry about. They went back to Delhi – things had turned topsy-turvy for everyone. Plans laid, futures imagined, the basic tenets of belief – 'of course this chair will be there in the morning' – all so much dust in the wind.

Valerie and Protima kept me afloat. Protima stayed with me for a week. And this is when she dragged me to every clairvoyant in town. Nothing helped.

~

One of those astrologers was Dr Vasant Kumar Pandit, who was very well-known at the time. This was his prescription: I must bathe and wear a pearl. At the end of the day, the pearl had to go into a little bowl of water, alongside some supari. The next morning, I had to drink two drops of the water and pour the rest of it into a flower pot. The supari had to be placed next to my money and my jewellery.

Rinse and repeat, so to speak.

I did it. That's how desperate I was. Not to have Alyque back. But for this pall to lift, for some kind of a change in my circumstances. I was living in glamourous penury – hand to mouth, every single day.

~

I told my story to these would-be saviours over and over again, through tears that never seemed to run dry. That was important to do, to tell it over and over. At least we bypassed denial.

I lie, perhaps.

Maybe I spent decades thinking about it. Over and over again. From every angle. Every possible outcome.

Maybe my son and I spent years piecing our lives back together.

Maybe I thought about every reason why.

Maybe I provoked Alyque into it. Those stories were his. *This* is my decision.

Maybe I believed that he'd never do it again.

I was his woman, I lived with him, we shared a house. I never demanded property, marriage, money, anything.

Only once, after Quasar was born, did I overhear him talking to Shama Zaidi and Javed Siddiqui. I heard the words 'Jamatkhana' and 'Maulvi'.

'If you want to do it,' I'd said to him, 'get a proper divorce and marry me.'

He never mentioned it again.

I never wanted to depend on Alyque for anything. We split the thirty-five hundred rupees straight down the middle. But he paid for the telephone, the newspaper, the car we used in the evenings. The day he left, I was penniless. Everything that came in went right back out. Sort of like the food I tried to eat that week.

Alyque was so extraordinarily persuasive. When he zeroed in on you, there was very little you could do. He brought all of his considerable charm to bear. He was like global warming – sooner or later, you'd melt.

He drove down from Regal to see my face. He had a brass band play 'Mere Sapno Ki Rani' under Sharon's window. It was impossible to resist.

Maybe he was drawn to youth? To that kind of energy?

You know what? It doesn't even matter anymore.

~

Somewhere in my diaries, I jotted down fragments:

'Not till the sun excludes you, do I exclude you.'

Walt Whitman said that. Given the poem is titled 'To a Common Prostitute', I think it's a fair reflection of what was going on in my mind at the time. Love. And hurt. Those constant companions.

'Ever has it been that love knows not its own depth till the hour of separation' was another. That's Gibran.

I was bereft. Nothing else can explain the utter lack of gravity I felt. I was a body in space, drifting.

And there was this final one. Some unattributed quote from a poster, a feminist slogan, which I later found was a line from a Judy Grahn poem, 'The common woman is as common as the best of bread/and will rise.'

~

A little while later, the Sudhir Patwardhan came back. Sharon didn't like it, I was told. But something went back on the wall. One thing. A single mark on a blank slate.

A few months after Alyque left, the phone rang. It was Pearl.

'The bloom is off the rose,' she sang. 'The bloom is off the rose …' Then she burst out laughing, in the way only Pearl could. It was infectious. And that's how the two of us got talking.

18

TWO MONTHS LATER, in July 1982, I put down the deposit for a flat in Versova – the flat where my parents would live, and where my son now lives. It was the first conscious, visible, tangible decision I made in my new life.

I wouldn't have to wait long for my luck to turn.

~

On the 17th of July 1982, Quasar and I attended a dinner for the Spastics Society of India at Raj Bhavan. Begum Bilkiz Lateef, the Governor's wife, was our patron. I couldn't leave Quasar at home, so Mithu Alur, founder of the Spastics Society and my friend from college, suggested I just bring him along.

So, I put Quasar in his kurta pyjama, and the two of us went.

After dinner, we shared a taxi with Lilian and Randhir Khare, who were Worli-bound. They'd drop us off at Pedder Road on their way home.

Randhir sat next to the driver. I sat behind Randhir with Quasar on my lap and Lilian to my right. It was raining that evening. The tarmac was wet and dark, a ribbon of black silk twisting down the hill.

Everything else I 'remember' has been pieced together from other people – policemen and family and friends, and from newspaper reports.

We hit a BEST bus head-on. The impact was so great that Quasar went *through* the windscreen and landed fifteen feet away. Miraculously, he was unscathed though very shaken.

A BEST Inspector on his way home at the end of his shift stopped to investigate because he saw that a company bus had been in an accident and three bodies were laid out in front of a small café. These were the taxi driver, Lilian and myself. Randhir sat on a stool, clutching his back.

I'm told the BEST Inspector recognized me from TV. He *then* remembered that I had some Alyque Padamsee connection. So he called Deryck Jeffereis, his deputy general manager. He knew that Deryck was Alyque's brother-in-law. It was now past midnight.

Deryck called Esmie's neighbour. It was the only number he had. He spoke to her and rushed to the scene of the accident. Esmie woke Brian Mascarehnas because Dennis was flying with Air India, and Brian drove her to Gamdevi Police Station. They burst through the doors close to 1 in the morning to discover Quasar perched on the desk shared by Inspectors Iqbal Sheikh and Joe Gaekwad.

I was in Nair hospital. Not that I was aware of it. Apparently, I kept muttering 'Jaslok'. I can only ascribe it to survival instinct – I knew some doctors there, Dr Shaila Welling in particular. And it was close to home.

The first thing that Esmie, Brian and Deryck did was transfer me to Jaslok.

Those initial few hours, I drifted in and out of consciousness. I asked for Jaslok. I asked for the gold chain I always wore. Someone had picked it up off the street and handed it over to the inspectors.

After that, just black.

~

I spent twelve days in a coma. I don't remember any of it. No long grey veil. No white light. No awareness that time passed. No despair for my child or my family. It's just approximately two hundred and eighty-eight hours of my life that I'm missing.

Deryck got word to Alyque, who was in Pune. Quasar lived with Esmie. My parents were in Bombay, so they helped look after him. Deryck and Brian were life-savers. And my Amazon Guard – Protima Bedi and Valerie Agha – formed a protective cordon around me.

It was only when I surfaced – slowly, ever so slowly, like a free diver coming up for air as the surface shimmered above me, just out of reach, for years and years – that I heard both Lilian and the cab driver had died in the accident. Randhir was in the room next to mine. Quasar had survived with nary a scratch. And I had twelve stitches just above my left eye.

Rationality tells us that another inch here or there, a kilometre faster or slower, a wetter road, and things may have been very different.

I could call it blind luck. I choose to call it destiny. I have no other explanation for still being on this rock.

~

Alyque and I had avoided each for the two months since the break-up; like the plague. Still, for what it was worth, he checked in on us the moment he was back in town. I wouldn't have expected any less, but it was good of him to get involved.

But this is a marker of how strained things had become – like our compasses had stopped functioning. Even someone as practical, as level-headed as Alyque made some inexplicable choices. Here's an example:

He walked into the hospital room at one point. Protima and Val were there. Alyque told me he was leaving. But he didn't know if he'd be seeing me again, soon. Or what the protocol in this situation was. Because he said the following: 'I say, Doll. You owe me two thousand rupees.' He'd just paid a bill or something.

Even *Alyque* looked like he couldn't believe the words that had just come out of his mouth. This is what we'd come to, then. At the end of thirteen volatile but mostly good years. We waited in silence for a while. Then Protima got up, pulled out some money from her handbag, counted out two thousand rupees and handed them to Alyque.

~

I felt the repercussions of that accident for a long time. This was just before television in colour was set to debut in India, and the Ministry of Information and Broadcasting was keen on a big splash. Both the Asian Games and the Commonwealth Heads of Government Meeting in Goa were to be telecast in colour.

Post the accident, the Sports Ministry and the I&B Ministry sent me a set of worried-sounding messages. Sardar Singh Dhillon, the sports minister, was dispatched to Bombay to see me. Many people were keen that I host the inauguration ceremony, at the very least, and subsequent programmes if able. But I had twelve stitches over my left eye. The wound would take four months to heal, and it would be a few *more* months before I could wear make-up under studio lights.

I could have done the radio broadcast, maybe. This was the other side to the accident. We survived, but things were never the same again.

In 1982, DD was centralized. The news was now delivered from Delhi. If you weren't physically *in* Delhi, you couldn't be on air. None of the Bombay crew moved. Not Nirmala Matthan, not Luku Sanyal, not I. It wasn't an option. I had a home and a child in Bombay. I had several careers.

~

Gandhi led to a lot of other casting work. None of it as memorable. But it became, as always, completely by chance, another facet of my career.

Kim was a ninety-minute BBC production of the Rudyard Kipling novel. For the title character they needed an Anglo-Indian kid, a boy who spoke Hindi because Kim grew up in the jungles of India. My first choice was a young man by the name of Ravi Sheth who lived close by. Ravi had an English mother and an Indian father, and he seemed perfect. The unit came down, met him, approved the choice and then said they needed alternatives.

Finding real Anglo-Indians, the ones who look 'correct' on screen has always been difficult. You need brown hair and light eyes *and* the boy needed to speak good Hindi. I went to Darjeeling and Northcote, and Bagdogra and Sikkim, and to the Woodstock School in Mussoorie.

I also found a small window to visit the Rumtek Monastery in Sikkim. This is where Freda, Kabir Bedi's mother, had lived for a time. She'd led an extraordinary life – an Englishwoman who married a Sikh man and, eventually, moved to India. She was a journalist and a teacher, and both husband and wife spent time in prison because of their support for the Indian freedom movement.

While in India, she discovered Buddhism and was the first western woman to become a fully ordained monastic. She became a scholar and translator of Tibetan texts. She'd been a social worker all her life.

Almost forty years later, Andrew Whitehead, journalist, editor and historian, would write a book about her – *The Lives of Freda*. As has become almost customary, especially if I know the people in question, I had everyone over for dinner after the launch of the book in Bombay. But it felt personal, because I'd traced some part of that journey myself.

I don't know what I hoped to achieve by that visit. It was a pilgrimage, really. But I wanted to imbibe some of that calm – that serene, indomitable spirit that had served Freda so well.

I travelled to Ooty and all the Anglo-Indian institutions there – Hebron and Blue Mountain and Good Shepherd. I returned from the trip with photos, names and contact details.

So, a few months later, the BBC went ahead and confirmed Ravi Sheth, who lived across the road from me.

In the interim, Ravi had joined the International School in Kodaikanal. The production unit wanted a lock of his hair so they could make a wig. Quasar and I flew to Coimbatore, hired a car and drove down to Kodi and stayed at the Carlton. I managed to turn the visit to Kodi into a little excursion for the two of us. We visited the Meenakshi temple. And I had a brief little flicker of the trips I'd taken with my parents, like the expedition to Aurangabad. Here we were, trying to recreate the small magic of my childhood.

We spent two days at the school and came back with a lock of Ravi's hair. I was quite impressed with the attention to detail.

I ultimately cast Jalal Agha and Nadira (of 'Mud Mud Ke Na Dekh' from *Shree 420*) and Keith Stevenson in *Kim* and shipped them off to Jodhpur for the shoot.

~

On the 13th of March 1983, I received possession of the apartment in Versova. And on the 31st of March, Mum and Daddy moved from Delhi to Bombay one final time. Whatever else, I had put my roots down in the city that had become my home.

It was as if Bombay recognized it. Both my life and my career leapt forward. Assignments from various quarters started to pour in, and kept coming.

~

Richard Neville, the producer of an Australian programme called *Dimension 70* got in touch with me in July of 1984. They were working on a series called *Women of Substance*, and they wanted to interview me and for me to set up a few other interviews. Social workers and activists and, inevitably, film stars. They filmed the interviews at the Taj and I served as a liaison between the crew and their subjects.

Rekha came to film her interview in a nondescript car. She was a huge star by then, but there were no assistants, no managers, no acolytes. She carried her vanity case in one hand and the 'good' saree on a hanger in the other. I was in the lobby, waiting for her and I scrambled to my feet. I'd expected the usual procession, an advance guard with a bouquet for 'madam' and so on. Instead, there was this down-to-earth woman who gave me a warm smile and *asked* if there was a place she could change. I went to the front desk and they gave us a room in seconds, like it was the most normal request in the world.

I kept her company as she got ready. She ironed the saree herself. And did her own make-up. She asked me about the decision to have a child out of wedlock. She listened, a little wistfully I thought, as I told her about my abortions and my determination to be a mother.

Most actresses I interacted with were curious about the live-in relationship, the backlash, the decision to have Quasar. Hema Malini and I were once on a flight to Delhi and she kept saying to me, 'How lucky you are!' A few months later, she and Dharmendra had announced their marriage and she was pregnant.

~

On the 24th of August 1984, Quasar was on stage for the first time, at Cathedral Junior School. The play was called *No Place Like Home*. And despite being a professional – actress and reviewer – I found that I had not a whit of objectivity, and I didn't care. My kid was on stage, and I was thrilled. I could only hope that it would afford him the joy it afforded me over the decades – a place of refuge, transcendence, rigour. A place to dream.

~

The television experiences would stand me in good stead, though. In the second half of the '80s, I worked as a communications consultant for O&M. I was their director of sponsored programmes. It was a strange marriage of two of my previous jobs – advertising and television. They had formalized a position to sell advertising. I sold ad slots for *Hum Log* and *Buniyaad* during the golden age of Indian television drama. I had to decide what brands would benefit from the association and had to dangle a connection with the serial.

In November 1985, I got involved in a project that I wish had seen the light of day. Ketan Anand, son of the legendary filmmaker Chetan Anand, wanted to make a film about Major Hari Pal Singh Ahluwalia. The Major had been the sixth Indian man, and the twenty-first overall, to scale Mount Everest in 1965, twelve years to the day after it had first been conquered.

Major Ahluwalia took a bullet to the spine in the India–Pakistan war. He has been confined to a wheelchair since. But, amazingly, it has not dimmed his appetite for adventure sport or life. He was part of the expedition that followed the great 'Silk Route', travelling over land to China, through Kazakhstan, and re-entering India through Tibet and Nepal. He became the face for young achievers with disabilities, and was the Chairperson of the Indian Spinal Injuries Centre. He has written a number of books, the first of which – *Higher Than Everest* – was the basis for this film.

I cast M.K. Raina. And we even shot at the Indian Military Academy, the training school for officers located in Dehradun. But *Higher Than Everest* wasn't to be, unfortunately. There was a falling-out between the producers, and we never finished the film.

~

I still read the news if I was in Delhi on work. But it became more and more difficult to do. Doordarshan had become very Indian, very bureaucratic. 'Give us a month's notice,' they grumbled. Most of my travel happened on a few days' notice.

I did six more broadcasts, maybe. And then my career as a news presenter was over.

I read the news from Delhi for the last time on 6 November 1985.

~

I look back and wonder, though. What if everything else had remained the same? Alyque coming and Alyque going, Quasar and me, but what if there had been no accident?

We were so close to the liberalization of the economy. Then came the glut of cable news. Then indigenous news. And before it turned into the seething mess it is today, before the fellowship of Prannoy Roy broke bad, before news turned into bulletins from *The Hunger Games*, it might have been a very interesting time to be a broadcast journalist.

Between 1987 and 1989, I worked with both M.J. Akbar and Vinod Dua. I was the production executive – setting up the interviews and venues, and consulting on every little hiccup. We worked on *Newsline*, *Aaj Tak* and also *Focus*, if my memory serves me correctly. We talked about process and protocol; after someone had agreed to participate, the whole day had to be timed in reverse so when the interviewee walked in through the door, you put them in a chair, gave them some water or a cup of tea, did a soundcheck and rolled tape. You couldn't make chief ministers wait around.

I think *if* I'd stayed in the game longer … if I'd gotten to do the Asian Games … then my life might have been very different.

I don't regret it. But, damn, sometimes I do think about it.

~

Quasar was in third standard at Cathedral School when Alyque began to seek him out.

Before that, I hadn't allowed father and son to meet. Quasar was all I had, and I was terrified that he might not remain mine anymore. And, then, there would be no point in carrying on.

We didn't speak, Alyque and I. At all. We didn't share parenting duties. At all. Alyque didn't come home, and even if he did, he never came upstairs. I didn't know that he'd started to visit Quasar until I got a phone call from the school.

Apparently, Alyque would get to Cathedral just as school let out. He'd then clamber onto the *school bus* and ride with Quasar to Pedder Road.

'We can't have Mr Padamsee doing this,' said the school.

'Well, tell Mr Padamsee,' I said.

For the longest time, I thought Alyque wanted nothing to do with Quasar. Perhaps I was wrong.

I must confess – my memory of this time isn't perfect. Only now, putting this down, talking to other people, do I realize that I don't remember a lot of it.

Once the school put a stop to the bus rides, Alyque started coming to the building. In the evenings, Quasar went downstairs to play with the other kids, accompanied by the maid. If Alyque had been travelling, especially out of the country, he'd bring Quasar fancy toys from Hamleys. I refused to allow Quasar to accept them unless it was his birthday, or Christmas. Perhaps Alyque thought the problem was the expensive nature of the gifts. So he started to bring Quasar glasses and watches, toys that made him happy. But I had to ask Quasar to stop accepting those gifts from his father as well, because they were more than I could afford.

Quasar has a memory of me dragging him away from his father on one such occasion.

He also remembers us arguing at home, before Alyque left.

Decades later, Quasar told me that if Alyque ever took him to a film on the weekend, I insisted that father and son ride back in a taxi because I didn't have a car. And I would check his ears to see if he'd been in air-conditioning, the surest giveaway.

I have no memory of these things. Just as I'm sure they happened.

I resented Alyque. I resented the time he spent with Quasar. I was terrified that it would be one more – the last – thing that he took from me. I'd staked claim to the one thing that was all mine.

I remember only the good things. Some kind of willed amnesia – a lot like love.

Every Sunday, I'd take Quasar to the Taj for either fish 'n' chips or a dosa. I didn't want him to feel deprived. It meant that I had to go without eating for a couple of days a week, to be able to afford that meal.

I didn't mind. I'd do it again if I had to. It was irrational, of course. But it was my only source of joy.

It was important for me to be able to do these things for Quasar. He travelled a lot in those years, before he left for United World College in Singapore. He went to Hong Kong, Australia and Los Angeles with Esmie and Dennis.

I didn't care what it cost. If he wanted something, I'd do all I could. My mission was to make it possible.

Alyque took Quasar to Alibaug sometimes. I thought, bitterly, that it was easy to be an excellent father when you had someone for just the weekend. I don't know what kind of rapport they had. I never asked. I didn't want to pry.

Quasar told me, much later, that he felt like he didn't really know his own father until he was about seventeen or so. We'd done it to ourselves, Alyque and I. Because I feel like Quasar and I never shared confidences either. He was always his own person, eerily self-contained.

During his childhood, repercussions, much like Michael Kohler, were inevitable. Quasar became very aggressive for a while. He got into fights regularly. The school called and said he was becoming unmanageable. So, I took him to a therapist for a few sessions. There were no major breakthroughs.

We had some healing to do yet.

19

LIFE WAS ORGANIZED mayhem. My friends saw me through, like they have done all my life. Devika Bhojwani and her mother, Titoo and Jamini Ahluwalia, and my Amazon Guard. They looked after Quasar when I needed them to. They dropped him off at school and picked him up. They covered for me whenever they could.

Otherwise, I dragged the kid to every meeting I had. He turned to me one day and asked: 'Can't I be a latchkey kid?'

He used to watch a cartoon – Wonder Boy, Wonder Kid, something like that, a little African-American child who was a latchkey baby. Quasar thought that might be the best possible outcome because (I quote): 'Your meetings are so boring.'

He was right. The situation was unsustainable in the long term. I couldn't give him the kind of life I wanted to if I didn't, ultimately, send him away. Work took up too much of my time.

~

The one constant was always the theatre. And with a new crop of directors, new horizons opened up. I acted in *Wings*, one of the many collaborations I had with Janak Toprani around that time. Written by Arthur Kopit, the play is about an aviator who suffers a stroke. Through the course of the show, and through lighting quick shifts between her internal state of mind, and the chaos and confusion of the outside world, she, very slowly, gains a tenuous grasp of speech all over again. Rajit Kapur was in it as well. The reviews were some of the best of my career.

Jiten Merchant and I had a close association for several years, *Electra* being a particular highlight. Jiten also did a series of staged readings, well in advance of it becoming a pandemic-driven Zoom trend, and they were a fabulous way to keep working in a low-investment fashion and yet grappling with the questions posed by those texts.

~

I did a lot of work with Anand Mahendroo, who later became synonymous with the popular TV series, *Dekh Bhai Dekh*. I think we worked on *Isi Bahane* or *Idhar Udhar*; my memory of those times isn't so good, there was just too much going on, and it *was* thirty-five years ago.

Rajat Sharma, who later went on to host *Aap Ki Adalat* and create India TV, became the editor of the *Daily* and one of my bosses. For the next decade, I wrote, and wrote and wrote some more. The *Daily* and *Pioneer* were personal columns. I wrote for the *Times of India*. For the *Afternoon Dispatch & Courier*. I reviewed television for the *Telegraph*, and English and Hindi theatre both for the *Indian Express*, and film and theatre for *Midday*. And, on occasion, personal columns for the *Telegraph* and *Khaleej Times*. I would've written recipes if someone needed them.

I scribbled columns at bus stops, every free moment I had. There was a girl who lived on the sixth floor, Pinky Vakil, to whom I'm deeply indebted. She'd type up my columns, until she moved away. I was at a loss about what to do next when my brother-in-law Hartley brought me an electric typewriter from Australia.

Almost half that roll-call of employers is gone now: some newspapers shut down. The friends who founded those papers have passed on. Times have changed. We are the ebb. And still, here and kicking.

~

I also had the chance, in a roundabout way, of being involved in a genuinely groundbreaking theatrical production – *Bottoms Up*. It was the brainchild of Bharat Dabholkar, who was a rising advertising talent at DaCunha Communications. And it could only really have been shepherded by Burjor Patel, a legendary actor and producer and someone who was always on the lookout for new ideas.

Bharat envisaged an out-and-out comedy, in the form of a musical, but that actually functioned as a continually evolving topical revue show – built around sketches that could be tweaked and updated ad nauseum. The script skewered everything – politicians, social norms, institutions. It seemed easy to do, but it was refined over months, and the comedy had been honed to a sharp edge.

I eventually took over a small bit that Pearl did – a TV newscaster being plagued by a fly during broadcast.

It wasn't the most challenging thing I ever did, but I do think that the show was revolutionary. It was the first time that something in 'Hinglish', with the tone and temperature of everyday references, was such a mainstream success. And, ever so slowly, playwrights began to work in a language that was identifiably theirs – English, but Indian. Would it have happened? Eventually? Of course. But I have no doubt that *Bottoms Up* was a tremendous catalyst. Also because it was a massive success – hundreds of packed houses and a slew of sequels.

Someone threw a rock at the ivory tower and it landed.

~

I was still visiting astrologers. I'd do so until about 1986. One of them told me that I needed to throw rice into the sea, followed by a coconut. I did it. I read my horoscope with keen attention. And I hurtled from one thing to another, trying to keep up, trying to stay afloat.

~

In January of 1987, while Michael and Erica were visiting, Quasar broke his arm. For a kid who liked – no, *loved* – running around as much as he did, this wasn't a surprise. The plaster came off at 10 a.m. one morning a few weeks later. By 5 p.m. that day, Quasar had broken the same arm again.

Kids get dinged up. It was no big deal.

But, in the almost-precarious state of finances that I found myself in regularly, these things were always slightly more ominous. They held greater significance for us, somehow. We felt just a little bit more vulnerable than everyone else around us, a little more susceptible to the vagaries of everyday life.

In the same month, Adi Marzban died. He was seventy-two, so not young. And he'd dealt with lung cancer, being a smoker most of his life. But it was a huge loss to the theatre.

I'd acted for Adi in three plays just after Alyque left me. It was almost as if I'd shifted 'camps'. He'd become a part of the landscape of my recovery. And I felt like I was saying goodbye to too many old friends, all of a sudden.

~

In the midst of all this, family re-entered centre stage. My brother Ritchie returned to India for the first time in nineteen years in December 1987. We turned it into a reunion. Pam and Hartley and their kids flew down from Australia. My parents were here. As were Esmie, Dennis and Zhya, and Quasar and myself. It was the first time all my parents' grandkids were in one place at the same time. It was a joyous little interlude. We were lucky enough to repeat it on a regular basis over the next few years, without needing to wait another two decades. It became, after all that time, something that I looked forward to – how my own were getting on in the world.

I think about it now – those grandkids have kids of their own. Time, as advertised, waits for no one.

~

Ritchie's life would take a turn for the better in 1996. He married Dolores Lyngdoh, a very beautiful woman who flew with Air India. Their romance was a modern-day fairy tale: Dolores followed Ritchie to Los Angeles on the back of a *four-day* courtship in Bombay. Their stars seemed aligned. Her father was a police commissioner in Shillong. Our father, of course, had been in the Defence Services. And Esmie and her husband Dennis flew for Air India as cabin crew.

They had a gorgeous daughter, Rahael, soon after. But they never quite knew each other well enough. The relationship spiralled – drinks, arguments, stubbornness. A separation followed, then divorce. Ritchie spent a few months being a single parent.

My brother is now married to Mary Caputi – a professor of political studies at the California State University, Long Beach. Pretty ironic for a man who rejected academics in his teens. Ritchie is finally happy and healthy. He went back to studying (!) medicine at the age of fifty-five. And after two years of nursing practice, he now teaches yoga and Thai yoga massage.

~

Shortly after Quasar was born, Alyque and I had registered him at a handful of educational institutions: Doon, Mayo, Sanawar, in that order. For ten years hence. He'd, eventually, have to go to boarding school. Our lives were far too busy.

At Dom Moraes' place one evening, Leela Naidu asked, 'Where is my son going to school?' Quasar was seven by then, and I trotted out the list. Leela shook her head.

'No,' she said. 'He's going to Rishi Valley.'

I'd never heard of the place.

~

Rishi Valley School was the unplanned but glorious child of the marriage between the Guindy School, based in Madras, and J. Krishnamurti's idea for a world college. The Guindy School, run on the principles of the Theosophical Society, was badly damaged by a cyclone in 1930 and had to relocate. The new institution was based in Rishi Valley, in southern Andhra Pradesh.

The school was built around one of the oldest and largest banyan trees in India. The grounds now occupy over three hundred acres. Over the years, the school and its students have managed to reforest the surrounding hills and establish a bird sanctuary. They're largely self-sufficient; they grow their own fruits and vegetables.

The whole enterprise was based on Annie Beasant's, and subsequently, Krishnamurti's ideas about education. They envisaged a new world and evolved men and women who could populate that world and be worthy of it. Rishi Valley is non-sectarian. There's an emphasis on community and nature and sport. The local population has been carefully integrated into the running of the school, a process that has had its challenges. Krishnamurti was a thinker and a philosopher, and his impact on education might be his most important legacy. His foundation enabled schools like Rishi Valley all around the world, and therefore a holistic education that empowers responsible citizens. An idea established and implemented much before it was fashionable to wonder about whether our schools were, in fact, imparting the right lessons. Much later, I learnt that they'd been in trouble with the British government because they were socialists and that just made me like them even more.

~

Unbeknownst to me, Leela had written to Rishi Valley, and I received a letter inviting us to come and see the school. So in February 1988, we paid a visit.

It was as if we'd stumbled onto an oasis. It was beautiful, pristine. Every nook and cranny emanated calm. It was a privilege to be there, to walk the grounds. The kids seemed safe, happy, busy in the best ways. It made me wish my parents had known of it when I was growing up.

We liked it. Very much. And as soon as she heard, Esmie sent off an application for Zhya. Students were traditionally admitted into the fourth and the eighth standard, to allow them enough time to acclimatize to a completely different educational philosophy. Quasar was moving up to the fifth and Zhya the ninth, and those were 'off' years. The school was kind enough to make the concession, and the cousins were admitted together.

The boys would be gone for four months at a time. The school year started every June, as opposed to July. They'd come back around Diwali and then head back on the 1st of December. Parents were only allowed to visit once a term. The school, once again, was very understanding. Quasar was allowed two visits a term. Alyque, Quasar and I were glad to be spared the awkwardness. Parents lived on campus; we couldn't take the kids out. And we had to be judicious with our choice of date, since the school could only put up a very limited set of parents at any given time.

~

A few months before Quasar left for Rishi Valley, Zohra Segal and Uzra Butt were in Bombay. They were people I revered and adored, and I had the privilege of knowing Zohra in London. So, I hosted a dinner for them. I invited everyone I could think of, because Zohra and Uzra had both been members of Prithvi Theatres, Prithviraj Kapoor's company, and Zohra had later joined IPTA. Shashi Kapoor was there at the dinner, as was Govind Nihalani and a host of the old-time theatre folk, as well as my regulars.

Towards the end of the evening, Zohra aapa, then already seventy-six years old, launched into a performance of 'Abhi Toh Main Jawan Hoon' on my converted balcony, where so much of this book has been written. And nine-year-old Quasar picked up a table lamp and focused the light on Zohra aapa's face for the duration of her performance.

The kid never really had a chance to consider a career in, say, chartered accountancy.

~

In June 1988, Quasar left for Rishi Valley.

I accompanied him that first time. We had to drive from Bangalore to Madanapalle, about three hours. Quasar greeted the school like an old friend – I lost him in minutes. This new world was just too big, too magical for him to stay by his mother's side. I drove back with Abhijeet Karnik's parents. He and Quasar would become close friends, a relationship that is still alive and well, into their forties. Abhijeet's parents were feeling low, as was I, and we shared that on the journey and that made it better. Parents always feel worse. The kids are in their preferred universe straight away. After that first time, Quasar would return to his friends and his other life. Meanwhile, we were looking at a quieter, less colourful world for the next four months.

Three days later, Zhya joined him at Rishi Valley. A week later, like clockwork, I received Quasar's first letter. This was going to be my new normal, then.

~

The gloom lasted a few days. Empty house, grey skies. And then work simply swept me away. It began with a real highlight.

I had the pleasure of accompanying Sunil Kothari to Shantiniketan. Sunil Kothari was perhaps the most eminent dance critic in this country, a man who had been awarded the Sangeet Natak Akademi and the Padma Shri, as well as being a member of the International Dance Council of UNESCO.

He was a dancer who transformed himself into a historian and researcher simply because he felt it needed to be done – largely at the expense of his time and energy. He loved dance for the purity of its expression; the human form in space, but also because it was intertwined with religion and music, to Indian life, really.

He passed away in December 2020. I believe it was a cardiac arrest after he'd suffered from COVID-19, another victim of that great thief, time. What I will remember is his warmth. And his joy and his passion. For years we were comrades on the cultural beat, visiting far-flung parts of the country. I shall miss him dearly.

Shantiniketan, about a hundred and fifty kilometres from Kolkata, became Rabindranath Tagore's spiritual home. He established the Visva-Bharati University in 1921 and turned it into the university-town it has now become.

But that's not why that trip was a highlight. We spent the evening with K.G. Subramanyan, one of the finest painters India has ever produced. K.G.S. had himself been a student at Shantiniketan and was a professor there for the duration of the '80s. That itself *should* have been a highlight.

Instead, I got to visit Ravindra Bhavan in the company of K.G.S. This is the heart of Visva-Bharati, and maybe Shantiniketan as a whole. It functions as a museum and a library. But it also contains the majority of Rabindranath Tagore's archive – manuscripts and correspondence, photographs and journals, all his books and collections of poems, and his paintings and sketches. And because I was there with K.G.S. – a painter of immense acclaim and a resident professor – the staff there began to pull the original Tagore paintings and sketches out of storage. I have very rarely felt awe like I did that afternoon. I was looking at a remarkable man's work in a way that few people have ever have the opportunity to. I will always remember it.

~

I worked on the *Son Et Lumiere* at Gwalior Fort in August of 1988. These were light and sound shows that served as a brief, dramatic introduction to the history of a monument. We cast Amitabh Bachchan as the narrator, the main voice of the show. Filling out the rest of the cast were Jalal Agha, Saeed Jaffrey, Gerson and Ronnie Screwvala. I served as the producer and the coordinator. I also voiced some bits as and when required. The project was directed by

Manohar Singh and guided by B.V. Karanth, one of the titans of Indian theatre and a former head of the NSD.

Of note were the fantastic lighting by Tapas Sen, India's greatest lighting designer, and the music. Over the course of the evening, we heard Kumar Gandharva, Pandit Bhimsen Joshi, Pandit Jasraj (whose son Shaarang Dev helped Karanth put the score together) and Ila Arun. That line-up alone was worth the price of the ticket.

~

With Quasar at school, there was nothing else to do but work. It was as if I'd begun to collect postcards – these little snapshots – just to be able to tell where I was, and what I was doing. Because, otherwise, life was a blur.

Here's a sample.

August 1988. On the 13th, Gallery Chemould turned twenty-five. There was a 'Dhansak' dinner at the Ripon Club in Kala Ghoda. It was the first time I'd been to that rickety old treasure. To this day it feels like it exists in a mysterious pocket of time from a different era. The food remains exquisite.

On the 20th, I went to Rishi Valley with Esmie to spend Quasar's birthday with him. We were allowed to stay for two nights.

Quasar and I went for a walk in the vegetable patch. And I decided that I was going to make this a habit. I'd visit the boys in August.

Even though I was at Rishi Valley, I'd sent him a note from Bombay.

'My star was highest on August 20th when Quasar shone for his mama and for all in his orbit. Kick off to a greater start, my champ. You have all my love.'

Sometimes you've said all you need to decades ago.

On the 22nd, we shifted to Bangalore. I met Shashi Deshpande. I was a huge fan of her first novel, *The Dark Holds No Terror*.

On the 23rd, I compèred a dance recital for Protima at the Windsor Manor. On the 25th, I had lunch with Dilip's parents – Mummy and Pappa Thakore. We'd stayed in touch over the years. On the

26th, I drove back to Rishi Valley to catch the school performance of *Antigone*. But before that, I took a class on *Julius Caesar* for the tenth standard – as a professional actor, you understand. I watched the show and was deeply impressed by a young Devika Shahani. I drove back to Bangalore after, getting home just past one in the morning.

On the 28th, Protima and I went to Craigmore Tea Estate in Coonoor. The plantation was owned by the Shivdasanis, who also run the Inlaks Foundation. Inlaks provided local and international grants and scholarships to deserving Indians across a wide range of disciplines, including the arts. Protima was performing there, but she was also trying to raise funds for Nrityagram. We were there for two days.

On the 30th, I returned to Bombay. On the flight from Bangalore, I sat next to H.D. Deve Gowda, then Minister for PWD, who was to later become the prime minister of India. We didn't have anything to say to each other, although I tried to strike up a conversation.

I was in Bombay very briefly. Then it was back down south, for the Soorya Festival of Music and Dance in the city formerly known as Trivandrum. This is one of the largest arts festivals anywhere in the world, running from September to January, and has been in existence for over thirty years. I was travelling with Protima, but also in my capacity as a culture columnist.

Highlights? I saw a magnificent Kalari performance. I bought a lifetime's supply of mundus from a store named Karalkada. I dined with Laurie Baker (who had remotely designed the complex in Lonavala) and Adoor Gopalkrishnan, the noted Malyali auteur. Even so, those encounters were topped by my encounter with Kamala Das – the poet and writer who blazed a trail for female sexuality much before it became the vogue. To my delight, she gave me a palm leaf reading – a Naadi horoscope. She had one of the oldest collection of palm leaf horoscopes in south India. I don't remember what she predicted. I was just thrilled to be there.

I also visited the Padmanabhaswamy temple, one of the oldest seats of Vaishnavism in the world. In 2011, the temple became the site of controversy after the Supreme Court directed that its hitherto unexplored vaults be opened. Suddenly, the treasure the investigating agencies found meant that the complex had become the wealthiest place of worship *anywhere in the world.*

That trip was also the first time that Protima performed with the sobriquet 'Gauri'. Her guru had christened her and she would now begin to use the name.

The spectacular and the mundane, the coincidental and the deliberate, the personal and the professional, all rolled into one. All I knew is that I wouldn't – *couldn't* – waste a moment of my time. It was onwards, always.

20

TRY AS I did to ignore it, the heart had its needs too. At one time, those were easily ignored. But one can't remain immune to attention for too long. And I was juggling several careers – in communications, PR and the theatre – and I was surrounded by some very interesting people.

One day, in late 1988, my friend Noel Rand called me. There was a small excursion to Elephanta, would I like to come?

I went. It was a good trip. October in Bombay meant the weather was just turning pleasant. And on the boat was a gentleman I'll call Peter Smith, because that's one of the most common male names in the UK. 'Peter', I later discovered, was someone senior at a large publishing company in England. Tall, grey beard, perfectly turned out, beautiful to look at and oh-so-sophisticated. We got talking.

On the way back to Bombay, Peter asked if we could have dinner. Sure, I said.

As I got home, my friend Barota, who lives around the corner, rang and said, 'Come for dinner.'

'I can't,' I said. 'I've got this friend coming over, and we're to go to dinner.'

'No problem,' she countered. 'Bring your friend, have a drink, and go to dinner after.'

The moment we rang the bell, Barota opened the door and her eyes widened. She looked Peter up and down and turned to me. 'Where did you find this gorgeous man?'

It was a lovely evening. He was welcomed with great warmth. We had a drink, then left for dinner at China Garden. When he dropped me home, we watched TV for a bit. It was very comfortable. I told Peter that I was scheduled to be in London in a month's time. He made me promise I'd look him up.

~

During the time I was picking up the pieces in the aftermath of the break-up, some people around me became part of my life out of their abundant concern and care. One such couple were Jinx and Anand Akerkar.

Anand was the president of the Bombay Chapter of the World Trade Centre, and he put me in charge of the cultural programmes in 1986. In November 1988, the Annual General Assembly of the World Trade Centre took place in Bombay. The functions were spread across the Taj and the Oberoi. It was a massive event.

I was very surprised to be asked to host something of that scale. It showed a great deal of faith in my abilities. And it became something that gave me much-needed confidence as I moved into a phase of my career punctuated by the almost ceaseless change.

It was also four days that marked me for life.

On the 16th of November, the General Assembly was declared open at the Homi Bhabha Auditorium, followed by dinner at the

Regal Room at the Oberoi. I was invited to sit at the table for presidents of Chapters from all around the world. While we were having dinner, Anand turned to me. 'Dolly, the president of one of the American WTCs wants to visit a slum. Can you do something about it?'

'Yes,' I said. I was involved in some social work in Dharavi and it was very easy to organize a trip.

I chatted with the gentleman in question through dinner. I'll call him R.N. He was charismatic, and a wonderful conversationalist. He was a Senator. He made you feel like there was no one else in the room. It helped that he was gorgeous, terrific to look at.

I told him that it was all fixed up and that he should leave at 10 the next morning. The next day, we duly went to Dharavi, and Kumbharvada and the Potter's Colony. Then we went on to the day's schedule.

Bizarrely, at some point that day, a collection of John Donne's love poems arrived at home. A gift from Peter Smith. There was something about the timing of it, though. Almost as if it were a sign.

The next night, as the WTC dinner was winding down, this tall and very beautiful girl came up to the table and announced that they were all heading to the Cellar, the nightclub at the Oberoi. R.N. turned to me and asked whether I'd like to come.

I demurred. I was pretty sure I wasn't invited, I explained.

'What rubbish,' he said. 'You're with me.'

So, we went. We danced. We had a lovely time. It was pretty clear that neither of us had eyes for anyone else. The only blot on the evening was that my bag got stolen. Alarmed by the crime on the streets and clubs of Bombay, R.N. insisted on dropping me home.

It turned into a whirlwind romance, a mysterious, powerful encounter. As a rule, I'm not attracted to white men. As a rule, I'm never swept off my feet.

I didn't want it to stop. I didn't want him to leave. We tried to meet, to bridge the divide between America and Bombay, but it wasn't to be. I have never forgotten him, though. It was like being ambushed by magic.

~

My sense of adventure had reawakened. I was suddenly eager to head to London the following month. I was working on a project with Anand Mahendroo, something to do with Indian rock musicians, I think. I sent word to Peter that I'd be arriving soon and that I'd be staying with my friend Sunder Lalvani.

Sunder owned the largest bookstore in Bombay at the time and, in all seriousness, dealt and dabbled in horses. He had a six-bedroom place in Bishop's Avenue.

Sunder's car met me at the airport. I got to the house, and Sunder accosted me. 'Dolly, what the hell have you done? There have been umpteen phone calls from a Peter something or the other. Where are you, when are you arriving, like an Indian mother.'

Even as Sunder ribbed me, the doorbell rang. Flowers and champagne. For Dolly Thakore, from Peter Smith. Sunder rolled his eyes and flung his hands up in exasperation. Shaking my head, but secretly very pleased, I rang Peter.

'Can I see you tomorrow morning? Because I leave for Holland around noon?' he asked.

'Sure,' I said.

The next morning, Sunder drove me to the Ritz in Piccadilly Circus. Peter was seated in the corner. He was easy to spot because he was carrying another giant bouquet of flowers. He said he had an 11.30 flight. Which suited me fine. I was supposed to have lunch with Farrukh Dhondy, who was head of Channel 4 at the time. After that, Froggy and I would head back to his place.

Peter and I chatted over breakfast. It was lovely, as it had been on the boat. I kept looking at my watch. Finally, I couldn't handle the pressure.

'Don't you have a flight to catch?' I asked.

He waved it away.

'I'll get the next one,' he said.

We chatted a little more. I looked at my watch again.

'Look,' I said. 'I have to meet my friend Farrukh for lunch.'

Peter volunteered to drop me off. We were to meet at a charming Italian restaurant opposite the Channel 4 offices. He waited with me until Farrukh got there. Peter and he were introduced and got into an animated conversation. Peter even stayed for lunch. Froggy took his leave and went back to work. Peter and I were still talking. He was still there at 5 in the evening, when Froggy came back to pick me up. He watched us for a bit. He looked at his watch.

'Look, Dolla,' he said finally. 'I have to go home.' And Froggy and I took our leave and that's when Peter said goodbye.

That was Monday.

On Wednesday, I was in a queue outside the Leicester Square Odeon, waiting to watch Dereck Jacobi in *Richard III*. All of a sudden, I felt a peck on my neck. I whirled around. There was Peter. I was stunned, a little shocked and delighted, all at once.

'What are you doing here?' I asked.

'Well, I rang Farrukh Dhondy. He said you'd be here so I've come to say hi.'

The matinee was about to start, so we had a quick coffee at the bar.

I was leaving on Saturday morning. I'd lined up lunch with Richard Attenborough on Friday at his home in Richmond. So, as a matter of course, Peter picked me up and drove me to Richard's house. But before he could leave, Richard's secretary came to the door.

'Dolly, Richard's had to run out for a meeting –' Channel 4 or Radio London or something, I forget '– but he's said to please come in and have lunch and wait for him …?'

Peter was still there. I said thank you very much, but my friend was already here and I'd go and have lunch with him. We drove to the lake in Richmond and sat in the car for two hours, eating store-bought ham sandwiches and drinking champagne as a gentle rain fell around us. It was incredibly romantic, but we just talked. I can't even remember what we talked about. Just stories. How we found ourselves at this point in our lives. Pain. And joy. Peter knew I was leaving the next day. Two hours later, he dropped me off.

Richard was back, and I spent some time with him. We reminisced about *Gandhi* and India. Then Richard's car dropped me to the show I was watching that evening – *Les Liaisons Dangereuses*, the original RSC production, transposed to the Ambassadors Theatre, West End. I got home, booked myself a minicab for the airport drop, packed, had dinner and went to bed. I had to be up by half four. The pickup was for six in the morning.

I was woken up by a gentle patter of stones against my window. Sunder had regaled me with warnings; there had recently been a spate of burglaries in the area and everyone was paranoid. I peeked through a gap in the curtains, trying my best not to be seen. And there was Peter in the middle of the lawn, spot-lit by a blaze of motion-controlled lights he'd triggered. Sleepy and a little sheepish, I wandered down the corridor and asked Sunder to let him in.

Sunder made Peter a cup of tea while I finished packing. Peter made me cancel the minicab so he could drop me to the airport. We exchanged phone numbers and a long, lingering hug. I boarded the flight intrigued and a little overwhelmed. It had been a wonderful encounter.

I got back to Bombay and dialled his London number a few times. There was no answer. Then I called Noel, the man who'd set all of this in motion by inviting me onto a boat less than two months ago. I described everything that had happened. And then I asked how I could get in touch with Peter, because I enjoyed my time with him very much, but when I called the number I had, no one would pick up …?

There was a lengthy silence.

'But, Dolly,' said Noel. 'Peter … I think Peter is gay.'

Ah. Tiny little detail, then. Perhaps the universe wasn't quite ready for me to date.

I never heard from Peter again.

~

Even if it wasn't a commissioned assignment, my diary was crowded with commitments of all sorts.

On my return, I travelled to Ahmedabad for the Shobha Yatra – a cultural outreach programme for the underprivileged. I worked with Pratibha Matkari, the artist, actress and producer. I also knew her husband, the well-known playwright Ratnakar Matkari. In 2013, I would direct a reading of his *1, Safdarjung*, a snapshot of the life of Indira Gandhi from the Emergency to her assassination. But the guiding light for the Shobha Yatra was Pupul Jayakar.

Pupul was a writer and an activist and, crucially, had the ear of three prime ministers – Pandit Nehru, Indira Gandhi and Rajiv Gandhi. She was the main reason for the state's interest in matters of art and craft. It's no surprise that support dwindled post-liberalization. It was the same across the world. Programmes of this nature first splintered – into state or region-based events, and then slowly became something that occurred because of the goodwill of one particular person. Someone with an interest in the arts. Or with a constituency that contained artisans. It became, quite literally, about the economics of it. Pupul was one of the handful of people (Rajeev Sethi is someone else who comes to mind) who held the tide at bay as long as she could.

~

On the first day of 1989, I went to Pune. The Film and Television Institute had invited me to come and facilitate a module for 'News Training'. And I was in Pune when I received news that Safdar Hashmi had been killed.

Hashmi was thirty-four years old. He was a liberal Marxist who had worked with a host of theatre companies (including IPTA, for whom he wrote the delightful *Moteram ka Satyagraha* with Habib Tanvir). He also founded JANAM (Jana Natya Manch – the People's Theatre). JANAM performed street theatre, mostly in working-class neighbourhoods and factories and the like, trying to foster direct engagement with leftist ideology. It goes without saying they were anti-establishment and anti-authoritarian. In a country that had lived through an Emergency, and then in the tightening vice of the Licence Raj, it was not a difficult position to adopt.

But Hashmi was also an artiste – not just an activist. He had a wide-ranging set of interests. He wrote for TV, created work for children, made documentaries. God only knows what a man like that might have achieved with something like the internet at his disposal.

On 1 January 1989, JANAM was performing *Halla Bol* near Delhi when they were attacked by a group of political goons. Just in case we harbour the belief that hooliganism and self-appointed vigilantism is a recent phenomenon. Safdar Hashmi was wounded and succumbed to his injuries the next day.

JANAM, led by Hashmi's wife Moloyshree, returned to the same spot on the 4th and finished the performance.

We were really stumbling into the '90s, I thought.

~

All around me, violence and discord. Vinod Dua and I travelled through Punjab in February 1989, during one of the darkest chapters of the Khalistan Movement.

Vinod had set up Vinod Dua Communications, separate from M.J. Akbar, who had drifted away from television. I continued to work with him as production executive. We met both Julio Ribero (who has been a friend ever since) and KPS Gill. The two men were legendary – and legendarily tough – police officers, Gill controversially so. Julio became a fixture in the latter part of my career because he dedicated his life post-retirement to a variety of social causes.

While setting up one of the interviews, the cameraman took a moment to inform me that he had studied my interview of Vijay Merchant at Jamia Millia as part of his curriculum. I was pleased and mortified, all at once. Vijay Merchant had been the president of the Cricket Club of India at the time, and he was so pleased with the interview that he arranged for me to become a member, a privilege I enjoy to this day.

It was a surreal trip. I couldn't make much sense of the world I saw. We travelled to Tarn Taran Sahib, perhaps the centre of the movement, home to a prominent Gurudwara of the same name. We passed through Jallianwala Bagh. And yet, the one memory I can't shake off is that of a fourteen-year-old Sikh boy behind bars. He was a freedom fighter. Or a militant. Depending on who you spoke to.

All I could think was that he hadn't grown a beard yet. Hadn't been *able* to grow a beard. That young.

Whatever remained of the Nehruvian dream was dissipating quickly. All around me, in my head and my heart, and in the country at large, we were grappling with unresolved rage. Our ghosts wouldn't lie quiet.

~

Work sometimes provided necessary relief. Early in 1989, a man by the name of Claudio Biondi got in touch with me, via my old friend Suresh Jindal. He was working on an Italian mini-series called *The Mysteries of the Black Jungle* and needed the main lead and also a young male actor. I duly shortlisted three young actors to accompany me to Delhi for a screen test.

We were on the 6 a.m. Indian Airlines flight to Delhi, my three wards and I. We were to meet at the airport at a quarter past five. Security took much less time back then. One of the three young men was late. I got the other two to check in. I then bullied the duty officer into keeping check-in open, while I called this Rajeev Bhatia.

I had thought *I* was panicked. Half-awake, the poor kid could suddenly see an opportunity to screen test for an Italian series slipping away.

'Ma'am! I thought it was 5.30 in the evening! Hold on, I'm coming. Please ma'am, I'm coming.'

He said he'd be there in fifteen minutes. He was in Lokhandwala, and that wasn't inconceivable. I talked the staff in letting him through even though the counters had closed. I sent the other two young men ahead, with my bags. I waited until the last possible minute.

Rajeev Bhatia appeared just as I was about to board. The ground staff let him check-in, but the pilot refused to let him on the aircraft. Rajeev stood around, looking dejected. I found my seat and sat down. Nothing happened. Then the pilot got on the intercom. A red Samsonite vanity case had been abandoned in the departure lounge, was anyone missing any luggage?

I turned to look at my other ward, one Salman Khan. He nodded. Then he registered what the pilot was saying.

'Oh, shit!'

I'd given my vanity case to Salman to carry while I waited for Rajeev. He'd put it down to pull out his boarding card or something and had forgotten to pick it up. Unsurprisingly, it was a red Samsonite.

I got up. Everyone knew I was the reason that the flight was delayed because I'd been the last person to board. I made the slow walk of shame down the aisle, off the plane. I picked up the orphaned vanity case. As I made my way back to my seat, every pair of eyes on board followed my progress. Except one. Salman was studying the safety instruction card with great concentration.

We screen-tested the whole day and then took the last flight back. The director cast a young actor from England. He wasn't very good. For the main lead, I cast Kabir Bedi.

A few months later, the doorbell rang. To my surprise, there was a huge bouquet from Asha Chandra, the renowned acting teacher. I didn't know her, and I thought there had been a mix-up. So, I called.

'No, Dolly,' she said. 'I have to thank you because everything you have touched has turned to gold for me.'

Young Salman had returned to Bombay and signed a film with a first-time director from an illustrious film family. The director was Sooraj Barjatya, and the film was *Maine Pyar Kiya*. Much better, I think, than playing a cursory brown man in *The Mysteries of the Black Jungle*.

Rajeev Bhatia metamorphosed into Akshay Kumar. Even today, if we're at the same social gathering, he'll make sure to take a moment to greet me.

~

A few months later, I went to watch *Natsamrat* in my capacity as reviewer. It featured Dr Shreeram Lagoo, quite possibly the finest stage actor this country has ever had. I'd cast him in *Gandhi* and, ironically, would later cast him in *Jinnah*. We knew each other well. He was the first person who ever gifted me a Dharwad saree.

I was at Ravindra Natya Mandir well in advance of the performance, so I went to see him backstage. He saw me in the green room mirror and smiled. And spoke a full line in Marathi, in that rich, unforgettable voice, knowing fully well that I didn't speak a word of the language.

I grinned back.

'Lagoo Saab,' I told him. 'You know I don't understand. But if you stood up and performed it the way you would in the show, I'll tell you exactly what it means.'

And he laughed. Because he knew it was true.

V

Act Three

21

MORE THAN THIRTY years later, going over my diaries for this book, I stumble on the words 'not a moment to spare' and 'no holiday' repeatedly. It's as difficult to explain those words as it is to explain what I felt reading them thirty years later. My memory isn't what it used to be – not even close. I've started to lose details, sometimes in the short-term as well. But this was like strapping myself to a roller coaster. I was shocked how quickly I was there – the smells, the colours, the touch and the temperature of a life that I thought I'd moved on from. It was exhausting and addictive – an onslaught of emotion that I wasn't ready for and couldn't get enough of. Very rarely does anyone get to relive their life, and I had the briefest glimpse – just a taste, a single drop of ink in a bucket of pellucid water, watching the seed blossom, spread its tentacles, become a different thing and then wink away.

And sometimes, it was the realization that my life was, in fact, crazy – a melange of the personal and the professional until the boundaries blurred and the only thing left was the sense of momentum. A bit like opening a play, over and over again.

In the early '90s, I did a lot of work with the Birlas. The first of these assignments was a seminar titled 'City of Joy and City of Despair' in January 1990, to mark the 300th year of Calcutta's founding.

The event was significant for a couple of reasons. First, the star wattage on the panel: R.K. Laxman, legendary humourist and cartoonist; Khushwant Singh, iconoclast by religion; Mulk Raj Anand, the Charles Dickens of India; Mrinal Sen, Bengali auteur; Prakash Tandon, the first Indian to head Hindustan Lever; Professor Nisith Ranjan Ray, historian, activist and founder of the Society for Preservation, (City of) Calcutta.

I flew out three days in advance, to do my research.

On the morning of the first day of the seminar, a worried-looking Kumar Mangalam Birla walked up to me.

'Dolly,' he began. Then he hesitated. 'Dolly, I'm very sorry to inform you that Alyque has turned up.' Alyque and I had been around each other in the past eight years. How could we not? We had a child together. We had crossed each other's paths in corridors and passages and theatres. But we studiously ignored each other.

Except for the one time I ran into Sharon and him at the airport. We were all on a flight back from Delhi. This was around 1985, I think. I walked up to her. I had a strange whistling sound in my ears. My heart was beating too fast and my blood ran cold. I felt fear and hate, and like I'd just dodged a bullet.

'I can't believe you've done this,' I said. 'As a Christian.'

How absurd that I should fall back on religion, at that exact time. I didn't know what else to say. I was still at a loss for words. The betrayal was still too big, too raw, too recent.

That was then. This was now. And I was stumped.

'We sent him an invitation,' continued Kumar. 'But he didn't respond. Otherwise I would never have put you in a situation like this.'

But, really. This was my son's father, who moved in the same professional and social circles as I did. I couldn't have avoided him forever. I should know. I tried very hard.

'It doesn't matter,' I said. 'It's not a problem.'

Alyque was on the panel. I went up, and I did my job.

When it was done and we were leaving the stage, Alyque ended up behind me in the queue.

'That was brilliantly moderated, Doll,' he said.

Amen. Khushwant Singh and R.K. Laxman got me through the rest of that trip, like champions. They walked me from my room, and they made sure to accompany me back to my room whenever we were done for the day. They wouldn't leave my side. They made sure I had a chaperone at all times.

~

In April of that year, I took Quasar to the Andamans. We flew to Port Blair. We began our stay elsewhere but shifted to the Fortune Resort Bay Island because it turned out I knew the manager.

I used to read Amar Chitra Katha comics to Quasar at bedtime. I was trying to introduce him to India's mythology and its history. And to some of my heroes. He was fascinated by the freedom struggle. When we read about Bhagat Singh and Chandrashekhar Azad, I decided to take him to the Andamans and the Cellular Jail.

The Cellular Jail was the reason the term 'Kala Pani' entered the lexicon. It was built along the lines of a panopticon. Theoretically, a single guard could watch over ninety-odd prisoners without them being aware that they were being watched. The construction, therefore, fascinated Quasar. It looked nothing like his idea of a jail. Instead, spokes radiated from a rotunda. He was also very intrigued by the gallows. And then there was the history of the place. The fact that Indians had been imprisoned there during the Raj, and during the freedom struggle. During the Second World War, the Japanese commandeered it, and Subhash Chandra Bose had hoisted the Indian flag. Even so, rumour has it that the Japanese attempted to drown seven hundred and fifty prisoners when they retreated from the island. Those that managed to make it back to the shore had to resort to cannibalism to survive. At least, that's how the legend goes.

I don't know how much of it Quasar absorbed. But that kind of grisly is always gold for a young boy.

I also met one of the three surviving 'cannibals', and the stories he told me reinforced my desire to visit 'Cowrie Baba' (although it might have been spelt 'Kauri') on Chidiya Tapu. This was a man who could divine your future using sea-shells. We ended up having a very different kind of adventure.

I no longer needed to visit astrologers like I once did, but it had become a habit I enjoyed because it meant I got to collect another story. This was borne out that afternoon. Quasar and I trekked to a remote part of the island. We met the Baba – a weird old man with a long beard. We'd been warned about making it back to the jetty before dark. We hadn't realized that the sun set at 4 p.m.

I was genuinely scared on the way back. The sun disappeared almost as soon as we began the return journey. I'm pretty sure we were lost at one point, stumbling through a dark jungle that got more ominous every passing minute. And I think it was just luck that we found the path. We were both a bit shaken.

There was more to the Andamans than the Cellular Jail, and we spent our days visiting the nooks and corners. Poor Quasar had to tag along, though his sole interest was the Kala Pani. The other adventure sports were less hair-raising. We went to the Jolly Bouy Island via the Wandoor Jetty. We took the glass-bottomed boat and went snorkelling in the coral. You floated for a moment in the sea and when you plunged your head under the water, it was like you'd casually drifted through a dimensional portal. Beauty, glittering at a slower frame rate. It really was something.

We also went to Ross Island, the site of colonial settlements in the Andamans, and walked through the ruins. This was like passing through a different kind of portal, a living monument and a reminder of what had once been. And still so beautiful.

~

On the 11th of May 1990, Protima's dream came true, a testament to her grit and gumption. Someone, somewhere – and I clearly forget who – described the ideal director as someone with a foot in the gutter, eyes on the stars and a hand on the hilt of a dagger.

That was my girl.

V.P. Singh, then prime minster of India, inaugurated Nrityagram – a residential dance village, thirty kilometres out of Bangalore. Protima opened it on a grant, and on love and faith.

I couldn't not have been there. I felt as invested in the creation of Nrityagram as I did in the campus in Lonavala. It was that personal. Through Protima, on those fundraising trips, I met her gurus: Kelucharan Mohapatra, of course; Kumudini Lakhia for Kathak;

and Bharati Shivaji for Mohiniattam. It was an extraordinary thing to witness – a friend who stumbled upon a true calling and had the guts and the cussedness to follow through on it. Well, if it was going to happen to anyone I knew…

Nrityagram occupied ten acres and seemed to have been there forever. Protima and I travelled to Trivandrum to ask the architect Laurie Baker if he would design the campus. The frail old man was more of a Keralite than anyone we'd met. He was married to a lady from Kerala and he had adopted the local lifestyle completely. He advised us and introduced us to his student and assistant, the architect Gerard da Cunha (no relation to Gerson).

It was Gerard who designed Nrityagram. He used local materials and artisans and the result is something that *feels* spectacular but is rough-hewn, and comforting to the touch. It feels like a village. There's a deep, deep hush. It is a place for hard work and for rest. There are some crazy dogs. Every year, they used to host the Vasanth Habba, a celebration of Indian classical forms. Crowds of up to twenty thousand people would gather around the stone amphitheatre. Nrityagram was the other half of Protima's soul: wise, ancient, peaceful.

The opening ceremony was put together by Shankar Nag. Shankar was married to our friend Arundathi – actress and national treasure. Aru, Protima, Lynne Fernandez and I would later form a clique of sorts. Lynne's story is deserving of its own book. She was a highly sought-after lighting designer in Delhi. She was also a friend of Pamela Rooks. And Pamela had just published her novel, *Miss Beatty's Children*, which she would make into a film over the course of the next two years. I would cast Protima in it, and Lynne and she would meet on the sets. Starting in 1995, Lynne began to do more and more work with Nrityagram, even leading their overseas tours. Stealthily, Protima groomed her to take over as administrative head of the dance village.

But all of that was still in the future. On this day, doyens from the world of dance descended from all over the country to Hesaragatta.

Shankar himself was a massive celebrity – a film star with a cult following and a filmmaker of rare distinction. He also, of course, created *Malgudi Days* for television. His life was tragically cut short at the age of thirty-five, in a car accident. Aru would go on to build the Ranga Shankara Auditorium in Bangalore in his honour.

Nrityagram was a similar labour of love.

After that, whenever I went to see Quasar at Rishi Valley, I'd go straight to Nrityagram. And that helped. Being around Protima was like jamming your arm into an electrical socket. She was a *soul*-socket.

~

In December of that year, I would moderate something called 'Spectrum', also for the Birlas. This was a function for the Birla schools in West Bengal. The event was always held at the Netaji Subhash Chandra Bose Indoor Stadium in Kolkata, for a total of twelve thousand kids. Dances, debates, elocution – an all-round celebration. I'd end up going three years running.

Malavika and Vir Sanghvi lived in Kolkata at the time. Vir was editor of the *Telegraph*. They were always on my list of people to see.

That first year, Sarala Birla, Basant Birla's wife, invited me home after we'd finished the school function.

'*Humare ghar mein hain, kam logon ke liye, khas logon ke liye.*' Here, she dangled a carrot or issued a warning, I couldn't tell. '*Advaniji bhi aa rahein hai.*' She was stern and warm, all at once, like the perfect mother. '*Toh aap zaroor aiyega, par time pe aiyega, please.*'

The Birlas were such wonderful hosts that it was difficult to say 'no'. So I went back to the hotel to change. While collecting my keys, a dapper gentleman introduced himself. This was Basant Dubey. He'd seen me at the Birla function and asked me to join him for a quick drink. He was India's first-tea taster and was on an assignment in Mauritius. He passed through Bombay regularly. We exchanged phone numbers. I freshened up, called Malavika and Vir, and told them that I'd be later than I'd thought and left.

At Birla House, a long open veranda ran across the facade, about a foot high. There was an arrangement of chairs at the foot of this platform, three rows deep. About 150 guests and, as far as I could tell, they were mostly Marwari. They had all been at the school function, and they'd gone home and changed into fabulous gold-edged dhotis and sarees.

Ashok Singhal popped up. He was the opening act, sent in to warm up the crowd. He said lots of flattering things about L.K. Advani. At that time, we thought of the BJP the way Dilip and I had once dismissed the Sena and Bombay bandhs. They were distant noise, elements on the fringe. They spouted an agenda that worried English-speaking, foreign-educated, left-leaning liberals. I think their agenda *should* have worried everyone. What has become clear in the intervening years is that they were speaking for *someone*, they voiced the thoughts and feelings of *some* part of the population. I just wish we'd listened.

L.K. Advani arrived, a little bit like Rajneesh. There was a hush. People had gathered to hear him speak. He joined his palms in a namaste. He regarded us for a moment.

'*Abhi jo mein aa raha tha …*' he began.

There is nothing I love more than someone who has a great voice and knows how to use it. Here he was, this iron man, this relentless organizer, this bane, this boon, this radical. And he had an absurdly high-pitched voice. He sounded like he was on helium. It was the damnedest thing. I nearly died.

'*… Simranjit Singh Maan ne mujhe phone kiya*,' he continued. He meant Simranjit Singh Mann, of the Shiromani Akali Dal. '*Aur unhone kaha ki mujhe aap se milna hai.*' He hit a higher note. '*Aur maine kaha, ki main to subhe ki flight se Calcutta jaa raha hoon.*'

Now, he assumed another voice. He was narrating Simranjit Singh Mann's side of the conversation.

'*Jab 1947 main azaadi mili, toh Hinduon ko–*' He interrupted himself. He'd come to his punchline. '*Maine usse roka! Hinduon ko kuch nahin mila. Hindustan ka batwara hua!* He looked around the gathering with gimlet eyes, like an old bird of prey.

'*Mussalmaano ko Pakistan bhejo. Aur Isaaiyon ko America bhejo.*'

My mouth went dry. I couldn't believe that anyone, let alone a politician, could be this explicit about their agenda. It wasn't … *decent.* I wanted to grab an arm and jab my fingernails deep. I was sitting between Karl Khandalawala, who was eighty-one, and Basant Birla, who was my host.

As soon as Advani was done, I went up to Saralaben, made my excuses and bade my hosts goodnight.

I was still fuming when I got to Vir and Malavika's. Saryu Doshi made up the fourth that evening. They heard me tell the story of the gathering at the Birlas. Malavika thought I should have thrown something at Advani. As if one could, sitting next to Basant Birla in his own home. We were all worked up, but we were disbelieving. We couldn't fathom the brazenness of it. And because it was so brazen, none of us could take it seriously, at face value.

Little did we know. What the BJP was, was a group of fantastic capitalists. They needed to move a majority. Unlike other political parties, they didn't waste their time or energy pandering to minorities, or liberals, or the left. Not even basic lip service. They didn't need to. The electoral math was on their side.

I wish we hadn't been disbelieving. What followed was perfectly credible.

And when I watched the rise of Trump, these last few years, I felt that same sense of horror. Of watching a twisted joke told in real-time. What's the joke? Cartoon evil. What's the twist? We're the punchline.

~

Back in Bombay, I was invited to do the commentaries for *Apna Utsav,* which was the umbrella term for the festivals celebrating Indian culture and Indian artisanal practices. I worked closely with the distinguished Marathi director, Kamlakar Sontakke. But the festival itself was, unsurprisingly, under the aegis of Pupul Jaykar.

I'd been a freelancer since the '70s, but I never quite had a span like that. I bounced from theatre productions to assignments, and then to the next. My varied interests meant constant excitement – every day, a new job.

I loved it all. I loved being asked, being singled out, being recognized. I loved the acknowledgement. I loved being asked to travel all over the country.

There was some financial gain, but I took whatever was offered. Never negotiated. It seems silly now, but it felt like it was against the spirit of the game – the same spirit that saw me juggling so much.

I had one rule, and one rule only. I would fly. The only person I ever took a train for was Protima. That wasn't work.

The rest of it, though? Where to begin?

In the '90s, I was on the Central Board for Film Certification. And I continued to record interviews and special features. I'd gone from being a broadcaster to a specialist. I always liked interviewing public figures: politicians and thinkers. Those were fun interviews. I loved talking to Khushwant Singh, but then he was exactly my type. Older, irreverent, caustic, brilliant.

I prepared well. I read up as much as I could about the interviewee and their work. When it came to the actual taping, I could focus on putting them at ease and really listening to them.

~

By far, my favourite interview was the one with Balasaheb Thackeray, in January of 1991. I was working on a programme with Vinod Dua, for Doordarshan. I've never been afraid of making phone calls, so when the interview was mooted, I just picked up the phone and dialled.

Balasaheb was a charmer.

'Dolly, my house is too small,' he said when I asked him about the interview. 'The cameras and everything won't fit here. *Toh hum aapke yahan aa sakte hain …*'

I don't know if it was hurdle #1. Ways to get out of an interview. Famous people usually have a set of strategies.

'No problem,' I said. 'Except I live in Pedder Road.'

'No problem,' he said. 'We are going to Mantralaya for a wedding, and we'll drop in after that.'

'Drop in.' I'd heard that phrase before, and since, and I've never quite thought of it the same way. No one else I knew has ever 'dropped in' with two jeeps full of gun-toting guards, Black Cat Commandos, the lot. The commotion travelled up the building a little before his actual arrival, like the onset of a storm. Then the doorbell rang, and there he was, wrapped in a white shawl. He came in and sat down.

I decided I could push my luck.

'Balasaheb,' I began. 'I don't speak Marathi and I'm not Maharashtrian and I don't quite believe in the things that you're saying and doing.'

He listened. He nodded his head. He smiled.

'How long have you lived in Bombay?' he asked.

'Since 1969,' I said.

'Then you're Maharashtrian.'

He'd specified a ten-minute chat. We talked for about two-and-a-half hours. Four commandoes squeezed into the little office I have, a converted balcony, right behind where I'm typing this. Balasaheb was surprisingly easy to talk to – warm, observant, ready to engage with almost anything. He spent some time looking at my paintings when he first arrived. 'No Maharashtrian painters,' he complained at one point, and I said that my favourite canvas was by Sudhir Patwardhan.

I could almost have been talking to a favourite uncle. Almost.

An interview with Balasaheb has unexpected benefits. Until that day, the building security had largely ignored me. From that day on, for years, they'd spring to their feet the moment they saw me. I had a cook and caretaker called Ramu at the time, and he asked Balasaheb if he could have a photo with him. He used to carry that photo around with him like an identity card.

In the mid-'90s, Aamir Raza Hussain and I went to Balasaheb's place to invite him to come and watch *The Legend of Ram*. The irony wasn't lost on me. Here was Aamir, a Muslim, director of a play called *The Legend of Ram*, about a historical figure who has been adopted by the Hindu nationalists as a symbol of India's Hindu antecedents, in the home of Balasaheb Thackeray, the lodestone of the Shiv Sena. Everyone was very civil. Some tea and/or water was drunk. We were introduced to a young, very shy Smita Thackeray.

To our amazement, Balasaheb came to watch the show. Aamir was in his Wagnerian phase. Those productions were massive, built into the side of a hill, with the audience on a moving platform that took them from location to location. I played Manthara, who opened the show. I'm not sure what Balasaheb thought.

I spoke to him once more. I was surprised when he answered the call.

The potters next to Mahim Church showed up for the first time in the early '90s. There were a few to begin with. Then, someone in a chauffeur-driven car stumbled across them. Suddenly, their wares were all the rage. All these ladies would drive up in their big, long cars. Within weeks, there was a full-blown colony of potters, and traffic was a mess.

'You're always talking about people being discriminated against, at the cost of the people of this city,' I said to Balasaheb. 'Well, what about these potters? Because they're making everyone's lives hell …'

'Do you think it's easy, Dolly?' he asked. 'They – those potters – have a representative in Parliament!'

~

I'd snatch any opportunity I'd get, in the middle of all the madness, to go and see Quasar. Especially I if could sneak around the two-days-a-term rule.

I went to Rishi Valley to attend the flag-hoisting ceremony for Republic Day. But my motives were slightly more nefarious. I had permission to whisk Quasar away for a day. We drove to Nrityagram, for that year's Vasanth Habba.

That night, we watched Zakir Hussain and Hariprasad Chaurasia. They played all the way through to the next morning. We caught a few hours of sleep, and I dropped him back to the school around 5 p.m. on Sunday. Then I drove back to Bangalore.

I stayed with Kiran Mazumdar (she hadn't married John Shaw back then). And got a tour of the Biocon facility the next day. Later, in Goa, on tour with *Rashomon*, I stayed with Mario Miranda in Loutolim (in the house that inspired Shyam Benegal's *Trikal*).

I'd spent all of my youth looking up and looking in from the margins. At some point, I'd wandered in through the door and picked a spot at the table. I waited for someone to come along and ask me to move, because I was a fraud, because I didn't belong there. It never happened.

I don't claim the accomplishments of the people I spent time with. But I'm glad I looked them in the eye, got to know them and became friends with some of them. And I didn't judge myself an impostor. That might be one of my greatest successes. To have excavated that self-belief. To have recognized the extraordinary circumstances and situations that I found myself in.

Things just … happened.

~

A strange companion piece to the Bal Thackeray interview was the one I did with Dadi Balsara in August 1991. Dadi was a worthy subject. Starting as a modest LIC clerk in Nagpur, he had managed to create a billion-dollar empire that spanned some sixty-odd countries. This is a man who, at the time of his death, had been living at the Taj Mansingh Hotel for over thirty-five years! It wasn't a great interview, to be honest. But I went and had lunch with him the day before the taping, just to get a sense of how the conversation might go. He was at the Taj at Apollo Bunder. He insisted on walking me down and sending the car home with me. We were at the main entrance, making small talk, when said vehicle drove in. It was, without exaggeration, the size of my living room. I don't remember the make and model, but when it pulled up to my apartment building, everyone gawked. And when the same car came to pick me up the next morning, a small crowd gathered downstairs. For the car, I hasten to add.

I also had the great privilege of interviewing Geoffrey Kendal, way back in 1984. I considered it a real highlight because he was one of my heroes. I mention it because it was around that time that I stepped in to cover for Pearl in a production of *Gaslight*, his favourite play. It was the only time I worked with him. The old man was a real character. And the chemistry that the cast had, as a direct result of his rehearsal process, was the best I'd ever experienced.

~

At some point, it dawned on me that I actually had four careers. I was a casting director, a media consultant, I worked in PR, and I was a columnist. Acting was what I did for fun. Momentum had started to build after Alyque left, and then had surged in earnest after the accident. In one sense, I had no choice. But I also wouldn't have wanted it any other way.

'My life has hurtled from assignment to assignment,' reads a diary entry. 'Each page has six appointments a day. From rehearsals to reviews to columns to corporate meetings throughout Bombay – from NCPA to Prithvi, and travel across India. Compèring, casting, coordinating. Not a moment's holiday or rest. But I have enjoyed every moment.'

Some of it was a consequence of being in the right place at the right time. I didn't know it then but, because I was multi-faceted, I had created – purely by accident, as always – a well-nigh perfect media profile for myself. I was visible, but I wasn't restricted to only one kind of job or presence. And this happened to me as media rounded into the age of the generalist. Someone who could advise on many things had suddenly become more valuable. Because you saved time, knowing that one meeting would cover 'several verticals' (I think that's the current corporate-speak.)

I became a communications Swiss-Army knife. And I could dip into a lot of life experiences – the theatre, being an Air Force kid, the things I'd hurled myself into all my life – without missing a beat because I was never nervous about trying anything.

I was having too much fun.

It sounds very well-considered, but I was basically making it up as I went along.

I had a stint as a Corporate Communications Consultant with P&G. They were launching the washing detergent Ariel at the time, and as anyone who grew up during the '70s and '80s will tell you, breaking the hegemony of Surf, Rin and Nirma was no mean task. It was a weirdly inverted version of the Miss India tour. I went to smaller towns and villages. I held press conferences and gave demonstrations. I attempted to get women to sample the product. For some reason, P&G thought the cachet of a news anchor would make a difference. I didn't mind. I got to travel again.

I also went to Delhi to plead with Margaret Alva and the director-general of Doordarshan to allow us to show 'wet' Whisper sanitary napkins on TV, but we were unsuccessful.

I got paid five thousand rupees to record an audiobook, something I'd been doing for the NAB for years. *Socialite Evenings* by Shobhaa De. And also *The Untouchables* by Mulk Raj Anand.

Miss Beatty's Children had begun to gather steam. This was the start of a long working relationship with Pamela. And I would run into Jenny Seagrove, who played the lead, many years later in London.

It was a hectic time. I travelled to Coorg for the recce. I needed to find some white actors as well as Anglo-Indians, so I spent time in Auroville, Pondicherry, Chennai, Coimbatore, and the schools in and around Ooty. And when Quasar had an appendectomy at Breach Candy Hospital, I had to leave for the shoot as soon as the operation was done. Quasar stayed with his grandparents and Esmie and Dennis.

~

In June 1992, Quasar returned from his first-ever overseas trip with Alyque. I was at the airport to receive him. And Alyque offered to drop us home. For the first time since 1982, this was an offer I accepted. Even then it felt like a small but significant moment – a step towards whatever normal we would eventually achieve.

We stayed up all night, Quasar and I, talking about his trip.

Six days later, Quasar was back at Rishi Valley.

'Life so rushed,' reads the entry in my diary.

22

I WENT TO Pune in September 1992 to compère the Pune Festival. It was the brainchild of Suresh Kalmadi. The annual Ganesh Utsav became the focal point of a festival that showcased art and culture – dance, particularly – as well as being proudly Maharashtrian. It began in 1989 and has continued to this day, growing in size and scope, going through several iterations. I worked on it for three years. President Shankar Dayal Sharma inaugurated the festival that year.

It was a pleasure being in Pune for the duration of the festival. The city has its own charm – a laidback university town, unhurried and wise.

I made a trip to Khadakwasla, to visit the NDA – the National Defence Academy. I could never shrug off being an Air Force kid. If I could, I'd visit the places I'd never been to as a child. I also never did anything as prosaic as telephone in advance. I just showed up. Usually, they let me in.

I also paid a visit to the Osho Ashram in Koregaon Park. I had an exhilarating evening of White Robe Meditation, one of the forms of active contemplation Osho (formerly known as Bhagwan Rajneesh) had popularized. It was well-nigh impossible for modern man, Osho posited, to sit still and meditate. Instead, he advocated an explosive path to tranquillity – high energy movement or dance, sustained for almost twenty minutes, followed by relaxation.

Getting out of your own way, basically.

~

Alyque and I had been to see Osho, when he was still known as Rajneesh, in May of 1978. Let me be clear: we thought he was a charlatan. But too many of our friends, and too many intelligent, talented people were putting aside their lives to either go and see him or spend time at his Ashram. Vinod Khanna and Mahesh Bhatt, to name but two. Neither of whom was unintelligent. What was all the fuss about?

We were admitted to the hall. Rajneesh was scheduled to speak. We received a series of instructions, on par with riders for a certain level of film star. Once Rajneesh had entered, you couldn't cough, couldn't go to the loo, couldn't leave the room. And there was no guarantee of how long he would speak for. He'd been known to hold forth for eight, ten, twelve hours if the mood took him.

'Look,' I said. 'Can I at least have a chair?'

I was in the sixth month of my pregnancy. I couldn't have sat on the floor, as directed, for an unspecified amount of time. They acquiesced. In a sea of mostly white people, I was the only person perched on a chair.

Rajneesh arrived. Everyone seemed to sigh. The energy in the room went through the roof. He seemed to glide to the little dais. He settled down in a black leather chair and looked about the room with benign good humour.

It all seemed faintly ridiculous.

And then he began to speak.

Enough has already been said about his voice – it was genuinely mesmeric. He could have been an extraordinary telemarketer. But it was *what* he said. Rarely have I heard someone make so much sense. He made it seem simple, trying to find the answers within ourselves. I listened, rapt, for the three hours that he spoke. When he finished, my hands raised themselves in a namaste automatically, without conscious thought. Like one of those magical mornings when waking up isn't an interruption. Instead, awareness slowly shifts its form and the adjustment is effortless.

Rajneesh left. Almost immediately, I received word that Ma Yoga Laxmi wanted to see me. This was a bit of a surprise, but I wasn't fazed. I also suspect the fact that I was a newsreader had something to do with it.

'Bhagwan wants to meet you,' she told me. 'When can you see him?'

'Right away,' I said with a smile. 'Because I have to leave.'

'No, no,' she said. 'You must stay for three days. At least. Bhagwan can't see you otherwise.'

'I'm sorry,' I said. 'I'm reading the news tomorrow evening. And I have to leave.'

That was that. We stayed for the rest of the evening. We danced to awaken the kundalini. And we ate some fabulous vegetarian food. Then we left for Bombay.

This visit in the '90s felt overdue. Rajneesh had passed on. But it was good to go nonetheless. That whole Pune trip was a bit like that – bringing something to a close, a cool hand on my brow, in the midst of running, running. I finished by watching Pandit Bhimsen Joshi singing at Saras Bagh at 6 in the morning. It felt like he'd sung the dawn into existence. I didn't feel alone or isolated. Just glad to be there.

~

The following month, Deepa Mehta introduced me to Paul Stephens. Paul ran a company called The Film Works. They were about to begin work on making a film of Rohinton Mistry's *Such a Long Journey*, a film that, in its torturous progress towards realization, would come to embody its title.

I also took on the role of corporate communications director and PR consultant with the Mehta Group, specifically for Saurashtra Cement and Gujarat Sidhee Cement. For the most part, I travelled to their various plants around the country in the company of Ashvin Gatha, the internationally renowned photojournalist and fashion photographer. In November of that year, we journeyed to Ranavav (in the Porbandar district) and Rajkot.

I mention it because the job was one of the constants at an extraordinary time in my life, when the boundaries between the political, professional and personal collapsed. This is the moment when social work assumed an even larger significance in my life.

~

Basant Dubey called. It was the 6th of December 1992. Protima was in Bombay. We were going to the Town Hall for a Remo Fernandes concert. Remo was a friend – he'd helped with the music score of *Jesus Christ Superstar* in 1974.

While we waited for the performance to begin, we heard an announcement that an agitated crowd from Mohammed Ali Road was on its way to the Town Hall. We should all go home as quickly as possible, the announcement stressed.

The rumour was a large crowd of Hindu Kar Sevaks – who had been gathering for days in the city of Ayodhya under the aegis of

L.K. Advani and his ilk – had demolished the sixteenth-century Babri Masjid that evening. Riots had erupted.

So Protima, Basant and I came home to Pedder Road. I rang my contacts in the police. They assured me that it was safe to drive to Juhu, for Protima, and to the airport for Basant, who was catching his flight back to Mauritius.

~

For five days, the city was in the grip of the 'first wave' of riots. And then, it seemed, things calmed down. It felt like order, and then common sense, could be made to prevail. That Bombay might have talked its way off the precipice once more.

It was not to be.

~

On the 20th and 21st of December, two Muslim men were locked in a room that was then set ablaze. And the bodies of two other men, one a Hindu and the other a Muslim policeman, were found in Behrampada.

Communal battle lines, never too far below the surface, had been drawn. Inflammatory rhetoric began to spout on either side. In the first week of January, there were a series of stabbings of both Hindus and Muslims. All of them looked to be the work of 'professionals'. The city was a tinderbox, and it was beginning to get warm.

~

On the 4th of January 1993, I was part of a meeting at Sheriff Khorakiwala's office. He was aware that the city was simmering on the brink of something, and he wanted to gather like-minded people and attempt to be proactive. Eventually, this would result in the creation of the 'Mohalla Committees', seventy-two of them, across the city. But that was later. Mostly, we were gripped by a gnawing sense of fear, an unknown horror that waited in the next lane. If a group of people could pull down a mosque, *because they felt like it*, and if people could react by killing innocents because they were the 'other', and if the politicians all around us just beat the drums, just beat the drums, so sense was drowned out, then what might happen?

We didn't have to wait long to find out.

~

I had to travel to Delhi for the twenty-fourth edition of the International Film Festival of India. At midnight on the 10th of January, we gathered in Shabana Azmi's room. The riots in Bombay had been getting worse. First the Muslim agitation and then the Hindu backlash. The police had lost control of the situation. The city was a war zone. It had descended into some guerrilla hellscape – automatic weapons and Molotov cocktails and acid balloons and swords and knives. Locality after locality, Hindu *and* Muslim, was being barricaded and set alight.

On the 10th, the government finally indicated that the army would be deployed to regain control of the situation.

~

The film festival rolled on, background noise to the death of a dream.

On the 12th, we gathered in Mithun Chakraborty's room. This was another collection of like-minded people, trying to find a way to mobilize, trying to pool their influence and their phonebooks in order to stem the flow of blood. Fifty-two police stations had been attacked or ransacked. On the 11th, the army had to fire at a mob in Dadar. Thankfully, there had been no casualties.

It was madness. In truth, the fugue has never lifted.

~

I flew back to Bombay on the 13th. The violence on the streets was already personal but it had come home in the most unexpected ways. Someone had marked Alyque's door with a cross – here lived a prominent Muslim, it indicated. Alyque, who wasn't religious in the least, responded in typical Alyque-fashion. He sent Sharon and their daughter Shazahn to live with someone else for a few days and sat back to see who might come calling.

I landed at 1.30 in the afternoon. I went straight to Mantralaya, where Sunil Dutt was on a fast, in protest, in solidarity, in horror. I hadn't yet understood where I might be of help, but I needed to be there, for my sake. From Mantralaya, I made the short trip to Flora Fountain, where my friend Titoo Ahluwalia was addressing a rally. Titoo was a market research genius who would take an early retirement to dedicate his life to social causes, partly triggered, I think, by the events of that time. He was married to Jamini, who was one of my closest friends, as well as being a wonderful jewellery designer. The two of them had been very kind to Quasar and me after Alyque left.

At 3.30 that afternoon, I received a call – doctors were urgently needed at the relief camps. I immediately called Dr L. Hiranandani, the famous ENT specialist and philanthropist. We knew each other vaguely, as a result of my compèring career.

Contact details and references of doctors started to trickle back to me by 7.30 that evening. My friend Vipula Kadri was coordinating the relief efforts. She had founded PRIDE India in 1982, to provide aid, equal opportunity and human rights advocacy for marginalized communities. PRIDE began with specific focus on rural areas in Maharashtra but had expanded its ambit to the whole country by this time.

I even enlisted Zhya. The doctors would gather at my home every morning, and Zhya would then take them to wherever they were needed.

~

On the 17th January, Citizens for Peace was born. It was a non-political organization that was formed as a direct result of the carnage we witnessed. Our immediate aim was to provide relief to whoever needed it. But the larger goal has always been to fight for a secular, liberal, cosmopolitan Bombay – the one that we grew up with. Some of the usual suspects were there – old friends like Devika Bhojwani and Julio Ribero. I made some new ones. I remain a trustee to this day. We continued to meet every day at Titoo's office, until the city achieved some degree of sanity.

By the 19th, we had set up a collection drive. Every morning, between 7 and 9 a.m., we encouraged everyone – ordinary citizens and corporates alike – to donate whatever they could. Clothes, food, medication, toys.

All of it would then travel to the basement of the Y.B. Chavan auditorium, where it would be sorted. And then it would be sent to the relief camps in Kesar Bagh, Mahim Dargah, Musafirkhana and Behrampada.

~

My work with the Mehta Group continued alongside. I made undue use of the car and driver, with impunity. I will always be grateful to Jay Mehta for being so understanding. They never said a word.

The personal, political and professional intertwined and became one thing, a single long corridor that flashed glimpses of my life back at me, so that I wouldn't miss them in the rush to the next thing during that awful time. I travelled to Jamnagar for work. I travelled to the NDA in Pune for a show of *Rashomon*.

In February, we witnessed 'Hands Across Bombay' – a human chain to show our appreciation and support for the secular character of Bombay, to show that we could heal ourselves, regardless of the scars.

~

On the 20th of February, I hosted the Sherriff's Religious Meet – another call for unity. It was a gathering of religious leaders from all across the country: Maulana Wahiduddin Khan, the scholar and activist; Swami Chinmayananda Saraswati, founder of the Chinmaya Mission; Acharya Sushil Kumar Maharaj, the Jain Monk and crusader for global peace; Cardinal Simon Pimenta, a man who understood the diverse character of Bombay better than most (he used Marathi, his mother tongue, whenever possible, and wouldn't allow Catholic schools to be English-only); Lama Lobzang, who would go on to guide the International Buddhist Conference; and Nani Palkhivala, the lawyer and eminent jurist.

It was a sombre occasion, but joyous too, because everyone was so willing to reach out. Sometimes, that's all it takes.

I was about to find out how wrong I was.

~

March came around. I compèred a Sitara Devi concert at Nehru auditorium. On the 12th, I had a lunch meeting with Sailesh Kothari, editor of the *Economic Times*. I remember it very clearly. We were at Ménage-a-Trois, at the Oberoi. We had settled down and the food had just arrived when we heard an explosion.

Twelve of them, over the span of two hours, like a mouldy string of crackers, detonated to some staccato internal rhythm.

Here was the 'revenge' for the events of three months ago.

Chief Minister Sharad Pawar later admitted to lying about the thirteenth incident. A made-up explosion in a Muslim area, so that he could try and ward off the inevitable communal tension.

Try, he did. Succeed, he did not. Some kind of mask had been ripped off in December of 1992, and we would be haunted by Bombay's true face for the rest of our days.

~

I kept abreast – through friends and through Citizens for Peace. Within a week, I was travelling again, this time through the Northeast. Again, for the Mehta group. I saw some wonderful sights – the Salonah Tea Estate they had recently purchased, and a trip to Kaziranga National Park. But it felt like I was running away from something like the plague. Something that I had no control over, but which affected me directly, every day, in insidious ways.

Of all the small expeditions, the one that has stayed is my visit to the Tezpur Air Force Base. The former airport was converted to a base in 1959. Its geographic location makes it strategically important. But it was another of those places I'd heard about as a child and always wanted to visit. Like a life-sized stamp collection.

I thought about how much more innocent the world had seemed back them. How hope hadn't become a jaded commodity, made spurious by the inner workings of a republic. I felt like being Indian had become adulterated.

~

The pall lifted finally in April, when Ritchie arrived. This time, all of us went to The Retreat on Madh Island. No one wanted the hassle of making beds and cooking for a dozen people. And my mother got her first massage, ever.

Love, travel, war. Those old companions.

How odd that I, who had always shied away from family, now found comfort in their company. Just past my fiftieth birthday, maybe I *was* getting old.

Shudder the thought.

~

I made my first trip to East Africa in October 1993, courtesy the Mehta Group. This time, I was accompanied by Raju Bisht and Pramod Desai, both of whom worked for *Business India*. It was weirdly nostalgic in some ways. Gerson was in Kampala, on a UNICEF posting. We had dinner at Fasaki, which was the first Ethiopian meal I had in my life. The next night, we went to see Mira Nair because she lives in Uganda for some part of the year. After which, we finally began the drive to Kenya.

On the way to Nairobi, we stopped at Nakuru. This is one of the biggest cities in Kenya. And situated by Lake Nakuru, home to one of the largest concentrations of flamingos anywhere in the world. They say if enough birds take flight, the sky turns pink.

My connection to Nakuru was more personal. This is where my in-laws, Dilip's parents, were from. We had always meant to travel to see them but life intervened. I stepped out of the car and took a moment. I did my 'namaste' like a good Indian bride, and I was overwhelmed. It wasn't the ritual. It was distance – how far we've come, I thought. And so far yet to go. The world seemed, for a moment, an impossibly large place. Multitudes and multitudes, just trying to find their path and their place. So many stories, all happening at once. I felt small, like the child I'd once been.

~

The rest of the Kenyan sojourn was along more familiar lines. After ten days of eating vegetarian food with my travel companions, I made a beeline for the famous Carnivore restaurant where I ate zebra, crocodile and antelope. I also took the mandatory trip to Masai Mara. I didn't sleep a wink. Something scratched outside my tent all night. I was convinced it was a leopard. On the game drive, I saw a pride of thirty-nine lions, and two cheetahs as well. My only regret was not taking the balloon safari. It was just too expensive. I should have done it, but I didn't.

~

I also had the great honour of interviewing the current – the 12th – Tai Situpa Rinpoche, one of the oldest lineages of Lamas in the Kagyu school of Buddhism. I travelled with the scholar Dipankar Khanna to Himachal Pradesh.

On a visit to Beijing in 1954 in the company of the Dalai Lama, the sixteenth Karmapa had a vision about the Tai Situpa. He described, in great detail, the place of his birth, and his parents, along with a number of highly unusual signs – a rainbow and an earthquake. It was, therefore, relatively easy to find and identify the current incarnation.

As a young boy of five, the Tai Situpa left Tibet and lived in Bhutan and Sikkim. He had to move to Darjeeling for his health.

On his return, he lived at the Rumtek monastery until it was time for him to found his own monastic seat. This was the Sherab Ling Monastery in Himachal Pradesh, where we met him.

I lived with his family that first night. The next day, I witnessed the Tai Situpa and seven other Rinpoches perform a set of ceremonies. I met and spoke with him later that afternoon. He is an author and a scholar, and speaks fluent English. As a result, he has spent much of his life on teaching tours of Europe and the US, and translating Buddhist texts. He is also a tireless crusader for peace. He founded the Maitreya Institute in 1983, a forum where myriad approaches to spiritual development were explored with no specific focus on any one religion. And he had also set off on a Pilgrimage for Active Peace in 1989, meeting religious leaders and humanists around the world.

I was humbled and a little awed in his company. He was soft-spoken and gracious. I accompanied him to McLeod Ganj, 'Little Lhasa', and spent a couple of days there. Didn't get to meet His Holiness the Dalai Lama there, though.

That would happen in Bombay, in the year 2000. Friends of Tibet and the Tibetan Youth Congress organized a 'Festival of Tibet', spread across a week and multiple venues – the Y.B. Chavan Centre, the Birla Matoshree auditorium, the Museum and Prithvi theatre. It was a week of book launches, speeches, film screenings and dance performances.

I got to meet His Holiness just after his speech. He exuded a wonderful sense of calm. It was a packed house, so the organizers put out chairs in the aisles. I found myself sitting next to him. We didn't talk much, but I was enchanted by his laugh as he reacted to the events on stage. He laughed like a child – a big belly-laugh, just free and uninhibited.

I met him again a few months later at an open-air function – crowds of thousands this time. I shuffled up to say 'hullo' and was delighted that he remembered me. I was as chuffed as when I caught Pandit Nehru's garland. That thrill has remained the same, no matter my age.

23

TOWARDS THE END of April 1994, Quasar and I were involved in a hysterical endeavour. Boman Irani, always a marvellous actor but also a superb photographer and perhaps Bombay's finest potato-chip maker, was deputed by *Health & Nutrition Magazine* to take some pictures of the two of us exercising at home. This was complicated by the fact that neither of us owned any exercise gear! We bullshitted our way through it. What else was the theatre good for?

Quasar left for United World College, Singapore, in August, after he finished his tenth standard at Rishi Valley. It marked the first time that Alyque played a key role in shaping Quasar's life choices. At some point during the school years, one of Alyque's secretaries called me and said that he'd split the school fees with me. And, starting in 1989, Alyque visited Quasar at Rishi Valley. He approached the school and made his own arrangements. But Singapore was different, a very conscious change of direction. He did it at Titoo Ahluwalia's insistence. Both of Titoo's children had gone to UWC and he recommended it strongly. Alyque paid for the tuition and I paid for the air tickets.

When Quasar eventually graduated from UWC Singapore, a lot of big universities came calling, but Alyque couldn't pay for Quasar to go to an undergraduate programme in the West.

Did Quasar resent it? I don't know. I know I do.

I accompanied Quasar that first time. We took a stroll around Orchard Street, the night before he was scheduled to start school. It was bittersweet for me. It was the first time the two of us had been out of the country together. I was pleased that I could do these things for my son, and that I could be there with him. But he was also moving further away – I couldn't just go and sneak him away to Nrityagram. It was a mental thing, I guess. This time, there were visas and flights and oceans involved.

And he was older. I knew he'd begin to drift away from me. It was natural. I hated the thought a little.

~

After the events of December 1992, Basant invariably called every two months as he journeyed from Calcutta to Mauritius and back. We met for dinner.

When I travelled to Calcutta, I stayed in his guest house. He, his wife Savitri and I had dinner at the Calcutta Club.

Basant shared a lot of his insecurities with me. At some point, it became apparent that he considered me more than a friend. I was wary, but I did not want to cut him out of my life entirely.

I even travelled to Bhuyanpir Tea Plantation in Orissa with him. It was there our friendship cooled a little. We had an argument about the rights of women labourers, and I discovered how feudal his thinking was. An urbane exterior didn't always mean an evolved mind. That mood infected my return. I was less than pleased to learn that there were no direct flights from Bhubaneshwar to Bombay. I had to change aircraft at Nagpur airport. And as I was attempting to deplane, carrying my bags and muttering under my breath, a young couple approached me. They used to listen to *Glaxo Bonny Baby Time*, they said. And they were big fans. They then took my bags from me and marched into the terminal. Slightly mollified, I followed them and spent a pleasant layover chatting with them.

~

Basant eventually introduced me to his three charming sons – Pratap, Bharat and Rana (Siddharth, author and activist). And though I hadn't met Basant for twenty years, we remained friends till he passed away in Coonoor. I still keep in touch with Rana.

~

In the '90s, I did a lot of Hindi theatre. The first of these productions was *Ekshuff*, a translation of *Equus*. The show starred Shafi Inamdar and Feroze Abbas Khan. I played the barrister. I even did *Ek Do Teen* with Salim Shah.

When *Tumhari Amrita*, the Hindi adaptation of A.R. Gurney's *Love Letters* opened in 1992, it immediately became one of my favourite pieces of theatre. It featured Farooq Sheikh and Shabana Azmi. I watched every single show I could possibly manage. At one point, Shabana suggested they give me some kind of award for having sat through it so many times.

I worked on *Tum Kya Jano Preet* with Dinesh Thakur, an adaptation of *Pygmalion*. It ran for three years, and we travelled to Calcutta and Delhi. That production was a challenge. I had to light up three times during the show. I'd quit smoking six years before that, and I was scared that smoking on stage would be the start of a long slippery slope back to a filthy habit. I'm happy to report that I made it look very convincing in performance but didn't go back to smoking in life.

Dinesh remained a friend right up until his death. I think there was great fondness. There was respect and regard. But it was a formal relationship. We never became close in the way I did with other cast-mates and directors, dropping in and out of each other's houses. Distance played a part in this; he lived in the suburbs.

Dinesh was a few years younger than me. I have great affection for his wife, Preeta Mathur. She was a very hard-working actress, and she played the lead in almost everything that Dinesh directed. I found their style of performance a little dated, but I'm sure that people feel that way about me. I was also very fond of Dinesh's first wife Minakshi, who was a brilliant actress and a complete natural.

Even though I made it to SNDT in Juhu for Dinesh's rehearsals, I never convinced Satyadev Dubey to cast me in a play.

'*Dolly ko toh medal dena chahiye*,' he'd say, every time he saw me at Prithvi. I was the only one in that age group who was at Prithvi consistently. I'd find him, and I'd sit and watch whatever he was doing, whether it was a reading or a rehearsal.

He was a brilliant man. A fantastic teacher. One of the people who dragged theatre in Bombay into the twentieth century. He was an essential conduit as performances trickled down from the prosceniums to Prithvi and the Experimental at the NCPA, via Chabildas – the little school auditorium in Dadar that became the playground where Bombay theatre reinvented itself. Dubey was a maverick, an iconoclast. He delighted in wrecking convention, in sowing chaos. Naturally, I loved him.

For the longest time, he hated the English theatre. He hated what it represented. He thought it was an exercise for the privileged few, by the privileged few. He thought our choice of scripts were a symptom of our colonial hangover. He had Jan Sangh leanings and was a card-carrying member of the RSS, so that made sense. He thought our methods and practices had very little to do with the theatre in Bombay, or in India, or – in fact – reality. And everyone who did theatre in this city was, for him, an amateur. Because no one made their living from it. You couldn't call it the professional theatre.

Did he soften? Nah. Never.

Dubey raged right until the end. He began to work on English texts, yes. But he remained an old rascal, blowing up middle-class perceptions about art.

When Prithvi honoured him with a festival, they printed a bunch of tee-shirts. 'NSD', they said. National School of Dubey.

His ashes were scattered, in part, over the property of Prithvi. Which is just as it should be.

~

The tension between Hindi and English theatre wasn't imagined, although Dubey was a great one for imagined slights. It was only towards the late '90s that Indian writers started to bend the English language to reflect what we heard and spoke in everyday life. If nothing else, it brought down the ivory tower.

Is it over? Done? Have we achieved parity? Fixed everything?

No. Of course not. We must remember, at all times, that India is an unparalleled thought experiment. These many languages and cultures and traditions and ideas? It's unprecedented. It's never been attempted before in the history of civilization. So, it's going to take some doing.

But, like I said. It's better than it ever was.

Mohan Agashe, recipient of the Thespo for Lifetime Achievement in 2017, said something interesting. 'When you work in English,' he said during his acceptance speech, 'it's international. When you work in Hindi, it's national. But, when you work in Marathi ...' – he paused – 'it's regional.'

I don't know how one fights this perception. That it exists is a fact.

I watch so much modern work, in so many languages, that is vital, and urgent, and topical and utterly unique. I feel like theatre in this day and age is remaking itself in new and interesting ways, in *arresting* ways. Both formally and in the stories it seeks to tell. And yet, good work gets pushed further and further towards the margins. It's a problem worldwide.

~

Somewhere in my diaries, towards the end of February 1995 it says, 'With all this travel, went straight to hospital to spend the night with Daddy.'

Daddy was discharged on the 6th of March. I can't even remember what it was – something relatively minor, I think. I remember the date because Jalal Agha died on the 5th. Heart attack. In Delhi. He was just fifty years old. Slightly younger than I was.

The actress Sarika and I, two of his closest friends, were at the airport to receive the body. We took it to the morgue at Cooper Hospital. The funeral was on the 6th. Even then, it was a whirlwind.

Got Daddy home, and picked up Jalal's son Saleem from the airport. Always rushed, time slipping away, away, away.

And just as I thought I had it bad, I travelled to Madras with Paul Stephens and Waris Hussein to meet Kamal Haasan. Waris was attached to direct *Such a Long Journey* at the time. Kamal said no – he was too busy for the next few years!

~

By 1996, Quasar was back in Bombay and a student at St. Xavier's College. And while I remained as busy as ever, I exhaled a little. My child had been away from home for almost eight years, and it was good to have him back.

Almost inevitably, my life began to drift a little – not driven on relentlessly any longer – towards the last, long bend in the river. The pace slowed. I was no longer paddling madly.

'Autumn,' reads a quote in my diary, courtesy William Cullen Bryant. 'The year's last, loveliest smile.'

The casting work slowly began to slip away. It wasn't deliberate. I'd always functioned in a niche. I never cast for Hindi cinema. Well, only *Deham* for Govind Nihalani. Back then, casting wasn't taken very seriously. It was always about dates and who was popular, who 'sold' and the rest were either a gallery of the usual suspects or friends and relatives of the people on the unit.

I haven't cast in about twenty years. I still get phone calls, though. They're usually of a sort:

'*Dollyji, hum Saurashtra se bol rahe hain. Hume do solah saal ki ladki chahiye …*'

Things like that. No script. I find polite ways to hang up.

For a newer generation of filmmakers, I was no longer the cutting edge. I didn't agree, but it wasn't my decision to make.

In June of 1996, one of the last projects I cast also became one of my favourites. Waris Hussein had dropped out of *Such a Long Journey* and was now attached to *Sixth Happiness*. Based on the book *Trying to Grow* by Firdaus Kanga, it was a heartwarming story of a young Parsi boy born with brittle bone disorder (his mother calls him 'Brit' because of this and because, well, she's Parsi). It was a coming-of-age tale. Also, how does someone who grows to a full four feet in height negotiate love and sex? And being attracted to both sexes?

It was beautifully told, with a series of glorious performances. Firdaus played the lead himself. It was a small film, but I was glad to be involved.

~

In 1997, tragedy struck. Protima's twenty-three-year-old son Siddharth died in Los Angeles. She was completely broken. But I was astonished by how she handled it. I went to see her off at the airport. She was surrounded by a media circus and a stream of well-meaning people who only wanted to offer their condolences. All they did was remind her of her loss, over and over.

I would have fled. Or struck out. Protima simply closed her eyes and meditated for a few seconds at a time. Again and again, she emerged from these little trances refreshed, able to accept sympathies and questions. Her grace under pressure was just short of miraculous. I saw how her inner peace had become a weapon.

Back in 1982, after Alyque left, Protima had advised vipassana for me. I never had the guts to do it then, the ten days in isolation and silence. I didn't want to go to Igatpuri, and I didn't know if I could afford it. I thought I'd have to hire a car and that it was expensive. Later, I paid a hundred and twenty-eight rupees in train fare and discovered that you could donate what you felt like. Plus, I'd heard all sorts of stories about drugs and the like. It was easy to say 'no' because I'd already made up my mind.

Watching Protima at the airport washed away the last of my doubts. I applied the very next day. Everyone warned me about a long waiting period but luck, it seems, was on my side. I was asked to report three weeks later.

Having gone the distance, I surrendered completely. I followed every rule: no reading or writing, no non-vegetarian food, no pills or alcohol, I bathed at the appointed times, no talking or eye contact, and no religious rituals. If anything, I fell into it as if I'd been waiting for an experience like this my whole life.

When I left ten days later, I wept and wept. I had a sense of clarity I'd never had before, of having been pared down to my essential self. I felt calm, untethered, balanced. I felt light, like I'd been purified.

I shared this with Protima. She wanted us to book ourselves into a session six months hence.

In February of 1998, Protima and I were given a room together. When I asked for my own room, like my previous visit, I was politely informed that we were 'serious practitioners'.

Protima had been through too great a tragedy to be able to observe all the rules. I allowed her to talk to me and reciprocated only by listening. On the eighth day, Protima told me she had carried magic mushrooms from America and that they elevated meditation to a sublime state of being.

We were allowed to speak after lunch on the ninth day, to be able to share our experiences. I agreed to try a single mushroom. Up until then, I'd only ever taken a drag or two from a joint. There's no one else I'd rather have shared that experience with.

As advertised, that last trance was divine.

~

Such a Long Journey finally began filming, with Sturla Gunnarsson as the director.

Later that month, I travelled to Shirdi as a guest of Sahara. They wanted me to see and perhaps market Aamby Valley, the township they had created as a luxury lifestyle getaway. It was located about twenty kilometres away from Lonavala, and I was delighted when they insisted I bring the kids from the Balgram. We had a fantastic weekend.

A couple of years after that, they took fifteen of my friends there for my birthday. We flew out by helicopter, and we were there for two nights. They organized a band and everything. It was all a bit much – a glimpse of the superstar lifestyle. Best enjoyed and forgotten. You couldn't get used to that. That would be asking for trouble.

~

In April 1998, Protima set off for the Himalayas. Siddharth's death had caused some subtle, fundamental shift in her. She had been slowly handing over her responsibilities at Nrityagram. She had also suffered a minor heart attack. None of the effects were debilitating or permanent but, for her, the signs had begun to pile up. She had always been a relentless seeker, and she felt that pull again. She was drawn to the mountains and, in particular, Lake Manasarovar – the axial point of four great rivers and four religions.

~

On the 27th of April 1998, I started writing this book in earnest, picking up the jottings from 1982 and trying to put them in coherent order. On the 30th, Protima left for Bangkok. She returned on the 9th of May and came straight to my house. She spent the night and left for Juhu the next morning, like she'd done a million times before.

And would again, surely. Like breathing.

~

Protima and I had dinner on the 14th of May. I came home and made a note about how much I disliked chapter four of my book.

Somewhere in the first week of August, Protima left for the Himalayas. I hadn't seen her since that dinner, but we'd been on the phone every other day.

I spoke to her again on 10 August. She was in Batch #12 for the Kailash Manasarovar Yatra.

~

At 3 a.m. on the morning of the 18th, there was a landslide that wiped away the entire village of Malpa, where the pilgrims had halted for the night. There had been a landslide on the 16th – in truth, actually the beginning of seismic activity that would last until the 21st – and three mules had died.

But this is India. Everyone ignored it.

Two hundred and twenty-one people were lost. Amongst them, sixty pilgrims.

Amongst them, well …

It was one of the worst landslides India has ever experienced. I know several people who lost family members.

Quasar and I rushed to Juhu on the 18th, to be with Pooja, Protima's daughter. On the 20th, Protima's sisters Bulbul and Mona, and Pooja and her husband Farhan, and Lynne and I flew to Bareilly. We then travelled to Dharchula, the base of the relief operations and the only place we could access the search-and-rescue helicopters. We were informed that the chopper could only accommodate two people after all of us showed up. So, Bulbul and Lynne took the helicopter ride.

We found Protima's passport and handbag a few days later, amongst several bodies. But we never saw her again. The mountain had claimed her. It was, perhaps, as she had wished.

~

On the 20th of September, I held a memorial for Protima at the All Saints Church followed by lunch for sixty people at my place. It was the best I could do until I see her again.

Her family has become my extended family. I'm very close to Pooja. She has her own life. She lives in Goa now. Her kids are grown up and working.

Total honesty and openness – that's what Protima and I gave each other. And I've never found it again in the same way.

24

I WAS INVITED to join the Rotary Club of Bombay in 2002. I was glad, and I've enjoyed my association with them. But here's *why* I was invited to join them.

They had an art auction, and they had a target of eight lakh. I managed to raise twenty-four lakh. There was a small Sabavala, an etching, with a base price of eight thousand. I got Nikhil Khatau to buy it for three times that much.

When and how did *that* happen?

I'd known Devika Bhojwani since *Jesus Christ Superstar*. Back then, she was a young girl with such a beautiful voice that Alyque had an original song composed for her, the only deviation from the West End score. She'd been a friend since, and one of the greatest pillars of support for Quasar and myself.

Devika called in early 1990. She was raising funds for the renovation of the Elephanta Caves. She wanted to auction art as part of that initiative. Guests would get on a boat from the Gateway of India and make the short trip to Elephanta and attend the auction there. A bespoke experience. Would I be interested in being the auctioneer?

I'd never done anything remotely like it. So, of course, I said 'yes'. And then I sat down and did some hurried research. I think I was the first person in India who auctioned art on a regular basis. This was before Sotheby's and Christie's came to town, and before Neville Tulli responded in kind with Osian's.

~

I first encountered the name 'Francis Souza' in London. A colleague at the BBC mentioned that he was her son-in-law. Until then, I had never heard of this enfant terrible of the art world. I interviewed him for the World Service.

In Bombay, Samovar became our second home, and we were suddenly 'in' with the art crowd. That's when I started collecting. Every single artwork that hangs on my walls has a story to tell. It belongs to a time in my life. Quasar calls it my art gallery, which is correct because my bedroom is my library.

~

Anjolie Ela Menon and I once shared a taxi home at 2 a.m., after the Times of India Sesquicentennial Anniversary Special Art Exhibition on the platform of Victoria Terminus. We were just talking, and I mentioned that though I was a fan, I didn't own any of her work. A painting had hung on my wall, yes. But that was Alyque's. When I dropped her home, she asked me to wait and ran up three flights of stairs because the lift wasn't working. She returned minutes later, out of breath, and handed me an 18" x 12" canvas of Christ's head.

'It's still wet,' she said. 'Leave it out for seven days and then frame it.'

I duly left it in my kitchen loft as I was leaving town at 7 a.m. the next day. When I returned, I had it framed at Chemould, and it has occupied pride of place on my wall ever since.

In 1993, Husain gave me a painting from his *Mother and Son* series because Alyque took his Husain with him. Husain, the artist, just asked me to pick the canvas I liked. We'd known each other for years. So, I did. Once at home, I realized it was unsigned. I mentioned this to him when we met at a book launch, three years later. He insisted on accompanying me home and then drew out his large brush and signed the canvas in front of Quasar and myself.

A group of women, all friends, including Indu Sen, started an Affordable Art Enterprise at the Artists Centre in Rampart Row, Kala Ghoda. The goal was to encourage young buyers of art. Every canvas on display was priced under 10,000 rupees. I spotted a two-and-a-half-foot painting of a raging bull in retreat and bought it immediately. I believe it changed the energy in my home the moment I hung it on the wall.

I grew to enjoy auctioneering very much. It was another job that married my interests. Before every auction, I studied the catalogue. I knew every entry, every work that was up for sale and I knew about the creator – what they'd done, why they'd done it, the medium, the choice of colours, whether it was mixed media, whether it was on canvas, whether it was a lithograph or a serigraph …

As for the auctioneering, I didn't have any formal training but my years in the theatre served me well. The job was the same – to get my (unknowing) co-actors, the attendees, to want something I had. My research helped me make the object in question as desirable as possible, a slow drip of facts, myths and features. You had to start small, the starting price *just* out of reach, slightly impractical but not nonsensical. And then you drove it up, little by little.

The highest I ever managed was 1.62 crore for a Raja Ravi Verma, at a time before crores became common franchise. That wasn't the most satisfying auction I ever had, though. That honour goes to the one for the Rotary Club of Bombay.

My interest in art deepened over the years. Some of it, like with Anjolie Ela Menon, were due to random acts of kindness. My orthopaedic specialist, Dr Farhad Taraporevala was a great collector. Suddenly one day, without any warning, he gifted me two lithographs by that rare genius Raja Ravi Verma; works that would have been way beyond my means.

I went to Delhi to auction for Nina Pillai at one point. Nina was the widow of Rajan Pillai – India's erstwhile 'Biscuit King'. After his death, Nina reinvented herself as an impossibly glamorous patron of the arts. I've auctioned for the Indian Merchant's Chamber. Pritish Nandy and I handled the auction for Richard Gere at the Oberoi, raising funds for AIDS Awareness. That was a huge event held in the Regal Room at the Oberoi, a rarefied, glitzy blend of social awareness and star power. Sanjay Dutt was in attendance and we managed to whip the bidding into a frenzy.

White people came, the big auction houses. First, they brought other white people and then they trained Mallika Sagar, who's very,

very good and who was much, much younger. She was Christie's first Indian auctioneer at the age of twenty-six.

Now, of course, no one can sell anything to anyone unless it's fronted by a Bollywood star or a cricketer. It was fun while it lasted. It allowed me to engage with one of my great passions while getting paid for it.

~

I launched Sudha Murthy's book, *Wise and Otherwise: A Salute to Life*, somewhere around 2002. It was at the old Crossword Bookstore, as far as I remember, the original one near the Mahalaxmi Temple. Sudha, of course, is the better half of Infosys. She's a remarkable woman. An engineer and the chairperson of the Infosys Foundation, which has done so much for social upliftment since its inception. She's also a prolific author in two languages – her native Kannada and English. The book in question was a quite lovely series of (I think) fifty-one vignettes of people she had met, and stories she had gathered in the course of social work.

So, of course, our little encounter resulted in another story.

We were both early. We finished checking whatever we had to check and seeing whatever we had to see. And we sat, waiting for the guests and the press to arrive, and we chatted.

Sudha ended up telling me about how the company – one of the largest IT firms in the world – came to be called Infosys. And, as with the best stories, that wasn't the big takeaway.

A very long time ago, Sudha and her husband went to a branch of the Bank of Baroda to ask for a loan to start the business. They arrived at the bank at 10 in the morning and were asked to come back at 3. They decided that they didn't want the hassle of going home and returning again in the afternoon, so they found a nearby park and sat underneath the tree and wondered what they'd call their company, if the branch manager asked.

Eventually, they came up with the name: Infosys. It was elegant – an amalgam of 'Information' and 'Systems'.

They went into their meeting and made their presentation. The manager asked if they had collateral. They didn't. And that was the meeting.

On their way out, at the door, Sudha had a flash of understanding about what their futures might be. She turned back.

'We *do* have collateral,' she called out to the manager. 'Our brains.' And she pointed to her husband, and then to herself.

The rest, as they say, was history.

~

In 2004, I worked on *Dance Like a Man* with Pamela Rooks. It was the last real casting job I had. Stray phone calls and recommendations continue, but that was it. There had been others in the '90s – *The Far Pavilions* and *Train to Pakistan*, but they were both standard fare.

We auditioned Arif Zakaria for *Dance Like a Man*. Pamela liked him but wasn't convinced.

'I wish,' she said, 'there was a way we could see his legs. He *is* playing a dancer.'

We were in my sitting room, where most of these films and TV shows were cast. I turned towards Arif expectantly.

Poor boy nodded and stripped down to his briefs.

That showed real commitment, I thought.

Later, I'd go on to direct Arif in a reading of Meher Pestonji's *Feeding Crows*.

~

The late '90s and early aughts were a surprisingly busy time for me, as an actor. In 1996, I was in *The Bacchae*, directed by Zubin Driver. I also continued a string of associations: *Keely and Du* with Janak Toprani, and *Sister Like You* with Jiten Merchant. I worked on *Antigone*. And in February 1997, I was in *Shikara*, an adaptation of *Of Mice and Men*, with Denzil Smith, Gary Richardson, Aly Khan and a very young Vivek Oberoi. The year 1998 would add to that tally – by chance, there was almost a retrospective, with the additions of *Gossamer Gyre* directed by Sujoy Sood from the US, and *Electra* with Jiten Merchant. And then, in 2001, *Taking Sides*, again with Jiten.

And in 2004, I came back to Harold Pinter's *The Birthday Party*, directed by Arghya Lahiri.

When Alyque directed me in the play in 1971 or 1972, I played Lulu, a twenty-six-year-old ingénue. Alyque saw her as an over-sexed kitten, in a short skirt and spaghetti straps. Thirty-two years later, I played the sixty-year-old Meg, the befuddled owner of the shabby little boarding house where all the action occurs. In contrast to Lulu, who thrust herself at every passing man, Meg was scandalized by the word 'succulent'. I was just thrilled to have experienced either side of the spectrum of that puzzling, hypnotic text.

Universality in the theatre is a hard-won thing. It seems easy, but for a play to stand the test of time, it needs to have something that resonates across its lifespan. And that's mostly what ordinary men and women want, and need, and fight for.

So, when I look back, which ones do I remember?

Death of a Salesman for one. I played Linda, opposite Alyque. Vijay Crishna and Ronnie Screwvala played my sons. We didn't adapt the play to India, as Satish Kaushik did with *Salesman Ramlal.* Our production followed the original text. And yet, there was not a dry eye in the house at the end of the play. We watched an ordinary man slowly crushed by the system. In one final heroic act, he makes the ultimate sacrifice for his family.

I felt like I understood that role, wholly. I understood what drove Linda to protect her man from the outside world and from his sons. She wasn't a stretch for me.

That last speech – '… why did you do it? I search and search and I search and I can't understand it …' – still rings in my heart and my head.

And I understand the pain I wrought in Pearl.

I remember exiting after that speech. Three-year-old Quasar would be waiting in the wings, and he'd hug me tight.

'Don't worry, Mama,' he'd say. 'I'll look after you.' He needed to remind me that I had him, even if my on-stage husband had died.

We did twenty-five shows. When Alyque revived the play a few years ago, he cast Sabira Merchant. In spite of everything that had happened, all the spilt milk, I was pissed off when he cast Sabira. That role was mine. We had worked together after he left me. I performed an extract of *Salesman* for the launch of his autobiography. We did some readings of Shakespeare. I thought it would've been right to cast me.

~

By way of the generational baton transfer, in 2001 Quasar directed me in *All My Sons*, also by Arthur Miller.

Time zones had changed. I was much older. And the approach to the theatre was very different. We'd start rehearsal at 9 in the evening. A lot of the kids in the cast had jobs. Everyone was always tired. We got to work tired. And Quasar and I clashed a lot. I was used to a different way of working. His rehearsals started with stretching and vocal warms-ups. I just wanted to pick up the script and go, get on stage and look at the scenes. I had worked like that for decades. And the more I struggled with it, the more I wished for the tried and tested.

That's how they work in the West. Actors report in the afternoon. They warm up. They get notes from the previous performance – things that were good, things they can better, things they might consider. The crew runs all their checks: costumes, sets, props, lighting, sound. It's a slow build-up to a show. This is what they do. This is their day at the office.

As opposed to the manic lurch to a show *that we somehow pull off by the skin of our teeth*, which is the norm here.

That said, I would have loved to work with Quasar again.

I suppose it's easier when you have an extended run. Not when you have one show every few weeks or months.

On my last trip to London, I was at the National, poring over their schedule, when I looked up. And there, on a poster, was Harish Patel. He was a Gujarati stage actor, who was in film and television a lot.

I wondered what the hell Harish Patel was doing in London, on a poster at the National? The answer, of course, was staring me in the face. He was in *Rafta Rafta*, directed by Meera Sayal. So, I went to watch it. It's a funny show: two families, a wedding, a great many misunderstandings, that sort of thing. I sent him a note to let him know I was in the audience. He sent a note back. Come backstage after the show, it said, and we'll get dinner after.

'*Dollyji, yahan to mitti-paleet kar dete hain yeh log*,' he said. The National had given him a flat. He didn't cook much, but he lived a simple life. Not that he had much time for adventure. He was in at 11 in the morning, every single day. The National even flew his family down to visit three times because he was there, ultimately, for about three years. The show ran six days a week, Mondays excepted. They had matinees three times a week. And he made enough money to allow him to move to England for three years, away from film and television jobs in at least two languages.

Ah, state-funding.

But that *is* the dream. That's what the life of a professional actor could be. I don't know if I had that kind of staying power. Also, I would've been bored to tears.

~

Sabira and I shared the stage in *A Streetcar Named Desire*, the Tennessee Williams classic. She had the author-backed role, the centrepiece. She played Blanche Dubois, and I played Stella opposite Dalip Tahil's Stanley Kowalski. Stella was quiet and timid, and utterly secure in her relationship. It's a bit of a thankless part because it's foil to two elemental characters.

Saby had all the rave reviews. But I thought I did well – it was a solid, technical, heartfelt performance. It didn't call attention to itself. Balwant Gargi, the critic and director, who later started the Chandigarh Drama School sent me a long letter of appreciation after he watched the show. It meant a great deal to me.

Our tilts at the classics remain my fondest memories. Mostly because we stumbled onto *what* made those plays so powerful. *Inherit the Wind*, *Look Back in Anger*, *Who's Afraid of Virginia Woolf?* All those plays have stayed relevant through the decades, adapted to changing scenarios in other languages.

I remember Alyque's version of *Julius Caesar*, soon after the emergency, in which Caesar was a woman. Usha Katrak played the lead. I played Portia. Gerson was Brutus, Pat Sharma was Marc Anthony and Alyque played Cassius.

The theatre, and life itself, moves in circles. Some of those plays became constants and touchstones: *Inherit the Wind*, that polemic about free speech and free thinking, was the first play my son directed; *Who's Afraid of Virginia Woolf?* is what Dilip and I might have become if we'd stayed … if we'd stayed in the same house.

~

Being on stage for such a long time means I get asked to be on juries. I serve on the selection committee for the Academy of Theatre Arts, Mumbai University. We review auditions, and discuss the respective merits of the applicants. That led to an invitation to be on the selection panel for the National School of Drama, Western Region. And that, in turn, led to an invitation to sit on the selection committee of the Bharat Rang Mahotsav, the NSD festival and the Theatre Olympics. It sounds fancy, and I consider it a great honour. But it's also a lot of work. There's anywhere between three to four hundred entries from all over India and a handful of foreign applications. About fifteen of us are split into five juries, on the basis of language. I mostly deal with English and Hindi productions. Sometimes I'm asked to serve on the committee for foreign productions. Most of the applications are on DVD or on video links. And then, on the last day, we sit down to pick the seventy-two-odd productions that comprise the festival, across the six auditoria. Quality trumps everything else, but we're also keen on a diverse range of work.

A couple of years ago, I got asked to serve on the judging panel for the Mahindra Excellence in Theatre Awards (META). We watched the shortlisted plays and debated nominations and winners.

Jury duty enables a key component of my life – watching new work. I don't have the energy or, frankly, the means to watch new work like I used to when I was younger. Jury duty means that, even at my age, with its accompanying little indignities, I'm still able to stay abreast of what's going on.

25

COMPARATIVELY LATE INTO my acting career, the film business came calling. In the 80s', the National Association for the Blind (NAB) used to take a whole train to Pune for the races, and I was very closely involved with NAB at the time. Dilip Kumar, Saira Banu, Soni Razdan and Mahesh Bhatt were on the train, and Mahesh spoke to me. He was an established director by then.

'I'm doing a film called *Naam*,' he said. 'Will you act in it?'

Act in a Hindi film? Me? A Delhi University snob? You must be joking!

I said 'no'. And he went ahead and cast Nutan. It was a peach of a role.

~

But Dolly still didn't learn her lesson. Dev Anand asked me to act in *Gambler*, and I said 'no'. That part went to Rekha. So, when

Jagmohan Mundra came calling for *Bawandar*, three weeks in Rajasthan in September 1999, I said 'yes!' straight away.

Three-and-a-half months later, they called on the 18th of December and asked if I could leave for Rajasthan *the next day*.

'You must be joking,' I said. I'd heard nothing for months. And I'd agreed to host a New Year's Eve show at the Race Course for ALERT India (Association for Leprosy Education, Rehabilitation and Treatment).

So, of course, someone else got the part.

~

I didn't think I was destined to be an actress in Hindi cinema. Until I got a call from Madhur Bhandarkar in 2004.

'Dolly, we're shooting at Mukesh Mills. Drop by if you can.'

I had a show of *The Vagina Monologues* at the NCPA that evening.

'But I'll be done by 8.30,' I told him. 'I'll call you after that.'

I called him post-show and asked if I should come. He said, no, we haven't started yet. So, off I went to the Dutch Consul-General's cocktail party on Altamont Road. I left there at 9.30 and made my way to Mukesh Mills. They were shooting a song, some sort of cabaret. They filmed me standing around, watching the performance. Madhur came up to me.

'Will you say something for the camera?' he asked.

'Sure,' I said.

So he got me to say 'truck driver song' while watching the performance. And that was that, I thought. I had a good time, I was treated well and I got to say a line.

Two days later, I got another phone call.

'Madam, there is shooting, please come.'

'You must be joking,' I said. I was being serious.

That 'little walk-on' turned into ten days of work.

Fifteen years later, I still get recognized at airports. People repeat my lines back to me – 'truck driver song' and 'show me something in white' from *Page 3*, which continues to run unabated on television.

That's when I began to understand the ubiquity, the all-pervasiveness of Bollywood in this country.

Thus, I had a bizarre little postscript to tag onto my myriad careers. I did *White Noise* for Vinta Nanda, with Rahul Bose and my old friend Partap Sharma. Pat played my husband. And then I hit, quite literally, the older actress 'mother'-lode. A daily soap for Balaji: *Kya Hoga Nimmo Ka*, in 2006. I played the grandmother, the matriarch of a family involved in a bewildering range of shenanigans. I had a blast. It was hard work, but fun. I liked the people I was working with. And Ekta and her team *really* looked after me. I was picked up and dropped home every single day, and they pampered me silly. I hoped it would turn into one of those gargantuan soaps that ran for years and years, but it never did. With the time-jumps that are in vogue, they would've probably had to kill off my character.

There have been bits and pieces since. I did a film for Raman Bharadwaj where I played a tarot-card reader. That never released. And I did *Mittal vs. Mittal* for my friend Karan Razdan. I liked the script, but the final product fell a little short of the mark. I've shot a pilot for a web series. I'll try anything really.

I find acting on screen easier now. I can't remember lines like I used to. I could look down at my cue card, in the days before teleprompters, and scan six or eight lines at once. That's why I looked natural reading the news. In the late '90s and early aughts, I discovered I couldn't do it anymore. Lines were difficult to remember. If it wasn't the lines, the order would shift about. More than anything else, it made me unsure and that's the worst thing that can happen to an actor.

I prefer readings now. And the security of takes.

I wouldn't rule out a play, though. All you need is ask.

~

Around 2000, Pat Sharma put me in touch with Lucky Dissanayake. She was an enterprising young Sri Lankan woman who was an early specialist in the dotcom space and started a publishing business in her spare time. She's a bit like that. It became apparent to her that the publishing world was a safer bet, so she sold her flat and invested the money in Dakini Books.

We worked together on a Bollywood coffee-table book that launched in 2002. She has become one of my closest friends. She's one of those restless, driven people who simply refuse to believe that there are limits on anything they can accomplish. I've never sought that type out actively, but I'm drawn to them like a moth to a flame.

In 2011, she launched a Biomass firm in her home country of Sri Lanka, inspired by a book she published on global warming. They have become pioneers in the field of renewable, sustainable energy, at the forefront of a greener, better way of living in countries that lack the resources of the First World. As I said, she's a bit like that.

For a while, I worked with Dakini Books. And that is what enabled my trip to England in 2007. I was able to make my dates coincide with Quasar's. At the time, he was working as the assistant director on *A Midsummer Night's Dream*, helmed by Tim Supple.

They travelled the world with that play, and I was lucky enough to see it on three different continents over the years.

But this visit was special.

~

It's been interesting to watch Quasar grow as a theatre person. The first time he was on stage was in kindergarten. I thought he was better than everyone else. Speaking as a critic, of course, and not his mother. He was in *The Glass Menagerie* at Rishi Valley when he was a teen. He played Tom, the narrator, the brother who got away. People still mention that performance to me.

In 1992, Deepa Mehta was making a television series called *Young Indy* – young Indiana Jones travels the world, meeting all sorts of historical figures. Deepa was very keen on casting Quasar as J. Krishnamurthy for the show. We even flew down to Bangalore to meet him. Eventually, she cast someone else. Quasar had an aptitude for both cricket and the theatre. He took cricket much more seriously, and I think it came more naturally to him. When he was in Singapore, he took theatre as a subject. He found the right teachers there. It had to have helped to be out of India. Here, both his parents were 'experts' and that must have weighed on him.

We only started talking theatre after he came back from Singapore. The first year at Xavier's, he acted in *The Crucible*, directed by Rehaan Engineer. And then he directed his first two plays: *Inherit the Wind* and *The Night Thoreau Spent in Jail.* Those conversations, the first we ever had about the theatre, were between practitioners. He wanted to talk staging. He wanted a bouncing board. And that was when he first asked me to come and watch his rehearsals about a week before opening night. I gave him and his cast feedback. Those remain some of the proudest moments of my life. I'm thrilled that he continues to call on me before opening every play, to this day. Something about that is just … perfect. It's our thing. We are mother and son. But we also share the theatre.

~

In 2007, in London, I lived with Quasar and some of the cast and crew at Scala House in Tottenham Court Road. They were playing at the Roundhouse.

Work done, I could give free rein to the things that mean London to me: theatre, theatre and more theatre.

But before that, I had one afternoon I will cherish for the rest of my life. Quasar could report late, so I took him on a tour of what used to be my beat: Chelsea Manor Gardens, Seymour Street, Sydney Place, and Sloane Square and High Street Kensington and Marble Arch and the Chelsea Potter Pub, the place where I had my first drink in England, still standing after all these years, much like me.

I don't know what Quasar made of it. Nostalgia, although I don't have much time for it, seems to be such an essential part of growing older. It also seeps into memory. These were my places, my spots. This, I told Quasar, was where I grew up.

And the distance I'd covered seemed incredible. From a young woman who'd never dreamt that she'd live and work outside of the country of her birth, to a woman walking the same paths with an almost thirty-year-old son.

I was overwhelmed, in the best way. It was bittersweet, because of a past that I couldn't ever have back again, and a future that I could not – did not – know. A future that would have its share of heartbreak. But that moment was perfect, and I was glad I was there with my son.

Things come a circle, and sometimes it's like going home.

~

The magic that has populated so much of my life stubbornly refuses to run out. I could call it chance, but I don't think that does it justice.

On my journeys in and out of Scala House during that time, I passed the Wyndham Theatre. I was a little startled to find Jenny Seagrove's name on the billboard, starring in a revival of Somerset Maugham's *The Letter*. Jenny and I worked together on *Miss Beatty's Children*. Jenny had come to film in Ooty. In the '80s, Jenny had been married to Madhav Sharma, an old actor friend from the days when we'd all been struggling extras scrounging for parts on British television.

They had an up-and-down marriage and an acrimonious divorce, but those little details, knowing each other's contexts, meant that Jenny and I became friends.

I sent word that I was in the house and promptly got a message asking me to meet her after the show.

We were very glad to see each other and hugged warmly. And before I had a chance to ask if she'd like to have dinner or a coffee, things took a turn for the surreal. It turns out that Jenny's partner was a man by the name of Bill Kenwright, the producer of the show, one of the West End's great impresarios and the chairman of Everton Football Club.

I was whisked away, absorbed into this high-powered little party. I was dressed in something totally ordinary, had no idea where the hell we were going or, indeed, what the plan was.

But when has that ever bothered me?

Bill treated us to a beautiful, hideously expensive dinner. The wine and the conversation flowed. Just when I thought things were winding down, and that I'd have to figure a way to get home, we finished the meal and Bill led us to a very exclusive casino near Hyde Park.

I went along. A man like Bill is impossible to say 'no' to. And I was having too much fun. This, one didn't get a lot of in Bombay.

My luck must have rubbed off on him because he won big. Big enough to lavish – purely as a gift – a thousand pounds on each and every member of that dinner and gambling party.

Jenny and Bill dropped me home at 2 in the morning. Quasar was pacing up and down, worried that I'd finally gotten lost, something I had threatened to do since my early twenties but that had never come to pass. Some of the people he was living with had known me for over ten years, friends of his from college and the theatre in Bombay. They were awake along with him, worried about Dolly Aunty.

And in she waltzed, grinning hugely, waving around a thousand pounds, having collected another story.

The kids had a cast party or something a few days after that, and I insisted on paying for as much of it as I could. That was Mummy and Daddy – the windfall had to be shared. I don't think I would have ended up in that casino if I hadn't fully embraced that dictum.

~

Kris Srinivasan and I had stayed in touch over the years. Ever so often, there'd be a furious exchange of letters and then weeks and months of silence.

When Alyque and I were living together, Kris passed through Bombay on a tour of India. By then, it was obvious that he was being groomed for bigger things at work.

I went to see him at the Taj. Alyque dropped me off. Within minutes, I had kicked off my shoes and was lying on the bed, chatting with him. I'd always been comfortable around him. We'd spent so much time together over the years. He drank copious amounts of gin, even during the day, and he paced. He paced around the bed again and again, which amused me. Finally, he stopped and looked at me.

'Dolly, I have to tell you … I'm getting married.'

My first reaction was to burst into tears. It wasn't love, or anything daft like that. It was possessiveness. He was *my* special friend.

'Why didn't you tell me?' he kept asking. 'That I meant something to you?'

How to tell him? That a long series of coincidences had prevented us from ever wanting the same thing at the same time? Or sharing confidences?

We had bad timing. That was it.

He got married. Letters came, letters went. Short, intense bursts.

I saw him, in 2017, at the IIC when I was in Delhi for some work. We said 'hullo' but that was about it. I saw him again in 2020 and we do stay in touch. But it's not like it was before. That's true of so much now. All around me, things continue to end, in a whimper.

26

I HAVE THESE constellations of memories: some bright, some not so much, some twinkling. Together, they form the shape of my life, etched out against the sky. If you're ever up somewhere where the sky is clear, really clear, and you look up, it takes your breath away.

And in memory, everything seems to happen to music. Tennessee Williams said that.

I don't often look back. It's not a part of how I approach my life. I've always been a doer, and I've always looked forward. Perhaps to my detriment. But contemplation is not a natural state of being for me. Even this book, in many ways, is a protest. I do it because it *should* be done. I do it for my son. I do it because time, like my Nani taught me, so long ago, is to be used. Always.

Yet, in March 2016, as I returned from the north Indian leg of the Laadli National Media Awards, I was in an oddly reflective mood. Some of it was that I'd started work on this book. And some of it was the experience of the day before.

The event in Delhi, just like the event in Mumbai, had been a tremendous success. Houseful, with people sitting in the aisles at the Islamic Centre. An evening of terrific stories, people recounting their experiences on the frontlines. It feels odd to be talking of gender sensitivity like a war. But it's a serious enterprise, and it takes considerable gumption and imagination. And charm helps.

I found myself being sought out by a lot of the journalists from smaller towns. They all wanted a photograph with me. I didn't mind the attention – I seldom do. But I was intrigued. I used to be on television, yes. And on radio. But that was a very long time ago. Longer than some of the awardees have been alive.

And yet, those few hours were gratifying and a little mystifying. The requests. The photograph with the awardee that made the front page of a newspaper. Being recognized in the lobby the next morning. Enough to make me sit back on the return flight and ask: How the hell did I get here?

~

I met Bobby Sista in the '70s. He conscripted me into hosting a series of awards and events – the Young Professional Business Awards, the

International Press Institute Programme, most of which used to be held at the Taj. We've been friends since. He ran a successful outfit called Sistas, which he later sold to Saatchi & Saatchi in 1998.

He sold the business, in part, because he wanted to dedicate all his time to social causes, a trait that seems to run through a lot of the successful men of that vintage. Dr A.L. Sharda, who's the director of Population First, the NGO that Bobby launched in 2002, once said that Bobby 'envisaged Corporate Social Responsibility before it was a buzzword'.

At its heart, Population First is an advocacy initiative for a balanced and stable population. The only way to achieve this is by gender sensitivity. As Christopher Hitchens noted more than once, the only way to eradicate poverty, anywhere in the world, is by the education and upliftment of women. Bobby reached out to me because he wanted me to help Population First in an advisory capacity.

Education, social awareness, societal responsibilities and opportunities for women – these are all things that I have fought for, for decades. To call it a 'cause' would be trite. This has been my way of life for over sixty years. There is no other way to make this world a better place.

In the late '80s, I took part in a number of solidarity marches (unrelated to Population First), trying to raise awareness about prenatal sex determination, dowry deaths and drought relief. In 2001, I would join Medha Patkar in a march against the Sardar Sarovar Dam. We travelled, first to Malegaon, and then to a tiny village called Domkhedi on the banks of the Narmada, to draw attention to the villagers who would be summarily displaced by 'development'.

Although I'd been passionate about politics since childhood, I never took to the streets for anything political. When it came to social causes, though, I have never hesitated. I never raised my voice against anyone. I have always raised my voice *for* something or someone. All my life, I've been on the side of the minority, the underdog. From Chakeri to London to Bombay. The fate of the people on the margins has always mattered to me, maybe because I've always thought of myself as one of them.

But change is difficult. Existing power structures are resilient. Almost inevitably, the idea needed to evolve and find its true form. For Population First, this became Laadli – a campaign for the girl child, a response to the ever-falling sex ratio in this country. The statistics reveal a disaster waiting to happen. And finally, in 2007, Population First launched the Laadli Media Awards, to honour gender sensitivity in media and advertising. I have been the National Coordinator since its inception.

As with any work of this nature – and this is not so much an event as it is a movement – it happens year-round. The awards themselves; the categories are announced a year in advance, all across the country, led by press conferences wherever possible – it's even more important to explain why these awards are necessary in the first place than the eventual ceremony itself. We also run workshops and offer fellowships.

Along with *The Vagina Monologues* – which shares so many of the same themes – this has been the major part of my life for almost fifteen years.

~

In 2001, I wrote a half-page review of Eve Ensler's *The Vagina Monologues* for the *Sunday Observer*, and I read about the production in *Time*. I was very keen on performing it. Coincidentally, Goldie Hawn was in Bombay around then as a guest of Parmeshwar Godrej's. Goldie had been one of the celebrities who'd been part of the show. I tried to get in touch with Goldie through Parmeshwar, hoping I'd be able to get my hands on the script and perhaps get Parmeshwar to produce the show. But Goldie didn't reply to my fax, and I thought that was that.

Fifteen months later, Mahabanoo Mody Kotwal came home and asked if I would be interested in performing the play with her. I told her that two old vaginas on their own might not be very appealing, so I called Avantika Akerkar who I was sure wouldn't baulk at it. The rest is history.

People ask me if it's my swansong. I'm damned if it is. But there are worse things to be remembered for. It's the only play I've ever done that has seen two generations of audiences. We've been running consistently for *eighteen* years. And it's an important show, maybe the most important one I've ever worked on. It feels necessary, especially in this country.

And then I look around the world, at this moment, and I think it's not just about India. We need to find parity. Between languages. Between genders. Between classes. Between races. Between differences.

~

From 2016 to 2017, I served as the head of the National Sponsorship Council. We supported twelve schools, with a total of six hundred students, with very little money. But money wasn't the object. The object was, and always is, to bring exposure into the system – to get these twelve principals to see that there's still a lot we can do, many, many ways in which we can affect the lives of these kids. Money's the easy bit. Always, in life, *will* is the hardest thing. The rest falls into place. I can claim seventy-eight years of having watched things fall into place. Is it easy? No. Is it always fair? No. But people are surprised by how much you can achieve if you picked up your bag, put away your fear and just tried to move forward.

~

Here's what I have learnt: Every single story matters.

I have my favourite memories, of course. And those are for very specific reasons. But every story matters. Each little experience adds to the mosaic. They constitute the atoms that create a living, breathing republic.

I've always thought of everything I do in terms of the theatre. It is the only other constant in my life, apart from these stories, spilling out of me, each one a lesson. And what the theatre teaches you is that, no matter the size of the role or the magnitude of the responsibility you wield on a production, *the show belongs to everyone*.

If it doesn't, you can tell immediately.

So, Laadli belongs to me, in the same way it belongs to Bobby Sista and Dr Sharda, and to every awardee, every participant, every little child that has passed through our lives during its existence.

I'm the national media coordinator for Laadli. But I'll find hotel rooms (for free, at the Taj) for the winners travelling to Mumbai. I'll compère a section of the show if needed. I'll highjack Pooja Bedi's life and get her to host the show at a pinch. I'll lend someone a saree. I'll talk to the chief minister's office and make sure the crew knows that they have to stop for the bomb squad to sweep the venue two hours before the performance. I will cajole and coax and manipulate and irritate and hector and bully and order and intimidate. I'll do what I have to. This is what I do.

I work around the clock, and I don't need more than three or four hours of sleep a day. Unfortunately, this means that quite a few people – because I'm usually working on about seventeen things at one go – receive emails and text messages at *very* odd hours. I don't expect replies at 4.30 in the morning, but I can't help it if your phone pings and wakes you. This is where being older – and mostly I *am* older than the people I'm dealing with – helps. I'd rather be eccentric than irritating.

Sometimes the shoe is on the other foot. In 2016, Jeannie Naoroji was the recipient of the Laadli Lifetime Achievement Award in recognition of her work as a choreographer and a designer (over four-and-a-half thousand shows from the '50s to the '90s), as well as mentor and trailblazer. The best possible tribute was to put together a fashion show and invite her favourite models to walk for her. A lot of them still feel like Jeannie made them who they are today. They came in their droves: Zeenat Aman and cancer survivor Esther

Daswani, both of whom modelled; Shobhaa De who came and spoke; Salome Roy Kapur, who handled the logistics of the show; Jeannie's favourite male models, Deepak Parasher and Azghar Ali; Meher Castelino, Marianne Rao, Lubna Adams, Anna Bredemeyer and Pheroza Modi; and Kiran Juneja and Nandini Sen. It reads like a murderer's row of the first Indian supermodels.

Now, this *seemed* like a wonderful idea. And it *was* a genuinely extraordinary couple of days. Even the rehearsal, as these (now) grown women giggled while Jeannie yelled at them like she did decades ago. Sam Kerawala, Ajit Shah and Kaizad Bhabha – all Jeannie's old collaborators – gave us sound and light equipment free for the show. And it was an emotional, joyous climax to the awards ceremony. But that same murderer's row is an *executioner's* row of schedules. Making that math work, with the plethora of commitments that an overwhelmingly successful group of people have, fell squarely on my shoulders. Secretaries and sisters and wives and managers and agents and dog-walkers – I had to call them all. With the added twist of several phone calls a day from Jeannie herself; one of the few times when the age card had been flipped. If a ninety-one-year-old is calling me, I'm the one who drops everything to field that call.

Laadli, for all the seriousness of its purpose, is not without its share of anecdotes. A few years ago, Sitara Devi, the recipient of the Lifetime Achievement Award that year, brought the show to a standstill. Once she'd been helped onto the stage, the side effects of a lifetime spent dancing, she thanked everyone present, turned to Prithviraj Chavan (then chief minister of Maharashtra and the guest of honour that year) in the third row and proceeded to heckle him for twenty-odd minutes. She had applied for a governmental grant, severally, to set up a dance academy. As with most things to do with the arts in this country, the proposal had been sucked into the machinery of the bureaucracy and … simply disappeared.

Sitara Devi had an audience, she had the chief minister in her sights, and she had a microphone, by God.

'Don't think,' she said, wagging a finger, jabbing it in the CM's direction repeatedly, 'don't think that just because there are people here and you smile and nod and say you'll look into it, that I'll let it go. *I want an answer tonight.*'

By minute five, Pooja was onstage, trying to coax Sitara Devi into giving up the mic. By minute seven, I was onstage. By minute thirteen, Usha Uthup, resplendent in the trademark Kanjivaram and sneakers and scheduled to perform *much* later (as a surprise), and an old, old friend of Sitara Devi's, was on along with the rest of us. Sitara Devi simply kept backing away, mic held out of reach, now circling around, never taking her eyes off the chief minister.

To me, she looked like an ageing boxer. Weaving, staggering a little. Maybe almost out on her feet. But still standing. Still defiant. It finally took four of us, in some sort of intimate scuffle, trying to smile for the audience, aware that the media were in full attendance (actress Rani Mukherjee was also presenting), to gently wrest the mic away from her.

Everyone breathed a sigh of relief, and the show went on. After all, we were also felicitating Homai Vyarawalla, India's first woman photojournalist, and Sindutai Sapkal, the iconic social worker who has nurtured and/or adopted over 1,500 children.

I, for one, was delighted by Sitara Devi's stand, awkwardness be damned. Even in the genteel environs of the National Centre for Performing Arts, on an evening that celebrated gender sensitivity, the old battle-axe went to war. Like she has done every single day of her life. *That* is also what it is to be a woman in this world.

To me, that is what Laadli is about. The people who win *aren't* people who regularly win awards. They aren't celebrities. They don't toss out well-rehearsed speeches peppered with anecdotes and just the right dose of self-deprecation. Gender sensitivity, maybe, is about the rough edges, and about finding a way through.

~

Some of the people I've mentioned in this book, people I loved and revered, have been called out in the recent past. I refer, of course, to #MeToo.

Predatory behaviour is unacceptable and unforgivable. It cannot become a systemic tool for exploitation.

And, yet, can we ask for nuance?

I have personally never been in an uncomfortable situation of this nature with anyone at any point in my life. I have neither felt forced to do something against my will nor felt that the power dynamic was insurmountable. But I am amongst the lucky few.

We live in a world where the onus lies with the women, and men are exempt by dint of biology. That can never be.

I'm glad that women are speaking up. I can only hope that it's not just about settling scores. Because that's what men do.

~

Being a senior citizen is also a minority.

So, it was with great delight that I accepted an unusual invitation from the Dignity Foundation towards the tail-end of the first COVID-19 lockdown.

In all my years, I've never lived through anything like the coronavirus pandemic. What an extraordinary moment in our lives. What an unprecedented event in our history. I'm lucky. For me, it has been nothing but an extended pause – another opportunity to go through diaries and journals and memories.

And, yet, so many people in the world are just scrambling for a sense of normalcy. Against sometimes insurmountable odds.

For senior citizens, it has been a different kind of horror – the kind of slow death that we've fought against all our lives. Locked in our homes, ostensibly for our safety, away from friends, family, human contact, watching the will and the momentum we have created over decades ebb away. Like a car losing power as it heads up a hill.

This is poison too. Because it kills. The challenge we've faced during this period is to reimagine ourselves. To reinvent ourselves. To reintegrate and retrench.

Let me tell you: every little bit counts. Because we're fighting for our independence. Once again, and still.

So when I got the opportunity to help in the tiniest possible way, I leapt at the chance.

The Dignity Foundation works with and for senior citizens. It believes strongly that life as a senior citizen doesn't mean a compromised existence and looks to engender that confidence in people. And it reaches out to those elderly people who lack the proper support structures.

Dignity wanted me to judge a fashion show. For senior citizens. During the lockdown. On Zoom. Two hundred and fifteen entries from people over the age of sixty-five, from all over the country. People modelling their own clothes, in their own homes, on Zoom.

It was an absolute thrill. I was pleased that a lot of these people knew who I was from my days on television. I spent a few hours in utter delight watching a bunch of supposed old fogeys (and I'm one of them now) cocking a snook at their age and the situation.

I was glad to be alive. So were they.

~

In the '70s, I had befriended a highly sought-after journalist by the name of Ashok Row Kavi. He worked for the *Indian Express*, but he'd also launched *Debonair*.

More interestingly, he hit me up to accompany him to a disco in Tardeo. There, he proceeded to distribute condoms to everyone present. A 'gay party' was scheduled for after.

The party never did happen. But we became fast friends.

I was invited to the HUMSAFAR office in Sakinaka for the launch of the premier issue of *Bombay Dost*, India's first gay magazine.

I was introduced to Ashok's friends and colleagues – Vijay Anand, Pallav Patankar and Shibu Thomas.

It was only after I met Ashok that I realized there was another critical battle for rights being waged by some of the most wonderful people I've had the privilege of knowing.

I've been a supporter ever since.

And when filmmaker Sridhar Rangayan founded *Kashish*, India's first queer film festival in 2010, I was thrilled to serve on the advisory committee as well as on the first few juries.

The festival itself was a response to the (two-step, ultimately) decriminalization of homosexuality in India in 2009. *Bombay Dost*, which had shut down in 2000, was relaunched in celebration, and *Kashish* followed suit.

Yes, I believe in equal rights and opportunity, regardless of gender, class, caste, colour and orientation. That goes without saying. But the LGBTQ community has broadened my horizons. There is so much talent. So many stories. So much potential.

And love should be for everyone. The right to love *is* freedom.

I know, because I've craved love all my life.

~

I have always craved love.

And because I did, I always gave completely of myself. Every fibre of my being went into each of those relationships.

Maybe that is why, in spite of everything that happened, the relationships endured.

Dilip and I just celebrated the fiftieth anniversary of our wedding. And he sent me a present.

Alyque and I, after ten years of not speaking to each other, slowly drifted back into each other's orbit. On the fringes, yes. But we were there. The relationship, in spite of everything, had endured.

~

In mid-January 2018, I was asked to spend a few nights at Christmas Eve. Alyque needed someone from the family to be around since his devoted attendant, Ida, was going to the village for her daughter's engagement.

At some point in the interim, the great thaw had occurred. Or maybe that's the advertising/theatre version of events. Alyque and I had slowly returned to the periphery of each other's lives. That's a better description.

Every once in a while, Alyque would call. He'd have tickets for a play or a film, and I was happy to accompany him. It wasn't a regular occurrence, but we did it a few times a year, and quite easily.

When we'd been together, I'd been very careful to not try and impose myself onto the Padamsees. I didn't want to be that person. I had a complex about my family. In retrospect, that's bizarre because I had the happiest childhood. I submit that it was completely in my head. When I was with Alyque, it didn't matter because I knew I had his wholehearted support.

But it plagued me. When we went to London in '74, we lived with Alyque's brother Chotu and his wife, Marguerite, in their lovely home in Hampstead Heath. It was a little awkward. I told myself that I wasn't close to the Padamsees. Hadn't ever sat down and had an intimate conversation. Was I eager to please? I might have been. Perhaps I wanted to be accepted by this family. Perhaps I didn't want anyone to see it.

Circumstances played into it, of course. When Alyque and I first got together, whether I'd be 'admitted' into the circle became a matter of vicious contention. When Alyque and Sharon got together, I made it a huge issue. I wish I hadn't, in retrospect. Too much was said, and you can't unsay things delivered in the heat and pain of the moment. They linger and fester, and the bitterness can haunt you.

Ten years after Alyque left, I wasn't as upset or uptight anymore. We had the little exchange in Kolkata. There were no visits or dropping-in unannounced. We never went out of our way to say 'hi'. But we could now be in the same room.

It was the Padamsees who reached out. Jerry, and her daughter Pooh, and Marguerite. Pooh, in particular, has been unfailingly gracious. It had to do with Quasar, I think. Pooh included me in the functions after Jerry's death, and it was a family occasion. It wasn't an earth-shattering gesture, but it felt unforced and natural.

Just before the launch of Alyque's autobiography, *A Double Life*, in 1999, he asked me if I'd play Linda in a reading at KC College. I was happy to. After that, I was part of the Padamsee family celebrations on Christmases, birthdays, occasions like that. We were present in each other's lives. Sometimes, we exchanged gifts. We were always very formal. If I was invited to his place, I'd go. There'd be hordes of friends. I'd chat, eat and come home. And vice versa; sometimes he'd come to my place in much the same way.

We never discussed the past, ever.

Randomly, I'd get phone calls from Annie, Alyque's secretary. Please send your medical bills to the office, she'd say. I was delighted by the development. It was some sort of gesture, for sure. I'm glad that it occurred to him.

Suddenly, one year, I got a message saying we were going for a health check-up – everyone, Quasar, Sharon, Shazahn, Alyque, myself. We all congregated at 8 in the morning at Hinduja hospital. We did this for three years. Then we went to Reliance Hospital for a couple of years. During that time, I was asked to send my medical bills to Alyque's office.

I was very glad of it. Was I overwhelmed? No. I looked upon it kindly. The financial crunch precipitated by his departure was never quite over. This wasn't his fault; we just went from a double-income household to a single-earning member. He shared the school fees and, later, the costs for Singapore. But I was always scrambling.

Alyque still had the capacity to surprise me. In the last three years of his life, he'd surprise me with the odd extravagant birthday gift. The gestures were always lovely, precisely because they were unexpected.

So, when the call came, I couldn't pretend the lack of a relationship.

~

Spending a night at Christmas Eve, though? *That* apartment?

It took me some time to agree. Alyque's health had been up and down, and the family felt that one of a handful of people needed to be there at all times, even though Ida had eventually returned. Ultimately, it was something Quasar asked of me.

From June of 2018, I spent two or three nights a week at Christmas Eve, splitting duties with Sharon, Shazahn and Quasar, depending on everyone's commitments.

The old push and pull resurfaced immediately. He requested his old favourites – Taheri and French toast and keema-aloo – and I was glad to cook for him after all this time, albeit with Ida's assistance, even though I hate kitchen-work now. It seemed worth it because the food cheered him up.

The next moment, I'd have to leave the room because someone had called. This ranged from his friends to doctors to accountants and biographers and publishers. Everything was still clearly 'top-secret'. As soon as he was done talking, he'd invite me back into the room to watch the news with him, or *House of Cards*.

There was no doubt about *who* was in charge. Everyone else, doctors included, were being told what to do. Alyque was still directing. Very much so. This time, it was his convalescence.

Very little of what we discussed was personal. In conversation, his life seemed to have begun post 1982, with Sharon. When he spoke of *Jesus Christ Superstar*, he referred to the production from a few years ago, not the one he'd done in 1974. Even *Gandhi* seemed to have dropped into his lap fully formed. I was nowhere in that picture. That was his choice, I guess.

I was surprised that it could still sting. Not like before, of course. But it was a measure, perhaps, of how entrenched, how important, we'd been in each other's lives.

Then, one evening in October, Alyque presented me with a black-and-silver linen saree. He'd seen it in Fabindia, he said. And it reminded him of me. He'd bought it, as a thank you for everything. That kind of loose, generic catch-all 'everything', and still it brought a tear to my eye.

Ever so slowly, his essential life force, that raging self-belief, started to dim. It wasn't noticeable day-to-day, and he still pulled out the old Alyque for trips to the theatre, the cinema and his public appearances. His real addiction had always been work, more than anything else. But it cost him now, that effort.

He was still active, still sharp, still worrying about Indian cricket when he was hospitalized the final time. Everyone thought it was a routine visit, that he'd be back in a few days, and that we'd be summoned home again and glad to be berated.

I went to see him on 16 November 2018. He was in the ICU, and the hospital was strict about visiting hours. I saw him at 11.30 in the morning. I fed him a few teaspoons of 'Prosure'. I put my hand on his forehead, trying to give him some comfort. He reached out and took my hand in his. He raised it to his lips, looked me straight in the eye and kissed it tenderly.

The next morning, he was gone.

~

Tributes and eulogies poured in. He was 'God', after all. He was a Titan of advertising; the Grand Old Man who managed to stay relevant for decades. Lintas put up a heartfelt billboard – he'd put the 'A' in 'Lintas'. Somewhere, I saw that old image of him as Moses, carrying a tabernacle that read 'The Ten Principles of Advertising'. He'd meant a great deal to a great many people.

A lot of the outpourings in the press left me cold. I was the odd one out. In the public coverage, there wasn't much mention of our life together. It hurt, yes. But I also understood. People were grieving. Old wounds were perhaps best avoided, for fear they opened up again.

~

I was glad to be included in everything the family did after his death. That first day, and then the funeral. We made a trip to Awas – bereft that Alyque would never accompany us again. The air was ripe with memory. Ghosts almost walked.

I found myself caught between grief and pain, wondering why it was that I couldn't embrace one or the other. Maybe that was *my* tribute. He was a complex man, and he elicited many, often contradictory, emotions.

Our paths had crossed, and we had both been fundamentally altered. We'd had a child together. I had turned my back on the world for this man. For him, I was happy to be an outcast.

And yet, so much pain lingered. So much hurt. So much left unresolved.

But Alyque left behind a link, a bond. Something that sustains Raell and Shazahn and Quasar. And, just maybe, Sharon and myself.

It has been almost three years since Alyque's passing as I type this. And in spite of everything, in spite of our twelve years together and our thirty-eight years apart, there hasn't been a single day I haven't thought of him.

He was an immense comfort and support to me when we first met. Of everyone I knew, he communicated the best. And he instilled confidence in me and in my way of thinking. I overcame my inhibitions – social, familial, cultural. He gave me the courage to traverse the unconventional.

In the world we live in, and the political climate of our time, I can only ascribe it to a similarity of thought. We were on the same wavelength about many things: religion, faith, honour, generosity, respect, relationships, theatre, books, films. We believed in liberal thought, word, deed, and commitment to community, causes, country.

That's my life, right there.

Both sides of my relationship with Alyque are valid. The things we agreed on, and the hurt and the bitterness.

It's like that line by Hemingway: 'There's no *one* thing that's true. It's all true.'

~

I think back to a handful of incidents. I don't do it often. I should.

The Flight Lieutenant in Palam. Trying to get to classrooms in Kanpur without feeling like we'd waded through a river of filth. The good-natured chest thumps in Delhi. A man on Colaba Causeway trying to put his finger in me.

Maybe if a man was writing this book, they'd be small incidents. Building blocks for character. Things that, you know, *happen*. Everyone goes through it, no? It's a rite of passage. It's how you know you've become a woman.

But when I think about it, I never trusted anyone. At all.

So, since 1982, when Alyque left, I've dressed differently. Every day. The image of Dolly Thakore – the saree and the pearls – came to be because I was single. Because I was alone.

When Alyque and I went somewhere, we had the car. After it ended, I took public transport for almost twenty years. I never wore anything form-fitting, anything that showed any skin, anything that made me feel attractive – because I didn't feel safe.

Being a single woman is another kind of minority. A minority within a minority.

And what kind of freedom, what equality, is this that you deny a part of yourself so completely?

Please understand, it's not about the clothes. It's about not feeling safe.

And if I didn't feel safe – Air Force kid, English-speaking, lived and worked in England, and then in Bombay, and was on television – if I didn't feel safe, what does that say about the majority of women in this country?

It boggles the mind.

That's why Laadli isn't a job. It isn't a cause. It's a necessity. Women matter. As much. Every day and every second. There can be no compromise about this. It is not possible. This is inalienable, inarguable, perfectly logical, and yet we've spent centuries trying to argue our case.

Let me put it to you this way: If you're not a feminist, you're a fascist. You don't believe, fundamentally, that people are equal.

The only way out of this is education. Educate the kids and the parents. Once you do, equal opportunity and financial parity will do the rest. And they will be easier to achieve because you'll have put in the work in the early years.

What are you afraid of?

27

IN 2004, I received an invitation to apply for a visa to attend the India-Pakistan cricket match in Lahore. I was thrilled. I'd never been to Pakistan. I accepted, but on one condition. I wanted my visa to allow me to visit Karachi, Islamabad and Kohat, in addition to Lahore. I knew that an endorsement for one city didn't allow travel to other cities.

My passport returned from Delhi with a visa for only Lahore.

By sheer chance, I happened to be in Delhi a few weeks later and happened to have carried my passport with me. I met the high commissioner of Pakistan at a Mehdi Hasan concert at the Ashoka and a glimmer of an opportunity presented itself.

So, I deposited myself at the gates of the High Commission and asked to see him. There was a round of hurried calls on the intercom and I was ushered in. The official who met me asked why I wanted to go to Kohat.

'Because I was born there,' I said.

He nodded. 'Me too,' he said. And stamped my passport for all the cities I wanted to visit.

~

I put down my thoughts about my trip to Pakistan in a column I wrote.

The response of most people when they heard I had gone to Pakistan alone was:

'Didn't you feel scared?'

'Only you have the guts.'

'You are so brave.'

There is so much misconception about the people who are a one-hour-and-twenty-minute flight away.

I was overwhelmed by how they reached out. I wasn't part of a cricketing delegation or a film-star brigade. And yet, when I walked past a fierce-looking, white kurta-salwar clad, strapping gun-toting security guard outside a jewellery shop in Lahore's Liberty Market, I did a double-take when I heard him say 'I love India'.

As part of the Indo-Pak Friendship Initiative, some twenty children from the Ryan International School in Delhi had brought a performance of '*Thumak thumak kar chali*', and had the four-hundred-strong audience of Pakistani adults dancing in the aisles to the rhythms of India, and shouting 'Sat Sri Akal!' in response to their 'Shab-e-khair'.

And when the flags of the two countries were brought onto stage by the children singing *We Believe*, there was not a dry eye in the house.

At the Anarkali shopping centre in Karachi – so similar to our Elco Arcade – I ran short by almost fifteen hundred rupees. Instead of allowing me to return what I had no money for, the shop assistant insisted I take it saying, 'There will be another time. You will come again now that our borders are open.'

Frantically searching for a ready-made white salwar, the man at the counter offered me the salwar from a set and refused to take any money for it.

Each time I wanted to tip a waiter or a driver, they only said: '*Aap toh hamare mehmaan hain*,' and refused.

This was the ordinary man-on-the-street.

The women were beautiful, with their heavily kohled eyes and fair complexions. But it was the symmetry of the salwar-kurta clad men that cut across barriers and lent dignity to the little beggar child, the bus driver, the shop keeper, and the feudal lord of the manor.

'*Salaam alaikum*', the greeting amongst domestic help, children, parents, siblings, husband and wife, friends, relatives, colleagues, telephone operators, receptionists, was disarmingly charming.

Feudal lifestyles still rule the roost in Pakistan, and I saw a lot of examples in my time there. These were the proverbial twenty-two families that had amassed great fortunes during other regimes. They atoned for their consciences in exile in London. But some of them have attempted to move with the times.

The ancestral Saigols of Karachi ran mandatory classes for fifteen of their domestic help in the expansive kitchen veranda. They receive instruction from 8 to 10 a.m. every day. I heard the head of the household, artist Shakil Saigol, reprimand them for non-attendance with salary cuts.

In Islamabad, Billo Ali Mahmood has constructed a school on her sprawling Banigala estate for some two hundred children of the underprivileged.

I did go to the old city in Karachi – albeit at midnight. But there were no sleeping bodies curled up on pavements.

I visited the sixth- or seventh-century shrine of Data Saheb and even offered flowers there; Yusuf Sali's Haveli; Shahi Masjid; the Gurudwara; the massive Lahore Fort; the Museum (where a ten-year-old finally picked up the courage to say '*Shahrukh Khan ko Osman Mirza ka salaam kehna*'); Kim's Zamzam Gun that guards the crossroads; Kinnaid College – home to many prominent Indian women of the pre-Independence era (including film star Kamini Kaushal); National College of Arts; Government College; Aitchison College with its ninety-lush-acres in the heart of the city; Beacon National University (headed by Saleema Hashmi – daughter of famed-poet Faiz Ahmed Faiz); even Lady Maclagan Girls High School, all in search of landmarks and places my aunt had teacher-trained at – the places that made Lahore the great seat of learning.

I noticed the absence of ambulances and asked. My hosts pointed at the many Suzuki vans with just a sliver of red or blue like the crescent moon. The red cross had been abandoned as it conjured alien Christian symbols.

The public transport buses were a kaleidoscope of colour, in the sunlight, and at night, lights glinting and mirrors reflecting as they streaked across the roads.

Food Street in Lahore is to die for – in spite of the familiar Bombay-type traffic snarl.

Education for girls is the top priority. And I attended the inauguration of a girls' school for the underprivileged – started by Raza Kazim some ten years ago – which had now moved to better premises in Sanjan Nagar, on Ferozepur Road. He insists English education be imparted to the underprivileged girl child to give her an equal opportunity on par with the elite.

A whole generation of people has been brought up without music, dance and theatre, all banned under the Zia-ul-Haq regime. Performing arts is a new culture.

The most touching experience I had was an invitation for tea by some ladies who had heard that I knew Kabir Bedi. Credentials established, Mujahida produced a framed work signed by Sister Palmo (Kabir's mother's Buddhist name) and related how her mother had had this hanging over her bed in New York, and told her who it belonged to. When she died in 1996, Mujahida felt it should be returned to its rightful owner. And I brought it home to Kabir.

~

My host in Karachi threw a small dinner in my honour and I had an excellent time with a group of journalists and actors. During the course of the evening, I mentioned that I was keen to visit Kohat. One of the guests did some digging and reported that Kohat would entail a ten-hour drive from Islamabad.

The previous year, Eve Ensler had visited India to perform *The Vagina Monologues*, and two actresses from Pakistan had accompanied her. We had done our best to look after the ladies, and they had extended an open invitation if we ever came across the border. One of them was Nighat Rizvi from Islamabad. I decided it was time to call in my favour. I landed up at her house (next to cricketer, and later prime minister, Imran Khan's!) and threw myself at her mercy.

Her frantic investigations revealed only one concrete fact: Their driver was from Kohat. That was good enough for me. So, the next day, we set off in their very comfortable car.

Mohsin Sayeed, a press contact and my host in Karachi, had given me the name and address of my point of contact in Kohat. As we drove into the city, an installation of a tribal lord on a huge horse greeted us. The driver explained that this was Kar Hussain Kuli Khan Khattak, the lord who had rescued the kidnapped daughter of the-then British commander from the clutches of tribals in Peshawar.

British soldiers, the story goes, had committed sacrilege and invaded a 'zenana'. In retaliation, the tribe attacked the British Residency. Hearing the commotion, the lady of the house came out to investigate. Unfortunately, she was in her pyjamas and sported a short haircut. The tribesmen mistook her for the Resident and killed her. They then kidnapped her daughter, an eight-year-old by the name of Alice. It took six years for Kar Hussain Kuli Khan Khattak to find the girl. Father and daughter were finally reunited in England.

In early 2000, at the age of eighty, Alice returned to Kohat to inaugurate a film festival that was screening a movie based on her life. She said she'd never been treated better, with as much love and respect, as during those six years she'd spent amongst tribal families.

Imagine my surprise when I reached my destination in Kohat to discover that I was being hosted by the grandson of Kar Hussain Kuli Khan! Since I was only there overnight, my hosts insisted on taking me to the highest point in the vicinity, so that I could get a bird's-eye view of the whole area. We climbed to the top of a water tower.

I thought it right to call my father from my cellphone. My father listened as I described where I was. He was silent for a long time.

'Beta, can you see an abandoned airfield?' he asked finally.

I could.

'At the edge of the airfield,' he continued, 'is a church. Can you see it?'

I could.

'That's where you were baptized,' he said. 'And beside it is the "sarai" where you were born.'

My hosts took me to both the places. The church had been replaced by a newer structure in 1962, but all the old photographs are preserved in the vestry.

Like I said, things come a circle. In the most unexpected ways.

~

I don't feel close to my family. Less every year. Esmie and I are there for each other, but we don't share things, we don't confide in each other.

There are two sides to it, as ever. I've always felt that Esmie has been far too critical of me and my choices. She says that I've always been about me. That it's 'I, I, I'. She's right, I guess, to some extent. But then again, I wasn't my mother's favourite. Esmie didn't have to spend her childhood being shoved away. And then she'd say that I never got sent away the way she did.

It never ends with family. I spent a long time trying to be a snob and couldn't wait to be rid of my family. From the age of two, I was with my grandparents. I adored my grandmother. And my Rani Aunty. I didn't care much for my grandfather. But the kids were always close. Cynthia and Cyril, and even Esmie, really. There was a sense of a unit, regardless of whether or not you *liked* the people in your family.

I don't feel that now. Dennis passed away in 2015. We're scattered all across the world. And when we meet, it's nice for a bit. It's not the life-affirming thing it should be. Perhaps it's me. Perhaps I'm selfish.

~

But we return to family because that is where we may find ourselves. Because those are the elements from where we fashion our identities, and find the things we value in the world.

I gained so much from my childhood that it's good to be reminded of it sometimes.

That same year, 2004, I was also in Ranthambore with my friend Lucky. Priyanka Gandhi Vadra was there at the same time, with her children. We didn't know each other. The only connection was my Rani Aunty. When Rajiv became prime minister, he and Sonia were advised to not send the kids to school any more. But they still needed a tutor. Sonia approached the Convent of Jesus and Mary School, and they were more than happy to recommend Miss Solomon, who'd just retired after thirty-five years of outstanding service.

I sent Priyanka a note, telling her I was also in Ranthambore. I was motivated by the same impulse that made me send her grandmother a note all those years ago. Just.

We crossed paths the next day. I was in a jeep. She was on an elephant. And she grinned. 'Miss Solomon!' she yelled.

That made my day. It put a huge smile on my face. I'm so proud of being her niece. I love that she was my idol growing up. And that's how I'd like to be remembered, once it's all done and dusted.

28

TEN YEARS AFTER Alyque and I had been, I took Quasar to Kashmir. We went by train and spent a night in Jammu before we went to Srinagar.

I was quite aware that Quasar and I were on a pilgrimage, passing through places Alyque and I had been to together. I'm not sure what made me want to do it. Perhaps I wanted to reclaim those places for the two of us.

We saw all the sights. It was the month of May, so we went to Gulmarg, where people ski. We walked to Khilanmarg – a valley overflowing with flowers in the spring and the site of the ski runs in the winter. We lived on a houseboat.

And, yet, like Kashmir, we were stuck between who we were, and who we might become. And that feeling ran through the middle of that holiday – mellow, not all-pervasive, but lingering, like faint grief.

I'll never forget this one memory: Quasar and I were in a room in a small hotel. The chimney was a huge, bronze cylinder in the middle of the cabin, and Quasar and I sat beside it, our faces a dull red, trying to stay warm. He was all of seven. It was odd, incomplete, perfect.

This is how we grieve. We wait. We go. We find the photographs and look at them. And we crack from the strain. Over and over. Until we feel we have enough distance. Until we feel 'yes, I've broken myself enough times to *be* broken'. Then we stop worrying about fixing ourselves. About *healing*. We get on with it.

This is the second time I've had to do that. I do not grieve. But there is always grief. Things lost, things unsaid, things taken from us.

Zhya Jacobs died on the 11th of November 2008.

Esmie's son, my nephew, Quasar's 'bhaiya', our boy. Too soon. Too early.

I have not recovered. I do not expect to recover.

~

I hadn't seen Zhya since the 13th of September 2006. He'd made a short trip to Bombay, after two years at Harvard. I couldn't believe it, how quickly our kids had grown. Time is a river. You move, whether you're aware of it or not.

We said a perfunctory goodbye after Esmie's birthday dinner at Out of the Blue in Bandra. Zhya expected to be back in a few weeks on a Harvard Student Mission to study the slums of Mumbai. And I would see him when he was back, of course.

Outwardly, Zhya had become everything I'd hoped for. The embodiment of every dream I had for myself. He was brilliant at what he did. He collected accolades for fun. He became an architect in India. Then he went to Berkeley. Came back to India. Wanted to be better still. Got his master's from Georgia Tech. *Then* he went to Harvard.

He was a faculty lecturer at Yale. He taught at Harvard.

He was kind and generous and wise.

Sometimes, I couldn't reconcile the two Zhyas – the little boy I used to babysit, the little boy who wore an upside-down pot while he pretended to be Don Quixote, and the towering, handsome man he'd become.

There were also two other Zhyas. Before his stint in Atlanta, he had a nervous breakdown. His faith helped him heal. Before long, that faith consumed him. He became a born-again Christian. But, unlike the younger Zhya, my refusal to embrace his faith became the cause of distance between us. His worldview had changed. I was still his Dolly Massi, but we weren't as close as we'd once been.

When he left for Atlanta, we both cried. He hugged me last. On the way back from the airport, after our goodbyes, Quasar said to me: 'Mama, bhaiya found it very difficult to say goodbye to you.'

Zhya was mine as much as he was his parents'. He was the firstborn of all my nieces or nephews. His parents travelled a great deal. We had each other. I pampered him silly. I took him everywhere.

This is the note I sent him for his first birthday at Rishi Valley:

'There is a flood,' it said, 'in my love and remembrances for you on your 14th birthday. Greater than the monsoon deluge. Thinking of Quasar and you'.

I remember him at my bedside, just after I'd delivered Quasar. Zhya was thrilled. He was fascinated by the little baby in my arms. He reached out and cupped Quasar's face. In that moment, he claimed Quasar in the way that I had claimed him. And I thought to myself that I'd be lucky if Quasar grew up like Zhya.

I was there at every event in school. Plays, sports days, it didn't matter. Zhya would look for me in the audience. And he was very rarely disappointed. So, when he joined Quasar at Rishi Valley, it just became a natural extension of the bond we already had. I knew Quasar would always be safe with Zhya around. And I always believed I had two kids at the school. At individual parent-teacher meetings, I'd ask after both boys. When I went to visit, the two nights in the year we were allowed, Quasar and Zhya both came to spend the night at the school's guest house. Alyque did the same. He always asked after Zhya. And when he spent the night, he'd always ask for permission for both boys.

I had two sons. Even Quasar will admit it. Sometimes I loved Zhya more. Quasar knew that.

We discussed every academic decision he ever made. Choice of course. Choice of institution. I accompanied him to his interview at Rachna Academy of Architecture. He invited me back to conduct a communications workshop for the students.

I visited him at his first job. He walked me around the office and introduced me to everyone. They must have thought him, and me, very uncool. He didn't care. When he and his partners launched their own firm, he showed me around the new office and then his own cabin. I sat there, in *Zhya's* office, and looked at the artwork for their logo. How the kids have grown, I thought. And they'd become these wonderful men. I could have died happy, right then. The future, for the first time in my life, felt secure. It felt like it was destined for the right hands – sure, steady, gentle.

He took me to the office of Grey Worldwide in Parel. He'd designed it. We went at midnight, because we could. He got security to switch on the floodlights, and we walked around the building. I could barely pay attention to what he was saying. I felt too proud of him to be able to concentrate.

Around the year 2000, things began to change. He got busier and busier. Then the troubles. And finally, the turn to a stronger faith.

His decision to pursue his master's at Georgia Tech was the first time he made an academic choice without consulting me, and that gave me pause. Was it just inevitable? As he grew into adulthood, I would get left behind. Was this it? Or were we no longer as close as we'd once been, because I wouldn't conform to his beliefs?

Still, I was thrilled. He was my kid. He chose to settle in Chicago over New York. I tried to convince him otherwise. But he felt strongly that Chicago was the city of the future.

He got a job with a firm he liked. He bought an apartment in the Lincoln Park Area, overlooking Lake Michigan. He seemed distant. He said he was happy.

I sent him things for his new place. A carpet, some kitchenware. He always thanked me, but he didn't have much to say beyond work and the church.

On the 11th of November 2008, he returned home after working all night at the office. He had lunch at about half past noon. And then he went out for a walk.

A little while later, a jogger noticed him in the water. Zhya was screaming for help. It was raining, and the water was at -3 degrees centigrade. The jogger called the police immediately. He stood there and watched as the current pulled Zhya deeper into the lake. He looked for life preservers, something the lakeside community had petitioned for. The same thing had happened earlier that year.

They fished Zhya out of the water forty minutes later. The death certificate reads death by accidental drowning.

He was tired. It was raining. He slipped. It was cold in the water. Below freezing.

He was close to the bank, but there was no way to climb up, and nothing to hold on to. He must have felt his strength drain away. Minute by minute, as the cold ate away at him.

He must have been so scared.

Quasar and Esmie and Dennis flew to Chicago that evening. A few days later, they flew back with the body.

Two weeks after he'd died, we buried my Zhya.

He looked calm, in death. Half a smile on his face.

I hope he's at peace. I have lost mine. I have a good life, and a wonderful son, and great friends. But I am incomplete. There is nothing in this world that hurts as much as burying your young.

Your Massi loves you and misses you, beta. Be well, wherever you are.

29

NOTHING WORKED OUT the way I'd thought. Nothing. Not one single thing.

And yet, my heart is full and the memories spill out of me, and away, carried by this restless breeze that never settles.

What a ride. Every good thing, and every bad thing, and all in the middle – where life is lived.

My son threw me a party for my seventy-fifth birthday. I got up and I danced. I danced the night away.

And they were all there. My Rani Aunty. And Pooja. And Protima's sisters. And Sharon and Shazahn and Raell and Alyque. And all my friends.

And Gerson.

And Quasar.

My favourite film has always been *Gone with the Wind*. And always remember: Tomorrow *is* another day.

We danced.

That is perhaps all there is to it.

~

And so, Dolly from Delhi, when you look back, what do you see?

~

In 1983, Quasar and I travelled to Hyderabad for *Glaxo Bonny Baby Time*. I hadn't been back to Hyderabad in something like thirty years. The last time was when I was in the sixth standard, at St. Anne's English High School.

I had to go visit. When I introduced myself, the nuns were very gracious. We walked around. Quasar sprinted through corridors. It was like meeting someone you'd once been very close to. I could see the shape of my memory buried wherever I looked, like déjà vu that lasts a long time.

In conversation, I mentioned that Sister Adrianne was the principal when I was in school. The staff were delighted. She was still at the school. She had retired, but was still on campus. She was bedridden and lived upstairs. It would have been impolite to clamber up into the nuns' quarters. The sisters were happy to send her a message from me.

'My name is Dolly Rawson,' I wrote. 'I was here thirty years ago. I left when I was in the sixth.'

To my surprise, I was asked to wait. And then Sister Adrianne was carried downstairs in a stretcher, to see her old student. I was delighted and a little moved. I'd like to think that I was a happy distraction for her, something out of the routine. We chatted for a while. About where life had taken me, and her experiences at the school, and of old students and teachers. I asked Sister Adrianne about one teacher in particular: Dolly Aranha. She was a very pretty Indian lady who had been my teacher in the sixth. I remembered her fondly. She was cheerful and she played fair. Everyone got treated the same. She also had very long hair, all the way to her ankles, which she tied in a single plait, folded up to her knees. There was no doubt about it. She was 'cool'. Her boyfriend was a pilot.

Dolly Aranha had decided to become a nun, Sister Adrianne said. Her boyfriend had died in an air crash, and she elected to serve the church. In those days, you had to go to Rome to be ordained a nun. But she returned to Hyderabad and became a teacher. She was now a director in the Ministry of Education. She'd given up the habit and wore a saree. And she had become a crusader – she worked to save young Muslim girls, in some cases as young as eight years old, who were being married off to Arab sheikhs.

She lived at the Race Course in Secunderabad, said Sister Adrianne, with her mother. If I wanted, I could go see her. Sister Adrianne gave me Dolly's address and sent a peon along with me.

Two Dollys met. It was lovely. My old teacher remembered me, and she was thrilled to see me and to meet Quasar. Her mother sat in a rocking chair, frail and ancient, like she was something out of *Great Expectations*. Quasar ran around the old, dilapidated mansion. Dolly and I swapped notes about love and loss, and careers and working with women and children. I felt I'd found an old friend.

Dolly was set to travel to Bombay in two months' time. I invited her to come and live with me. We promised each other we'd meet.

One day, a few months after our trip to Hyderabad, I picked Quasar up from school and brought him to the CCI for his tennis lessons. I struck up a conversation with a lady who had brought along her grandson to play tennis as well. Her name was Betty Aranha.

'What a coincidence,' I said. 'I knew someone called Dolly Aranha. She's supposed to come stay with me soon. She normally lives with Joe Aranha, the commissioner of police, but she said she'd stay with me this time.'

The lady simply stared at me.

'Haven't you heard?' she asked finally.

'Heard what?'

'A week or ten days ago, she was attacked by a gang. The police think it's because of the work she was doing, with the young girls.'

'Attacked?' I asked.

'They killed her on the spot. They cut her into four-inch pieces.'

I was silent for a long time.

I thought about circumstance. About how we'd met all of a sudden, after all those years. And I thought about how random fate was. How reckless and violent life can be. She was trying to do a good thing. She took on some very powerful people.

And now, after all this time, I also wonder what happened to her mother.

We really can't control anything. The best we can do is soldier on in the face of our powerlessness.

~

In spite of my ambivalence towards my parents, going through my diaries, I see the entry 'night in Versova' almost four times a week if I was in the city.

It surprised me. I suppose it is at the heart of the parent/child dynamic. We're not close, until we suddenly realize we are.

When Mummy passed away in 2003, I wasn't by her bedside. I drove into the compound just after she breathed her last. Quasar went away to live in Versova with his grandfather.

I loved my father more. It wasn't a secret. We weren't the sort to share great confidences, but we did play Scrabble almost every time we were together.

6 August 2003: 'Daddy scored a triple letter, and a grand slam of 50 …'

We didn't share confidences. So, I don't know how emotional it was for him when Esmie, Dennis, Quasar and I took him to Awas in 2004, for the first time since 1982.

The house got built, Daddy. Even your kids got old. And the last time we played Scrabble was on the 30th of August 2004. As usual, you thumped me.

I never got to say goodbye to him either. I stayed busy until it was too late. I was on my way to the NCPA on the 11th of September 2004 when Quasar called in the afternoon to say that I should change my plans and come to Versova.

I missed him by a few minutes.

And now, seventeen years after she passed away, looking for my diaries, I discovered that my mother had collected everything to do with me, starting from *1958.* Every speech and every debate. Clippings of every column I was featured in, every column I wrote.

Our secret hearts remain hidden from plain view. I didn't know, ever, that those things had meant so much to her.

For that, and everything else, I'm sorry.

Sorry, mum. Sorry, dad.

They lived long and active lives and were devoted to each other until the end. I miss them because they were my parents, because they were part of the fabric of my life. But they weren't friends of mine.

I transferred that onto my son. That's what I feel, on most mornings. We're not close, Quasar and I. We hardly see each other. He is so, so busy. And when we *do* get a chance to speak, most of the time I've forgotten what I wanted to say. But we don't share things. He's forty-two years old now, so perhaps that's natural.

Or perhaps it happened because I sent him to boarding school. Because boarding school can make kids independent in ways that their parents come to regret. We don't speak of personal things. Well ... he doesn't share a lot with me. He knows of most of my life, although I'm sure there are things I've shared in this book that may surprise him. He used to call Jaimini Ahluwalia, Kamal Mulla and me 'the first wives club'. He'd come home, see the three of us and chuckle. I'm glad he could see the funny side of it, but I don't know how much of that he carries with him.

I know he's proud of me. He's a dutiful son, in the way I was a dutiful daughter. He's uncomplaining. And he's patient. Which is something I struggle with. I adore Rani Aunty, who's now the tender age of ninety-seven. I look after her. But I can't go and see her, spend time with her, take her to the doctor. Esmie does that. She is very good at it. If my aunt came and lived with me, I'd be restless. I'm not the family type.

In my view, Quasar can do no wrong. As he's said publicly, more than a few times: 'Mama, even if I farted, you'd say it was perfume.'

He's not mistaken.

But he's a good guy. This I know. He's very close to Esmie. He's very close to his cousins, scattered as they are across the globe. I've never had to worry about drink and drugs. He's a responsible young man. He worked with Alyque once, on an ill-fated *Romeo and Juliet*, and said he'd never work with him again. That is not a dynamic they could share. But he was a dutiful son to his father. Until the end, if his father called, and his father called often, Quasar was there, any time of night or day.

He saw his father be erratic. He saw me be erratic. I never had a great poker face. Around Alyque, I used to be a different person. My body language would change. The expression on my face would change.

Quasar made his peace with it. Somehow. I don't know how. He's never said a word about it.

But I'm not half the person he is.

As advertised, I have some resentments. I have no regrets.

~

I do wonder about some things, though. Those moments that, in hindsight, were pivotal. Points where the river changed course.

What if I'd gotten on the flight back to London?

What if I'd never met Alyque?

What if I'd never had Quasar?

And then I think, no. Am I glad that some of those things happened? No. I wouldn't want anyone to live through some of those things.

But I got my child out of it.

Pain is a scar. It is a sign of the wound.

The wound, says Rumi, is the place where the light enters.

The scars are what remind me that I was there, that I fought for every *particle* that comprises the whole of my life.

I'm aware that we're in the final act. Somewhere, and it could be ten, fifteen years from now or it could be much sooner, the final curtain is ready. We're running through the lines of the last few scenes. There's a fat lady in the wings, doing her vocal warm-ups.

I cannot divine if it'll be a long, lingering fade. Or a snap blackout. Those things are not for us to know.

~

I've been ready to die for a long time. I think Bobby, in retrospect, wounded me in some fundamental way. He left me with a hole in my heart. And ever since then, there's been a half-acknowledged desire to kill myself.

I felt like that when Alyque left, but I had a little man to take care of.

When Zhya went, I knew I had turned the final corner. That the finishing line was somewhere down the straight.

And that's okay. It's okay to be melancholy. I've had a great life. I wish I'd made more money, but who doesn't?

I've wanted death, always. I'm not scared of it. I'm ready to go. I'm not buying new furniture or new clothes. I really believe my time's nearly done. When people die, I'm relieved for them. They've been spared. They can move on.

My Protima died. Sometimes I envy her, because she was in her prime, at the top of her game.

These days, these last days, there's nothing I look forward to.

It's perhaps a pessimist's view of the world. But here's the flip-side: If there aren't any expectations, chances are that everything that follows has the potential for delight.

That is what I choose to believe.

~

In the '80s, in the aftermath, I was smoking forty Rothmans a day.

Every time I stepped out, every time I was at a theatre, every interval at every show, I could feel people looking at me. Sometimes it was one person, or three. If I was at Prithvi, for the opening of a new play, it was a gaggle of people, all looking. Some of the looks were sympathetic, some hostile, most just curious. And a cigarette was something to hold, something to do, security at the end of your arm, a way to become the statuesque lady in the corner, smoke curling out of your nostrils.

I was loyal to my brand. I never mixed cigarettes. My voice was my signature, my instrument. My livelihood depended on it.

Once, I went to a conference in Delhi. On the third day, I ran out of the cigarettes I'd carried from Bombay. I immediately rang room service. They said they didn't have Rothmans. Unlike Bombay, you couldn't buy Rothmans at the street corner.

As soon as I landed in Bombay, almost thirty-six hours later, I instructed my cab-driver to stop at the Kalanagar kiosk, the first available store on the highway. It was 10 at night, and I noticed a few seedy-looking men lurking nearby. I decided not to tempt fate and drove on.

On the 2nd of August 1986, the first thing I did when I woke up was to reach out for the phone to dial my supplier. And something occurred to me.

I had gone forty-eight hours without smoking. That habit cost me a hundred and seventy rupees a day.

I just wanted to see how much longer I could hold out.

I have never smoked since.

~

A few months after that, Quasar and I were talking.

It was the era of the Angry Young Man. And in Quasar's hands, every projectile turned into a weapon. Every pencil, ruler, straw would become a sword or a gun. He'd inherited his father's temper. And he used to get into fights in school. Except, on this day, he said, 'Mama, have you noticed you've stopped smoking?'

I was at a loss for words, so he continued.

'I stopped fighting, Mama,' he said. 'You stopped smoking and I stopped fighting.'

We were healing. In spite of ourselves.

~

For years now, I thought I hadn't done enough with my life.

For a long time, I really missed having a car.

Alyque had a car on call. When he left, it was back to cabs for another decade and a half. Then, towards the turn of the century, I finally had my little Alto. But it's difficult to drive in this city. It's impossible to park. Even though Quasar bought me another car a few years ago, I don't take it out unless I have a driver for the day. So, I'm back to taxis and Uber.

Well into my sixties, I was out every night, multiple engagements; a new play, a show, a consular shindig, no problem. I can't do that anymore.

I don't go out much. I'd rather not.

A lot of it has to do with money. Maybe it's because I'm obsessed with deprivation.

The economic impact of a break-up is something that never gets talked about. It was a severe financial crunch – and it lasts to this day.

I loved working. I hate having nothing to do.

I've never asked anyone for work. I won't do it.

At this point in my life, I don't have assignments. I have appointments. But they're not work assignments. Work has dwindled in the last three or four years – and not because I don't want to work.

But I'm older, I think that people are a little more reluctant, and I don't have the energy for that stuff anymore.

There's never been a moment when I thought I didn't have to work. I enjoyed work.

Perhaps it was drilled into us? That we had to earn our living and pay our bills. But I was one of the lucky ones who got to do what she liked. Always this mad patchwork of jobs.

When I was young, time passed slowly between the highlights. At some point, in my thirties, in my forties, time started to blur. Years became weeks, and decades went by in a blink.

~

And then Quasar sat me down.

'You bought your parents a flat,' he said. 'In Bombay. A flat I now live in.'

I had, yes.

'And look at your walls, Mama. *Look* at them.'

Once I came home to walls that were bare; then populated during a relationship I had. They were left bare again.

And now these walls have no room to spare. Because these are the stories I have collected. These are the lives I have lived. These are the lives I held, close to mine.

Over these fifty years, I found myself.

You *can* have everything. It doesn't last.

You learn you don't *need* everything.

Here is one more truth. In order to move forward, sometimes you look back.

Another entry from my diary:

'Not wasted a moment of one's life. Going through my diaries – each name, each appointment, flashes memories of different jobs, assignments, interests, people I've enjoyed. Names and faces leap out of every page.'

Like *Gandhi*, I'm glad I was there. I'm glad I lived it. I'm so glad I got to remember all of it, perhaps one last time.

This gallery of faces. These stories. These overcrowded walls.

That is my legacy, beta.

~

And even in the midst of this inexplicable year and a half – through this strange quasi-apocalypse that we're *still* living through, there are things to see, to read, to *do*.

I learned how to use Zoom. And to attend webinars. And to act on hurried messages of 'please mute yourself'.

I acted. In the pandemic. I did readings. I performed.

The fire may have dimmed. Of course it has. That's the passage of time. But the appetite still exists.

I look around me, I look at the young women around me. I see them – so poised, so knowledgeable, so eager. I see the situation they have inherited. It was so much more innocent when I barged through the door and tried to make a place for myself.

And I feel a thrumming – in the ground beneath my feet, and under my fingers. So much power. So much potential.

The fear will come. It always does.

But there is always tomorrow. There is always another opportunity. The world waits to be made in your image, every day.

You can do it all. That is what I'm here to tell you. You can dream up a career and do the things you love, and have a child and be a single mother, and take tragedy on the chin, over and over again and just plain survive. And still live a life of honour and integrity and grace and humour that will fill your days with love and laughter and wave after wave of memories.

Just ask yourself: what do I want?

And have no regrets about the rest.

None.

~

In 1988, we visited Rishi Valley for the first time. It was our first morning on the campus, we'd just arrived. The rooms were only available after 12 p.m. So we walked around the property. Quasar found a tree that had fallen over and perched on it. He swung his legs. He was all of eight, a thin little man with big eyes. He grinned.

'Mama, the vibes are right!' he announced. And that was that, as far as we were concerned. That sealed the deal.

My name is Dolly Thakore. I'm seventy-eight years old, and the vibes are still right.

4 June 2021

List of Performances

A selection of stage roles performed across fifty years:

1955 *Pickwick Papers* by Charles Dickens

1956 Lady Pilkington in *Pied Piper of Hamelin Town* by Robert Browning

1956 Miss Havisham in *Great Expectations* by Charles Dickens

1957 Pitti Sing in *Mikado* by Guilbert and Sullivan

1957 Betsey Trotwood in *David Copperfield* by Charles Dickens

1957 Maid in *Policeman's Serenade*, written and directed by Santosh Mahendrajit Singh

1957 Lady Macbeth in *Macbeth* by William Shakespeare

1959 Ella Delahey in *Charlie's Aunt* by Brandon Thomas

1959 *Square Pegs in a Round Hole*

1961 *Trikon Ka Chautha Kon* by Gyandev Agnihotri

1962 Antioche, Queen of the Amazons in *Rape of the Belt* by Ben Levy, directed by Krishna Esalof

1966 *Shoonya* by J.P. Dikshit, directed by Vinod Pandey

1966 Washerwoman (Chorus) in *Yerma* by Fredrico Garcia Lorca

1970 *Power Play* by Partap Sharma, directed by Arun Sachdev

1971 Suraksha in *A Touch of Brightness*, written and directed by Partap Sharma

1971 Udabai in *Mira* by Gurcharan Das, directed by Alyque Padamsee

1971 Geraldine Barclay in *What the Butler Saw* by Joe Orton, directed by Arun Sachdev

1973 Lulu in *The Birthday Party* by Harold Pinter, directed by Alyque Padamsee

1974 *Suddenly Last Summer* by Tennessee Williams, directed by Adi Marzban

1975 Honey in *Who's Afraid of Virginia Woolf* by Edward Albee, directed by Alyque Padamsee

1976 Rachel Brown in *Inherit the Wind* by Jerome Lawrence and Robert E. Lee, directed by Alyque Padamsee

1976 Juliet in *Exit the King* by Eugene Ionesco, directed by Alyque Padamsee

1978 Emily Stilson in *Wings* by Arthur Kopit, directed by Janak Toprani

1979 Sally Scudamore in *Farrukh of Finchley* by John Chapman, directed by Adi Marzban

1979 Portia in *Julius Caesar* by William Shakespeare, directed by Alyque Padamsee

1980 Linda Loman in *Death of a Salesman* by Arthur Miller, directed by Alyque Padamsee

1980 Stella Kowalski in *A Streetcar Named Desire* by Tennessee Williams, directed by Alyque Padamsee

1981 Newsreader in *I Love Bombay*, written and directed by Sylvester da Cunha

1985 Mausi in *Evam Indrajit* by Badal Sircar, directed by Protap Roy

1985 Parveen in *Yes, Mother Dear!* by Kamala Ramchandani, directed by Adi Marzban

1986 *Bottoms Up*, written and directed by Bharat Dabholkar

1986 Esther Saloman in *Equus* by Peter Shaffer, directed by Varun Khanna

1987 Mother in *Six Characters in Search of an Author* by Luigi Pirandello, directed by Vickram Kapadia

1989 Amy Ruskin in *Special Occasions* by Bernard Slade, directed by Janak Toprani

1990 Magistrate in *Ekshuff* (*Equus* in Hindi) by Peter Shaffer, directed by Mahendra Joshi

1990 Mrs Zero in *Ek Do Teen* (*The Adding Machine* in Hindi) written by Elmer Rice, and directed by Salim Shah

1991 Mother in *Rashomon* by Fay and Michael Kanin, directed by Janak Toprani

1993 Elizabeth in *Gaslight* by Patrick Hamilton, directed by Geoffrey Kendal

1994 Agave in *The Bacchae* by Euripides directed by Zubin Driver

1995 Phoopi in *Tum Kya Jaano Preet* (*Pygmalion* in Hindi) by George Bernard Shaw, directed by Dinesh Thakur

1996 Her Ladyship in *The Dresser* by Ronald Harwood, directed by Jiten Merchant

1996 Shanti Desai in *A Sister Like You* by Dina Mehta, directed by Jiten Merchant

1996 Mantra in *Legend of Ram*, written and directed by Amir Raza Hussain

1996 Du in *Keely & Du* by Jane Martin, directed by Janak Toprani

1997 Buddhist Lady in *Shikara* (adaptation of *Of Mice and Men*) by Gary Richardson, directed by Aly Khan

1997 Nurse in *Antigone* by Jean Anouilh, directed by Jiten Merchant

1996 *Workshop on Crime*, written and directed by Kalpana Swaminathan

1998 Clytemnestra in *Elektra* by Richard Strauss, directed by Jiten Merchant

1999 Mother in *Mirror*, written and directed by Zubin Driver

1999 Eleanor in *Gossamer Gyre*, written and directed by Sujoy Sood

2000 Kate Keller in *All My Sons* by Arthur Miller, directed by Quasar Thakore Padamsee

2000 Tamara Sachs in *Taking Sides* by Ronald Harwood, directed by Jiten Merchant

2000 Dip in *Dip & Dop*, written and directed by Shanta Gokhale

2003 *The Vagina Monologues* by Eve Ensler, directed by Mahabano Mody-Kotwal and Kaizaad Navroze Kotwal

2004 Meg in *The Birthday Party* by Harold Pinter, directed by Arghya Lahiri

2005 Manik in *Vultures* by Vijay Tendulkar, directed by Alyque Padamsee

2006 *Much Ado About Nothing* by William Shakespeare, directed by Imogen Butler-Cole

2006 Lady on a Chair in *Loving Silence* (part of *Flawless*), written and directed by Shomshukla Das

2007 The Wicked Witch of the West in *The Wizard Of Oz* by Frank L. Baum, directed by Divya Palat

2007 Wife in *Small Is Beautiful* (part of *Unspoken Dialogues*) by Anish Trivedi, directed by Alyque Padamsee

2007 *Kissa Yoni Ka* (Hindi version of *The Vagina Monologues*) by Eve Ensler, directed by Mahabano Mody-Kotwal and Kaizad Navroze Kotwal

2008 'A' in *Three Ladies of Ibsen* by Ramu Ramanathan, directed by Arghya Lahiri

2013 Sati in *Sati* (part of *Devi*), written and directed by Zubin Driver

2013 Nurse in *Antigone* by Jean Anouilh, directed by Alyque Padamsee

2015 Gertrude in *Rosemary for Remembrance* by Shanta Gokhale, directed by Arghya Lahiri

Some productions directed:

1976 *Shankar* for Nirmala Niketan and All India Radio

1976 *Sava Ser Genhu* by Premchand for Nirmala Niketan and All India Radio

1976 *Emperor's New Clothes* by Hans Christian Anderson for the Spastics Society of India

1986 *Wiser Counsel & Heavens Above* by Kamala Ramchandani for Cathedral & John Conon School

2007, 2014 *Feeding Crows* by Meher Pestonji

2013 *1 Safdarjung* by Ratnakar Matkari

Acknowledgements

In spite of the army of friends and family who made these stories – and so much of my life – possible, this book would not exist without some people.

Arghya Lahiri, my collaborator and second son, who persevered in making this book a reality, by being incredibly patient and supportive. There is no one I would rather have been on this journey with.

Shanta Gokhale, who has read iterations of this book over decades and, more importantly, been a friend, philosopher, guide and a hero of mine for even longer.

Jerry Pinto, who refused to give up on this book and on me.

Sathya Saran, who fanned the flame back to life.

Farzana Contractor, for her friendship of decades and the cover photograph I never knew existed.

Swati Chopra, my editor extraordinaire, who piloted us home.

Margaret Peacock, Siddharth Dube and Toral Shah, who read the book and were so gracious with their time and their attention.

Farrukh Dhondy, for being a friend for over sixty years and always a phone call away.

Kanishka Gupta, who was in our corner from start to finish and whose faith in this book remained undimmed through the thick and the thin.

Arjun Gaind, Dibakar Ghosh and Gulnar Mistry, whose expertise and patience we could call on repeatedly.

Tanima Saha, who gave the manuscript such minute attention; and everyone at HarperCollins for the care they have lavished upon us.

And, Tara Khandelwal, who spotted a diamond in the rough.

I thank you.

Acknowledgements

About the Author

Dolly Thakore is a veteran actor, newscaster, columnist and casting director who has worked in advertising, communications and public relations. She is also a staunch social activist, particularly for children and destitute women, and for Citizens for Peace.

Arghya Lahiri is a writer, theatre director, lighting designer and filmmaker. He has worked in the theatre, in every capacity he can lay his hands on, for over twenty years. This is his second book.